To Comfort and To Challenge

To Comfort
and To Challenge

A DILEMMA OF THE CONTEMPORARY CHURCH

BY

CHARLES Y. GLOCK

BENJAMIN B. RINGER

EARL R. BABBIE

A Joint Contribution from the Survey Research Center,
University of California, Berkeley, and the
Bureau of Applied Social Research, Columbia University

1967

Berkeley and Los Angeles

UNIVERSITY OF CALIFORNIA PRESS

University of California Press
Berkeley and Los Angeles, California
Cambridge University Press, London, England
Copyright © 1967 by the Regents of the University of California
Library of Congress Catalog Card Number 67-15560
Printed in the United States of America

To Mickey, Rosalind, and Sheila

PREFACE

In 1952, the Bureau of Applied Social Research of Columbia University was invited by the Department of Christian Social Relations of the National Council of the Protestant Episcopal Church to assist it in organizing and executing a research study of the Church's clergy and lay membership. The study had a three-fold purpose. First, it was to provide an evaluation of the Church's Social Education and Community Action Program —a program developed to foster in local congregations activities (forums, lectures, study groups) which would serve to inform parishioners about public affairs and to encourage them to participate more fully in the life of their local communities. Second, the study was to contribute a portrait of prevailing sentiment among parishioners and clergy on a range of social, political, and economic questions on which resolutions had been passed by Triennial Conventions of the Church. Third, it was to discover the kind of role which the clergy and laity would like to have the Church play in social education and community action.

The Columbia Bureau responded favorably to the Church's invitation, and Patricia L. Kendall and I were assigned to be the Bureau's representatives on the study. On the Church's side, primary responsibility for the study was carried by the Rev. Dr. M. Moran Weston, then on the staff of the Department of Christian Social Relations, under the supervision of the Director of the Department, the Rev. Dr. Almon R. Pepper.

The study produced out of this collaboration involved the administering of the questionnaire reproduced in Appendix C to all bishops of the Church and to a sample of parish priests and laity. The priests were also asked to complete a second questionnaire, called a Parish Inventory, the purpose of which was to collect background information on the sample of parishes in which the first questionnaire was administered.

The results of this study were then presented to the Church in two reports: one concentrating on the data collected from bishops, priests, and parishioners, and the other on the information contained in the Parish Inventories. These reports, prepared by Rev. Weston, were written to satisfy the primary purposes for which the research was underwritten.

By way of acknowledging its gratitude for the assistance rendered, the Church deposited a set of the data in the archives of the Columbia Bureau for such further analysis as its personnel might wish to undertake. Then a budding young sociologist with a primary interest in religion, I conceived the idea that a secondary analysis of the data could contribute to an understanding of the meaning, sources, and consequences of church involvement, a subject about which very little was known at that time.

I recruited Benjamin B. Ringer, then a Research Assistant at the Bureau, as a collaborator and we began work on the analysis in 1954. Funds were limited, and we were occupied full time on other assignments, but we managed to work intermittently on the manuscript evenings and weekends. By 1957, a first draft was in hand. A year at the Center for Advanced Study in the Behavioral Sciences provided an opportunity to move the book closer to completion, but by the end of that idyllic year, the manuscript was still incomplete.

Beginning in 1958, Ringer and I took new jobs which simply prevented further work on the manuscript and both of us were by then of a mind to give up on the enterprise in light of the time which had elapsed since the data were collected. The manuscript lay fallow until 1964.

Our interest in it was revived in the sixties by the appearance in the literature of a number of new studies of the church. These studies, which are reviewed in the Introduction, were essentially critical essays on the state of the church. While penetrating and insightful, they omitted, in our judgment, a consideration of the conditions giving rise to the kind of church they described. Our own study seemed nicely to fill the gap and we decided to reconsider, once again, bringing the manuscript to completion.

This called for a reappraisal of the contemporary significance of the data which by then, 1964, were twelve years old. Neither of us was disposed to think that the data were any longer descriptively accurate. Episcopalians today probably hold different views on public affairs than they did back in 1952. However, the primary thrust of our study was explanation, not description. It was unlikely, we thought, that the factors which lead people to be deeply committed to their church would be significantly different in the sixties than in the fifties. Neither did we feel that the consequences of differential involvement would be significantly changed. Even if subsequent studies should show that changes have taken place in these regards, it seemed of historical moment to report the situation in the fifties.

In 1964, again working evenings and weekends, but now with the assistance of Earl R. Babbie, a graduate research sociologist at the Survey Research Center of the University of California, work on the manuscript was started once again. This book is the result.

Institutionally, the book is to be considered a joint product of the Bureau of Applied Social Research where the work began and the Survey Research Center where it was completed. Acknowledgment is also due the Center for Advanced Study in the Behavioral Sciences which provided the setting for moving the project along in midstream. We are grateful for the major contribution of the Rev. Dr. Weston in the initiation, design, and execution of the study and for the support and encouragement of the Rev. Dr. Pepper. Recognition is also due Patricia L. Kendall for her collaboration on the construction of the questionnaire and to Hanan Selvin who designed the sample. The preparation of the book was facilitated by grants from the American Philosophical Society and the Institute of Social Sciences of the University of California, Berkeley. Neither the Society nor the Institute assume responsibility for any statement made or any point of view expressed in the book, of course. We are pleased, however, gratefully to acknowledge their support.

CHARLES Y. GLOCK

Berkeley, California
November 1, 1966

CONTENTS

INTRODUCTION

At no time in their history have the Christian churches in America been as much the subject of critical appraisal as they are today. Since 1960, an unprecedented flow of popular and scholarly books and articles have appeared demeaning the significance of the church in contemporary life, and challenging church leaders to articulate a meaningful role for religion in the modern world. While every generation has produced critics who proclaimed the ultimate irrelevance of religion in society, the voices heard in today's confrontation are of a different genre. By and large, these latter critics defend the continued relevancy of religion in society but despair that the institutional church, as they see it, has abdicated its responsibility to promote this relationship. Their call is not for the church's demise, but for its renewal. The proponents of this position may be found within the church as well as outside it; they include sociologists, historians, and journalists, but also theologians, clergymen, and laymen of the church.

The primary thrust of criticism, then, does not represent so much a quarrel with basic Christian beliefs and values as an intense concern that the church has betrayed its moral obligation to seek the implementation of those beliefs and values in everyday life. To understand this viewpoint, it is necessary to appreciate the context in which it appears. The belief that the church has failed as a moral force is intimately related to the pressing social issues of the sixties: civil rights, poverty, and peace.

Social movements formed around these issues may very well prove to be the prime feature of the second half of the twentieth century in America. The issues share one thing in

1

common: they are based essentially on the discrepancy between man's social condition and the society's proclaimed social values. Racial discrimination is conceived as a direct violation of religious and political values of brotherhood and equality, inbred poverty is seen as wholly incompatible with the proclaimed values of individual opportunity and the pursuit of happiness, and the existence or threat of war is proclaimed to contradict the religious sanctity of human life and American ideals of peace and tranquility.

The mood of the criticism, different from in the past, is one of disenchantment rather than disavowal. Michael Harrington, writing in the *New Republic*,[1] contrasts the radicals of earlier generations with the "New Left" students of today. Radicalism in the thirties was nearly synonymous with the search for new values with which wholly to supplant what was seen as an evil system. By contrast, Harrington suggests, the contemporary rebels have, by and large, maintained a commitment to the proclaimed ideals of American society, and have directed their attack at what they consider the hypocritical betrayal of those ideals by the leaders and institutions of the Establishment. Fulfillment rather than replacement is the motif of the "New Left."

The values, beliefs and moral principles which a people share represent an ideal picture of society as they feel it ought to be. Whenever social ideals and social conditions are visibly out of phase, demands for social change may be expected to arise; this seems to represent the situation in America today. Racial discrimination, war and poverty are but three of the more visible aspects of contemporary conditions which have mobilized men to demand social change. Such demands have come from many sectors of society, but a recurrent question may be heard from the platforms and picket lines: "Where is the church?"

This question reflects the religious roots of many American social ideals. Historically, the values and principles which define the desired society may derive from many sources. A nation's political history and heritage may provide many ideals; a revered social or political leader may sketch the utopian image which men will strive to attain for generations. In most societies, re-

[1] Michael Harrington, "Radicals, Old and New," *New Republic*, July 3, 1965.

ligions have helped provide the inspirations and ideals which constitute the rules of proper social conduct and humane social organization. The impact of Christianity on the founding of America has been discussed by many authors and need not be elaborated here. From our earliest colonial origins, the Christian ethics and the Christian churches which the settlers brought to the New World left their mark on the values and social structures which have survived to this day. While the social values derived from Christianity were not unique to that religion, Christian—and particularly Protestant—churches and church members provided the most direct sources of religious values employed in nation-building.

This is the starting point for today's critics of the church. They contend that the Christian message contains the basic values of peace, brotherhood, human dignity, compassion and equality implicit in the nation's origins and which should characterize American society today. Furthermore, they reason, whenever these values are violated in the life of the nation, the first wounded cry should come from a vigorous and morally concerned Christian church. In the judgment of many, this does not happen. They suggest the church has grown tired, complacent and myopic in the defense and advancement of its own proclaimed values. Many critics—both within the church and outside it—have demanded social change on behalf of Christian values, and have discovered the institutional church, at best, a slow and reluctant follower, or, at worst, an active opponent.

This reaction is the crux of the present criticism of the American churches. Ironically, one finds non-Christians and even agnostics demanding that the Christian churches stand up and fight for Christian ideals. While the voices joined in this demand are numerous, there are five writers in particular whose indictments typify the main themes of criticism: Peter Berger, Harvey Cox, Gibson Winter, Pierre Berton and Martin Marty.

Common to their criticism is the contention that the church has become overwhelmingly aligned with the secular status quo in America. In his *The Noise of Solemn Assemblies*,[2] Peter Berger, one of the earliest of the critics, effectively expresses the

[2] Peter L. Berger, *The Noise of Solemn Assemblies* (Garden City. N.Y.: Doubleday, 1961).

theme in concluding that the church no longer generates its own values, but, like many secular institutions, merely supports and sanctifies the values and conditions of the general community. Thus rather than helping to define and seek what *ought to be*, the church merely defends and perpetuates what *is*.

Berger sees two evils in the church's commitment to the status quo. First, he argues, it involves a renunciation of the basic values of Christianity itself. To the extent that existing social conditions do not truly reflect Christian ideals, the church's support of those conditions is anti-Christian; when it actively opposes those who demand social change in accord with Christian ideals, its betrayal is compounded.

In addition to betraying its own basic values, the church's posture, Berger suggests, betrays its own members by hardening the cast of social parochialism. This latter point is elaborated in *The Precarious Vision*.[3] Here, Berger examines the unreality and delusion inherent in the social milieu of the man who is convinced that his truth is The Truth. This inflexibility of perspective prevents man from knowing himself, let alone others, and the church's veneration of the status quo contributes to the malady. By committing men to a particularistic and time-bound image of society, the church denies them the ability to understand and respond satisfactorily to any society.

The need for flexibility in social outlook is also a central theme in Harvey Cox's *The Secular City*.[4] Cox suggests that all men "see the world from a particular socially and historically conditioned point of view," [5] but points out that modern men are in a position to realize that their outlook is limited, while their tribal predecessors could not. This awareness of one's own particularistic viewpoint is, for Cox as for Berger, an important ingredient in the Christian understanding and acceptance of others. The opposing orientation is one of static dogmatism. From a theological perspective, Cox contends that the Christian churches are obligated to point out the relativity and precariousness of worldly things, and to continually readjust the application of Christian ideals to an ever-changing society.

[3] Peter L. Berger, *The Precarious Vision* (Garden City, N.Y.: Doubleday, 1961).

[4] Harvey Cox, *The Secular City* (New York: Macmillan, 1965).

[5] *Ibid.*, p. 30.

Cox, like Berger and other critics, is repulsed by the church's veneration of static formulas for life. As social conditions change, he feels the Christian formulas must change also, if they are to have any meaning. The obligation of the church is to generate new and relevant formulas for life, and through them, to direct modern man toward a social organization which accords closely with Christian social values. Rather than opposing social change, the church should understand and guide it; if social change is demanded by Christian values, the church should seek it out.

Implicit in these commentaries is the notion that the church has an obligation to shape men's relations with one another. From this perspective, religious institutions should be relevant to politics, to social problems, and indeed, to the entire society. The contrasting image of the church is to conceive it as having primarily a responsibility for the individual and his personal relation to God. From this alternative viewpoint, religion is a private matter, and has little direct bearing on social conditions. Gibson Winter suggests this is the predominant orientation of the contemporary church in the modern suburban community.[6] After examining the flight of the white middle classes from the inner city—leaving behind those too poor to move and those denied access to the suburbs because of race or ethnic origins— Winter discusses the new suburban values of cordiality, bridge clubs and well-behaved children. Like Berger, Winter finds the contemporary churches concerned more with social adjustment than with social justice. The function of the church in this setting is not one of telling men what society should be ultimately, but one of helping them to live harmoniously with society as it is. This latter charge constitutes the second major theme of current criticism.

In 1963, the Anglican Church of Canada asked Pierre Berton, a journalist, to prepare a book of criticism of the contemporary church which would provide stimulating Lenten reading for parishioners. *The Comfortable Pew*[7] was his response. Berton, like the earlier critics, portrays the church as being overwhelmingly committed to the status quo—even when such commitment

[6] Gibson Winter, *The Suburban Captivity of the Churches* (New York: Macmillan, 1962).

[7] Pierre Berton, *The Comfortable Pew* (Toronto: McClelland and Stewart, 1965).

seems to deny the most basic values which the Christian churches have preached for two thousand years. He contrasts the Christian ideal of "peace on earth" with the near fanaticism of some church leaders in justifying and promoting nationalistic wars. In the face of Christian proclamations of brotherhood, he notes the outright opposition to Civil Rights by Southern churches and the weak and ineffectual support and sometimes apathy which characterize the response of churches and clergymen in the North. He compares sermons on Christian conduct with the church turning its back on the questionable business practices of its members.

Berton agrees with Winter that contemporary Christianity has become strictly a personal matter. The "comfortable pew" is warmed, weekly, by those church members who need comfort and consolation when the cares of secular society become oppressive. "Institutional Christianity, in short, has become a comfortable creed, a useful tool for Peace of Mind and Positive Thinking, a kind of sugar-coated pill that soothes those who fear to face the traditional Christian concerns of evil, suffering and death. . . ." [8]

In Berton's eyes, the contemporary church has tended to soothe consciences, rather than stir them up; it has set about to *salve* human misery rather than to *solve* it. As an institution, the church has lost sight of that past era when it confronted secular society and demanded that matters of value and principle be placed above those of comfort and self-interest. "It has all but been forgotten that Christianity began as a revolutionary religion whose followers embraced an entirely different set of values from those held by other members of society. Those original values are still in conflict with the values of contemporary society; yet religion today has become as conservative a force as the force the original Christians were in conflict with." [9]

Martin Marty, in essential agreement, attributes the situation to the amalgamation of religions in America and to their convergence with secular society.[10] From Tocqueville to the present

[8] *Ibid.*, pp. 95–96.
[9] *Ibid.*, p. 94.
[10] Martin Marty, *The New Shape of American Religion* (New York: Harper, 1959).

many foreign observers have noted the religiosity of Americans. Everyone in America is religious; virtually everyone professes belief in God. Yet, Marty points out, religion has also become Americanized; the God in whom all Americans believe is the God of Religion-in-General. He is the God "in whom we trust" and under whom national allegiance is sworn. To be religious in contemporary America can scarcely be distinguished from being a "good American." Contemporary religiosity is characterized by respectability rather than fervor. The much-touted religious revival of the fifties was not an attempt to bring the nation to its knees in religious witness, but an affirmation of harmony with Religion-in-General. In Marty's view, it is this harmonious collusion between Religion-in-General and the secular society which has rendered the churches incapable of fulfilling their moral obligations.

These writers all agree that the church must somehow break away from its commitment to the secular society, and become again an independent force in shaping the structure of society and the lives of individuals. Although they differ on many specifics, the general themes of the criticism are clear, and quite convincing. Nevertheless, their commentaries are, for the most part, impressionistic. The careful reader, however sympathetic to the line of criticism, may feel somewhat uneasy in accepting opinion in place of facts. Furthermore, there is an important line of inquiry which most of the critics have failed to deal with directly.

Basically, the critics have failed to devote sufficient attention to the nature of religious involvement—particularly as this is defined by church members themselves. They call upon the church to lead, but provide no convincing evidence that church members stand ready to follow. When Berton notes that clergymen preach Christian conduct, but fail to enforce it among their businessmen church members, he assumes the church possesses some lever for shaping the actions of its parishioners. Whether such a lever exists is an empirical question, an answer to which is needed to round out the body and character of contemporary criticism.

The present report is aimed at an empirical examination of this question of leverage and more generally, at testing with evidence the critics' portrait of the contemporary church. As already noted in the Preface, the data are drawn from a national survey of Episcopalian bishops, priests, and parishioners conducted in 1952. The details of the survey are reported in Appendix A. Suffice it here to repeat that it involved the administering of the questionnaire reproduced in Appendix C to all of the bishops of the Church, and to a representative sample of priests and parishioners. In total, 100 completed questionnaires were received from bishops, 259 from priests, and 1,530 from parishioners.[11]

Episcopalians do not represent all American church members, of course. They are typical, however, of those at whom the current wave of criticism is directed. Most of the present critics have, at least temporarily, given up on the more conservative denominations and sects in American Christianity. Their appeal is aimed more directly at the relatively liberal, "mainline" denominations—Congregationalists (United Church of Christ), Episcopalians, Presbyterians, and Methodists—whose membership is so largely made up of urban and suburban, middle-class Americans. Although an analysis of Episcopalian parishioners cannot be taken as a definitive statement on religion in America, it can provide significant insights into the state of many Christian churches and allow a realistic assessment of their needs and potential for renewal.

This book is addressed essentially to two questions about the contemporary church member. Recognizing that church members differ in the strength of their ties to the church, the initial question asked is why this should be so; why do some parishioners become more deeply involved in the church than others? Part One reports on the analysis pursued to answer this question. Following Chapter 1, which confronts the task of measuring differential church involvement, Chapters 2 through 4 are devoted to an examination of sex, the life cycle, family status, and social class as they affect involvement in the church. Chapter 5, then, presents a theoretical overview of the observed relations reported in the preceding empirical chapters. It is here that a theory of the sources of church involvement is outlined.

[11] The data collected from a second instrument, the Parish Inventory, are not included in the present analysis.

The second question, addressed in Part Two, asks what difference church involvement makes; do the deeply committed hold significantly different religious and social values than those with marginal and weak church ties? Chapter 6 answers this question with respect to the role which the more and less involved would have the church play in attempting to have Christian values inform the larger society. Does greater involvement produce greater support or greater opposition to a politically active church? Chapter 7 follows the same theme by examining the significance of differential involvement for parishioners' acceptance of the social values promulgated by the church. Are church-approved social values more likely to be accepted or to be rejected by the deeply committed? In Chapter 8 a parallel analysis focuses on the relation between church involvement and attitudes on a number of specifically religious issues.

The concluding chapter brings the empirical findings and theoretical contentions of the book together to produce an informed perspective from which to evaluate the current criticism of the church. Through better understanding of the meaning of church involvement, it is hoped that the situation which has given rise to the criticism may be more fully appreciated, and that the prospects for the future of the church in America may thereby be clarified.

PART ONE

THE SOURCES OF CHURCH
INVOLVEMENT

Chapter 1

Involvement in Church Life

The mere assertion that men differ in their orientations to religion is scarcely sufficient to evoke great popular controversy or to set in motion any profound theological debate. Few people are likely to quarrel with the contention that no two men are exactly alike in their religious beliefs, attitudes and behaviors. Yet it follows from this observation that the standards which one man would use in judging the religiosity of his neighbor would differ somewhat from the standards used by any other man. Throughout the course of history, the attempt to distinguish the religious man from the back-slider, apostate and heretic has split religious bodies, shed blood and turned men against their neighbors. Ultimately, who can say what characterizes the *truly* religious man?

The reader who seeks a definitive answer to this question will be sorely disappointed by the present book. The authors can claim no special gift or revelation in this regard. Yet any study which seeks to investigate the sources and consequences of religious involvement must begin by facing up to the knotty problem of measuring religiosity. In lieu of a definitive answer, we shall offer one which is clear and precise, although necessarily arbitrary.

The process of defining a concept as generally vague as religiosity for the purposes of an empirical study is a compromise between two requirements. On the one hand, the definition must closely approximate generally accepted meanings of the term as it is used in the natural language. While the reader may choose to disagree with particular aspects of the definition, he should come away from the discussion with the feeling that he and the

13

authors are thinking about essentially the same phenomenon. On the other hand, the definition must be one which can be understood clearly and precisely enough to permit an exact replication by another investigator. This latter requirement is necessary for the coherent development of any area of inquiry.

In a secondary analysis of data which have already been collected, there are further restrictions on the sorts of definitions which can be used. In the first place, we are limited by the information provided by the questions asked in the original questionnaire. Thus while more acceptable measures of religiosity might be conceived, our efforts must be restricted by the material at hand. Furthermore, the definitions used must of necessity be somewhat tailored to the nature of the people being studied. Insofar as all the subjects in the study are members of Episcopalian parishes, the definitions and measurements must be constructed within that framework. Therefore, it cannot be expected that the variations in religiosity among Episcopalians will be as great as those which exist within the population at large. But although a narrower spectrum of variation will be found among these respondents, it is clear that Episcopalians are not all equally religious. What then are the differences, and are they systematic enough to warrant distinguishing the more religious from the less religious parishioners?

Despite the implicit notions which individuals may hold, there are few clear precedents within or outside the social sciences for trying to distinguish the religious commitments of church members. The distinctions which are made in everyday conversation are generally vague, and the churches themselves have neither sought to establish formal classes of membership, nor have they encouraged the systematization of informal distinctions in any way. And where religion has been studied by social scientists, only rarely have they sought to elaborate the types and extent of religious commitment.

To the extent that people discuss a man's religious life at all, they are generally content to describe him in terms of his denominational affiliation; that is, as an Episcopalian, a Catholic, a Lutheran, a Jew, and so forth. We occasionally speak of someone as a "regular church-goer," implying that he is different from an "irregular" one, or individuals may be described as "practicing" Christians or Jews in contrast to "non-practicing" or "nominal" ones. In general, however, when these distinctions are made, they are marked by both a lack of precision and a lack of agreement as to their meanings.

The churches, for the most part, have not shown a concern about the absence of formal distinctions nor about the imprecision of informal ones. There seems a natural disinclination to make distinctions which might be interpreted invidiously. Such caution may reflect the multi-denominational organization of religion in America and the consequent competition for membership recruitment which this encourages. The churches are understandably hesitant to impose rigid membership requirements which might alienate rather than attract potential recruits.

The churches face, in addition, the practical difficulty of discovering the extent to which an individual church member measures up to whatever standards might be explicitly stated or implicitly understood. This is most apparent with respect to the member's acceptance of dogma and specific religious beliefs. What a person believes tends to be a private matter. There are few occasions for his beliefs to be publicly communicated, much less measured. Conformity to other standards—those bearing on ritual observance and participation in the organizational life of the parish, for example—are inherently more amenable to measurement in the sense that the relevant behavior is observable. However, for the church to maintain records of attendance at worship services would not only be a troublesome task, but would probably not be well received, especially by the more "marginal" members of the church. Even were there a simple and unobtrusive way to classify parishioners, it is unlikely that it would be widely adopted or encouraged by the churches. Probably the feeling that this is an area where the final judgment should be left to God, not man, would ultimately prevail.

The preceding observations are clearly more applicable to religious groups approximating the "church" rather than the "sect" end of the well-known "church-sect" continuum. Because they are less concerned about identifying with the larger society, sects (the Jehovah's Witnesses, for example) are inclined to impose more explicit requirements for membership. However, the distinctions made between the saved and unsaved, for example, are not applicable to Protestantism in general, nor to the Protestant Episcopal Church in particular.

There seem to be good and sufficient reasons, then, why the churches themselves have not evolved what would amount to a classification of church members. But what of the social sciences? Presumably social scientists are not under the same restrictions as the churches about making such distinctions. Furthermore, in order to understand a variety of problems bearing on the postulated functions of religion for the society and the personality, there seem to be sound intellectual grounds for wanting to contrast individuals in terms of their orientations to religion.

Taking into account the degree to which religion has been the focus of scientific inquiry, it is perhaps surprising that little has been done to evolve a method for making meaningful "religious" distinctions among people. In addition, the attention which has been given to this problem has tended to focus on extreme or abnormal forms of religious expression. Around the turn of the last century, some effort was expended by psychologists, most notably William James,[1] to distinguish types of religious experience. Neither James' work nor that of his contemporaries, however, is particularly relevant to our present purposes. First, such investigations only allow us to talk about individuals who have or have not had certain extreme religious experiences, without further differentiating among those who have not. Second, these studies do not provide a set of exact criteria by which we might readily make the same distinctions in other populations. In the ensuing years, psychological interest in religion has remained at a relatively low key and no recent work to our knowledge has attacked the problem of typologizing or ordering religious experience.[2]

In sociology, the work of Joseph L. Fichter still represents an important attempt to deal with the problem, and also one which is directly relevant to our present investigation. Fichter was con-

---

[1] William James, *The Varieties of Religious Experience* (New York: Mentor Books, 1958; first published in 1902).

[2] For a more recent theoretical discussion of religious experience, see Charles Y. Glock and Rodney Stark, *Religion and Society in Tension* (Chicago: Rand McNally, 1965), chaps. 3 and 8.

cerned with classifying the members of a Roman Catholic parish[3] with respect to the strength of their attachment to the parish church. His typology distinguishes four types of parishioners— nuclear parishioners (the most involved), modal parishioners, marginal Catholics, and dormant ones (the non-involved).

In developing this typology, Fichter introduces three "personal" indicators—*intention:* the individual's self-perception of his interest in the parish; *religious adherence:* the degree of his participation in the prescribed rituals of the church; and *social participation:* his involvement in the organizational life of the parish. Unfortunately, Fichter is not explicit in stating how he uses these indicators to classify parish members into his four types. Judging from his discussion, however, it appears that parishioners were classified impressionistically on the basis of information collected on the three "personal" indicators of involvement in the parish.

This conclusion would seem to be supported by his definition of the four types. He says:

> We have tentatively classified the urban White Catholics of this study into four general groupings: (a) *nuclear,* who are the most active participants and the most faithful believers; (b) *modal,* who are the normal "practicing" Catholics constituting the great mass of identifiable Catholic laymen; (c) *marginal,* who are conforming to a bare, arbitrary minimum of the patterns expected in the religious institution; and (d) *dormant,* who have in practice "given up" Catholicism but have not joined another religious denomination.[4]

We can only assume that to be classified in the nuclear category, a parishioner must score high on ritual observance, be active in the organizational life of the parish, and express his strong adherence to the faith. There is an implication of a high correspondence among parishioners' scores on each of the three indicators. Fichter himself hints that the association is quite high, although he acknowledges that exceptions do exist without specifying how they were classified.

[3] Joseph H. Fichter, *Social Relations in the Urban Parish* (Chicago: University of Chicago Press, 1954)

[4] *Ibid.,* p. 22.

What are the implications, then, of Fichter's study for the present examination of Episcopal parishioners? Obviously, we are not able wholly to adopt his classification procedure. In the first place, there are important differences between the Roman Catholic and Episcopal situations—particularly with respect to definitions of what constitutes a parishioner. More important, however, it is simply impossible to mirror Fichter's procedure. We are neither told the exact measurements which are to be made on each of these indicators, nor the procedure by which they are combined in classifying individuals according to his four types. In short, replication of the study by an independent investigator is not possible. Nonetheless, the study does offer some insights into the types of indicators which might be used to determine differential involvement among church members.

Gerhard Lenski's *The Religious Factor*[5] represents a more recent attempt to measure religious involvement. Part of Lenski's conceptual scheme was derived from Will Herberg's[6] treatment of American religious groups as socio-cultural communities. In the light of Herberg's discussion, Lenski distinguished between *communal* and *associational* involvement. The former referred to an individual's participation in primary groups composed of his fellow religionists. Thus, the number of friends and relatives sharing the respondent's religious affiliation determined his score on communal involvement. Associational involvement, on the other hand, referred to church attendance and participation in church-related activities.

Lenski also considered the dimensions of *doctrinal orthodoxy* and *devotionalism*. As its name indicates, the former measured the degree to which a person held the major beliefs of his faith. The latter dimension was based on the frequency of his prayers and the extent to which he asked God's advice on important decisions. Throughout his investigation, Lenski stressed that the various dimensions of religious involvement were independent of one another and should be treated separately. Essentially the

[5] Gerhard Lenski, *The Religious Factor* (Garden City, N.Y.: Doubleday, 1955).

[6] Will Herberg, *Protestant, Catholic and Jew* (Garden City, N.Y.: Doubleday, 1955).

same point has been made elsewhere by Yoshio Fukuyama[7] who suggests that religiosity expressed in one form does not guarantee that the same person will be equally expressive in some other form.

The basic concept of religiosity as a multidimensional phenomenon was discussed at length by the senior author in an article dealing with the measurement of religious commitment.[8] In that examination, five dimensions of religious commitment were postulated: ritual, ideological, experiential, intellectual and consequential. *Ritual involvement,* as its name suggests, refers to a person's observance of the prescribed ritual activities of his religion. For Christians, this would include attendance at Sunday services, the taking of Communion, and so forth. The *ideological dimension* involves the belief component; to what extent does an individual personally believe the traditional teachings and dogmas of his religion? The *experiential dimension* taps the "feeling" aspect of religion. A religious experience may be as mild as feeling that one is in the presence of a divine being, or as strong as having an actual vision or seizure. *Intellectual involvement* refers to a person's knowledge about his religion; how much does he know of its history and teachings? Finally, the *consequential dimension* was suggested as a measure of the "effect" which an individual's religion might have on his life. As the name suggests, this dimension represents the consequences of a person's religious knowledge, activities, beliefs, and feelings for the way he actually lives his life.

This examination was in the form of a theoretical discussion and no attempt was made to empirically test the independence, interaction or even the validity of the five dimensions. While the data available to the present study do not permit an examination of all five of the postulated dimensions, the analysis is clearly informed by the notion of religiosity as a multidimensional phe-

[7] Yoshio Fukuyama, "The Major Dimensions of Church Membership," *Review of Religious Research* (Spring, 1951).

[8] Charles Y. Glock, "On the Study of Religious Commitment," Research Supplement to the July–August, 1962, issue of *Religious Education.* A more recent revision of the article may be found in Glock and Stark, *op. cit.,* chap. 2.

nomenon. For while the data do not provide all the information which might be desired, they do permit an approximation of three analytically distinct aspects of religious life.

The first dimension for which the data do not permit an examination is the belief, or ideological, component.[9] There is no information regarding the content and intensity of Episcopalians' conceptions of the divine and of divine will. Secondly, there is no way of examining the experiential dimension; no determination can be made pertaining to the religious experiences which Episcopalians have had, either as a consequence of, or as a complement to their beliefs. As a result, the belief and feeling components cannot be considered at all in the present study.

The information which is available bears more on practice than on belief or experience; the data describe what Episcopalians do rather than what they think or feel. It is possible then to derive several measures of the closeness of Episcopalians' ties to their church. These measures bear on ritual observance, participation in church organizations, and the parishioner's reliance on religious sources for information and advice in everyday life. For purposes of analysis, these will be called ritual, organizational and intellectual involvement. All three are primarily objective rather than subjective measures of a parishioner's involvement. Implicit in the utilization of these three measures is the assumption that the degree to which the parishioner participates in these aspects of his religion is a reflection of its overall saliency to him. Regular attendance at worship services, active participation in church activities and dependence on the church for direction in one's life will all be taken as manifesting a certain degree of attachment to the church. However, it should be emphasized once more that the available indicators deal primarily with parishioners' involvement in the institutionalized aspects of religious life. While it has been suggested that the components of religious belief and experience are conceptually independent from those which will be examined in this study, their empirical independence cannot be tested. Therefore, it should be clear

---

[9] It is of historical interest that the sponsors of the 1952 study felt questions pertaining to religious beliefs might offend respondents. Perhaps it is a sign of changing attitudes that most contemporary studies of religion include such questions without hesitation.

from the outset that no relationship between the dimensions studied and those neglected is either assumed or denied in the ensuing analysis.[10]

RITUAL INVOLVEMENT

Viewed from a multidimensional perspective, Episcopalians differ markedly in the extent and kinds of ties they have to their church. Their most extensive contact, as might be expected, is with its ritual life. Two-thirds—66 percent—say that they attend church services almost every Sunday, while only 9 percent say that they hardly ever attend except on Christmas and Easter. About four out of five say that they take Holy Communion at least once a month; 13 percent claim that they do so about once a week or more often.

Table 1 reports this evidence in detail and also shows the inter-relationship between attendance at worship services and taking Holy Communion. The high correspondence between participation in the two forms of ritual activity is, of course, scarcely surprising since taking Holy Communion automatically involves attendance at worship services.

In areas of church life which do not bear directly on worship and ritual, and which compete more directly with secular interests and values, parishioners' ties to their church are much weaker and less extensive. This is true of their participation in the "organizational" and "intellectual" life of the church.

ORGANIZATIONAL INVOLVEMENT

Aside from attending worship services, the principal formal contact that the average parishioner can have with his church is participation in its organizational life. The array of organizations operated by the typical Episcopal parish church afford opportunities to meet and interact with other parishioners in a wide variety of activities. Some, such as Altar Guilds, brotherhoods, and sisterhoods, are constituted primarily to enroll parishioners as workers

[10] Research currently underway in the Survey Research Center's *Research Program in Religion and Society* is directed specifically at an examination of the several dimensions of religious involvement and the interrelationships among them.

TABLE 1

As Might Be Expected, Parishioners Who Attend Church the Most Frequently Are Also More Likely to Take Holy Communion[a]

Frequency of taking Holy Communion	Attendance at Sunday worship services				
	Almost every Sunday	About twice/month	About once/month	Hardly ever except Christmas and Easter	Total[b]
More than once/week	5%	0%	0%	0%	3%
About once/week	15	1	0	0	10
Two or three times/month	27	20	1	1	21
About once/month	48	59	42	2	45
Less than once/month	2	11	26	23	8
Every three or four months	3	9	32	74	12
100%[c] =	962	190	171	88	1411[b]
No answer	17	6	6	53	82
Total number[b]	979	196	177	141	1493[b]
Distribution of responses on church attendance:	66%	13%	12%	9%	100%

[a] Throughout the book, the significance of statistical associations has been evaluated on the grounds of face validity and internal consistency. Formal tests of statistical significance have not been used for reasons similar to those presented in Seymour M. Lipset, Martin A. Trow and James S. Coleman, *Union Democracy: The Inside Politics of the International Typographical Union* (Glencoe, Ill.: The Free Press, 1956), pp. 427–432.

[b] Thirty-seven respondents did not answer the question pertaining to the frequency of church attendance; therefore the last row of percentages in the table is based on the 1,493 respondents who did answer the question. Similarly, only 1,411 parishioners answered both questions; the percentages in the main body of the table are based on those who did so. In most of the tables which follow, a small number of respondents did not answer the questions being examined. In each case, the percentages computed will be based on those parishioners who provided answers and the remainder will be omitted from the applicable tables.

[c] This designation (100%=) is used in this and subsequent tables to indicate the number of cases upon which percentages are based. All percentage computations have been rounded to the nearest whole percent, however, and the reader will note that the rounding procedure occasionally results in a column of percentages adding to 99 or 101 rather than exactly 100 percent.

in one or another aspect of the church's program. Others, such as Women's Auxiliaries, young people's and couples' clubs, afford opportunities, in some combination, for service, for education and simply for social interaction.

The parishioner is clearly under less constraint, either explicitly or implicitly, to participate in the church's organizational life than to attend worship services. The act of becoming a church member is, in effect, a commitment to participate in ritual observances to at least a minimum extent, but joining church organizations is a relatively more voluntary act. It is not surprising, therefore, that while all parishioners attend worship services to some extent, 43 percent have no organizational ties to their church. Among those who are members of church organizations, most—63 percent— belong to only one organization, 28 percent to two, and the remainder—9 percent—to three or more.

In one sense, the number of organizational connections that a parishioner has with his church may be interpreted as a measure of his attachment to the church—the more affiliations, the greater the attachment. However, such an interpretation doesn't take into account the fact that people differ in their general propensity toward belonging. Thus, it might be more significant that an "organization-phobe" belongs to one church organization than that an "organization-phile" belongs to three.

A superior measure of organizational involvement in the church, therefore, is one which specifies the degree to which a given parishioner's total organizational connections are church related. In this way, varying dispositions toward "joining" in general could be accounted for and parishioners would be distinguished in terms of the proportion of their organizational energy which is given to the church.

Since parishioners in the study were asked to list all the organizations to which they belonged, it was possible to score each on the proportion of his organizational memberships which were religious. This measure will be called the Index of Organizational Involvement. The distribution of parishioners on the index is presented in Table 2.

This new way of looking at the data permits some refinements in what has already been said about the organizational affiliations of church members. The 43 percent found to have no organizational ties with the church now can be further distinguished according to their secular affiliations. Eleven percent, it turns out, have no secular affiliations either, while 32 percent do belong to secular organizations. The 57 percent who belong to one or more church organizations differ markedly in the degree to which these memberships account for their total organizational

TABLE 2

DISTRIBUTION OF PARISHIONERS ACCORDING TO EXTENT OF THEIR
DEPENDENCE ON THE CHURCH AS A FOCUS FOR ORGANIZATIONAL LIFE

	Proportion of total organizations which are church related					
	100–75%	74–50%	49–25%	24–1%	0%	No group affiliations
Percentage of parishioners 100% = 1433[a]	12	19	18	8	32	11

[a] Ninety-seven parishioners provided insufficient information regarding their organizational activities and it was not possible to assign them valid scores on this index.

activities. Thirty-one percent belong to more church than secular organizations, while for 26 percent, the opposite is true.

INTELLECTUAL INVOLVEMENT

It would seem reasonable to suppose that parishioners who are deeply involved in the church's ritual and organizational life will be more likely to perceive the world through the eyes of the church. It is conceivable, however that some parishioners may be deeply committed to their church ritually and organizationally but still not find the church or religion to be particularly salient in their everyday lives. Their church activity may have very little relevance for what they think and do outside the walls of the church.

This possibility led to the development of an index of saliency which would be separate from ritual and organizational involvement. It was decided, in the absence of more satisfactory alternatives, to develop the index around a parishioner's responses to three questions: one pertaining to his magazine reading habits, a second relating to his perception of the church's influence on his ideas, and a third having to do with the sources to which he turns in a time of stress.

The Protestant Episcopal Church, like many churches, carries on an extensive publication program. It supports a book publishing operation and publishes a variety of periodicals at the diocesan and national levels. There are also a number of magazines of Episcopalian persuasion which are published unofficially. The parishioner therefore has considerable sources available to him if he wishes to become better informed about the intellectual life of his church. The extent to which a parishioner takes ad- , vantage of the religious magazines available to him will constitute part of what we shall call intellectual involvement.[11] A failure to read church periodicals cannot be interpreted, of course, as denoting an absence of intellectual concern about one's church. To do so would involve so classifying the 77 percent of Episcopalians who do not read church journals. Nevertheless, the 23 percent who are readers are making an investment of their time and energy which is prima facie evidence of relatively greater interest and concern. And, among these readers, the more their magazine selections are limited to church periodicals the greater their interest would seem to be.

It turns out that only 5 percent of all parishioners depend primarily on church publications for their magazine diet—50 percent or more of the magazines they read are church related. The balance of the subscribers, constituting 18 percent of all parishioners, read more secular than religious periodicals.

Taken alone, this information on magazine reading habits would scarcely constitute a sufficient basis for distinguishing Episcopalians according to their overall intellectual interest in the church. Nonetheless, combining it with other indicators of this dimension does create a useable index. The additional evidence of intellectual involvement was taken from the responses to two questions.

> If you wanted advice or information about a difficult community problem (not necessarily a family problem), would you do any of the following?
>
> ——Go to your minister ——Read the Bible
> ——Pray ——Read a religious book
> ——Go to Communion more ——None of these
> often

[11] It should be noted that the present use of this term differs from the meaning assigned it in the senior author's theoretical discussion. Nothing in the questionnaire adequately tapped the extent of parishioners' knowledge about their church, but the three questions now under consideration do afford an opportunity to measure an aspect of involvement which differs from both the ritual and organizational aspects. For that reason, it is important to take advantage of this additional dimension for purposes of the present study; the term intellectual involvement will be used only for lack of a better label.

Everyone's ideas change from time to time. Would you say that your Church has played any part in changing your opinions?

———Yes, the Church has changed my opinions a great deal.
———Yes, the Church has changed my opinions somewhat.
———I don't know whether the Church has changed my opinions.
———No, I don't think the Church has changed my opinions.

There is a reasonably strong relationship between magazine reading habits and the answers to these two questions. Parishioners who depend heavily on church periodicals are much more likely to refer to the Bible or other religious books in answering the first question, and/or to respond "Yes, the Church has changed my opinions a great deal" in answer to the second. Those parishioners who depend on church periodicals only moderately or not at all are considerably less likely to choose these responses (see Table 3).

TABLE 3

PARISHIONERS WHO ARE HIGHLY DEPENDENT ON CHURCH MAGAZINES ACKNOWLEDGE A GREATER INFLUENCE OF THE CHURCH AND/OR RELIGIOUS BOOKS ON THEIR IDEAS

	Proportion of total magazine fare which is church related[a]		
	100–50%	49–1%	0%
Percentage who claim church is an important influence on their ideas and/or rely on religious books for meeting problems	54 (64)	41 (245)	26 (1032)

[a] Parishioners who do not report reading any magazines are omitted from this table.

The relationship revealed in Table 3 does not in any sense approach a perfect correlation. If it did, we would be justified in using only one of the indicators as a measure of intellectual involvement in itself. In view of the observed relationship, we have combined all three aspects to create a rudimentary, but still useful, index of intellectual involvement. Parishioners whose reading of church-related magazines comprise 50 percent or more of their total magazine consumption, and/or those who consider the church a major influence on their ideas and rely on religious literature for meeting problems have been designated as exhibiting "high" intellectual involvement. Those who have none of these characteristics are classified as having "low" intellectual involvement in the church. Parishioners giving mixed responses are classified between the two extremes. (A detailed description of the construction of this index is to be found in Appendix B.)

TABLE 4

DISTRIBUTION OF PARISHIONERS ON INDEX OF
INTELLECTUAL INVOLVEMENT IN THE CHURCH

	Level of intellectual involvement			
	High	Moderately high	Moderately low	Low
Percentage of parishioners 100% = 1424	10	8	28	55

The majority of parishioners—55 percent—are classified at the lowest point on the index (Table 4). A much smaller proportion—10 percent—are placed at its highest point. These figures have to be interpreted, of course, in relative rather than absolute terms. We cannot say just how much intellectual involvement is represented by each score in the index. We can infer, however, that within the framework of the indicators used, the higher the score, the greater the involvement.[12]

12 The reader should understand this line of reasoning, since much of the subsequent analysis will be based on measures of this type. The meaning implicit in the measures of ritual and organizational involvement is direct and clear. Parishioners who attend worship services every Sunday, for example, obviously have a higher ritual involvement than those who do not. Yet in many instances it is more useful to create a measure of some phenomenon through the combination of several types of relevant information, as has been done in the case of intellectual involvement. In such a case, it is useful to think of the two "ideal types" of response patterns: those who appear "highly" involved on all of the items, and those who appear "low" on all. Parishioners giving mixed responses on the several items may be viewed as relatively "high" or "low," in terms of their tendency toward one or the other of the ideal types.

THE PATTERNING OF INVOLVEMENT

The analysis, thus far, has shown that parishioners can be distinguished in terms of the extent of their involvement in the ritual and organizational life of their church and in the degree of their intellectual interest in it as well. The indicators used produce a considerably higher proportion observing ritual than participating in church organizations, with fewer still appearing to be intellectually involved in their church.

The obvious next step is to explore the relationships between these different measures of involvement. As might be expected, they are highly related. Parishioners who score "high" on the indices of organizational involvement or intellectual involvement,

TABLE 5

THE MORE ORGANIZATIONALLY OR INTELLECTUALLY INVOLVED A PARISHIONER
IS IN HIS CHURCH, THE MORE LIKELY HE IS TO OBSERVE RITUAL REGULARLY

	Level of organizational involvement[a]			
	High	Moderately high	Moderately low	Low
Percentage of parishioners who observe ritual regularly[b]	82	80	71	51
	(165)[c]	(268)	(382)	(455)

	Level of intellectual involvement[a]			
	High	Moderately high	Moderately low	Low
Percentage of parishioners who observe ritual regularly[b]	88	83	77	55
	(135)	(106)	(387)	(796)

[a] The four levels of involvement ("high," "moderately high," etc.) for the organizational and intellectual dimensions are defined in Appendix B. Persons for whom no organizational involvement scores could be computed have been omitted from the first half of the table. Those who could not be scored on intellectual involvement have been omitted from the second half. The omissions include, respectively, those who reported no organizational activities, and those who do not read any magazines.

[b] "High" ritual involvement or "regular" observation of ritual will be defined as attending church "almost every Sunday." Those parishioners who reported attending less frequently will be scored "low" on ritual involvement.

[c] The figures in parentheses in this and following tables indicate the number of relevant cases upon which the percentages are computed. For example, of 165 parishioners who were scored "high" on organizational involvement, 82% reported attending church regularly. Of the 796 parishioners who were scored "low" on intellectual involvement, 55% reported regular church attendance.

INVOLVEMENT IN CHURCH LIFE   29

for example, are much more likely to attend worship services regularly than those who score "low" on these indices (Table 5).

The likelihood of observing ritual regularly is heightened even further if the parishioner is both organizationally and intellectually involved in his church (Table 6).

TABLE 6

RITUAL OBSERVANCE IS HIGHLY SENSITIVE TO ORGANIZATIONAL
AND INTELLECTUAL INVOLVEMENT IN THE CHURCH[a]

Level of intellectual involvement	Percentage of parishioners who observe ritual regularly[a]		
	Level of organizational involvement		
	High or moderately high	Moderately low	Low
High or moderately high	94 (107)	85 (59)	75 (42)
Moderately low	85 (135)	82 (116)	66 (92)
Low	71 (170)	60 (195)	43 (285)

[a] Periodically throughout the analysis, we shall want to examine the simultaneous interrelationships of three or more variables. Table 6 shows the format for such an examination. This table presents a nine-cell matrix created by cross-tabulating parishioners' scores on organizational and intellectual involvement. For each of the nine cells, the proportion of parishioners who are also scored "high" on ritual involvement is computed. For example, in the upper left corner of the table, we note that 107 parishioners were scored either "high" or "moderately high" on both organizational and intellectual involvement; the number in parenthesis indicates the size of the cell. Of these parishioners, 94% were also scored "high" on ritual involvement. By contrast, we note that 285 parishioners were scored "low" on both organizational and intellectual involvement; of these, only 43% were scored "high" on ritual.

Virtually all parishioners who score "high" on both the indices of organizational and intellectual involvement observe ritual regularly. Those who score "low" on both indices are least likely to observe ritual regularly, with a difference of 51 percentage points separating the two extremes. Although organizational and intellectual involvement are themselves interrelated, each produces an independent effect on ritual observance. Note the descending order of probability of observing ritual regularly as we move from the top to bottom of each column in Table 6 and from left to right in each row.

Thus in reading across the rows of the table, it is clear that whatever the level of parishioners' intellectual involvement, organizational involvement is still related to ritual observance. Similarly, in reading down the columns of the tables, it is apparent that for each level of organizational involvement, the association between intellectual and ritual involvement is still in evidence. Finally, if a diagonal line is drawn connecting the upper-left and the lower-right corners of the table, we note that the percentages on opposite sides of the line are reasonably close to one another if not exactly the same. This indicates that the relative strengths of intellectual and organizational involvement in predicting ritual involvement are roughly the same when the three variables are examined simultaneously.

Organizational and intellectual involvement, both separately and in combination, then, are associated with the parishioner's ritual involvement in his parish church. However, this tells us nothing about the time order of the various types of involvement. The data themselves cannot provide this information. It seems reasonable to infer, nonetheless, that the first "real" expression of commitment to the church is manifested in ritual observance. This leads then to involvement in church organizations and a heightening of the church's intellectual saliency. This, in turn, may feed back to intensify the commitment to ritual observance. In other words, the three aspects of involvement mutually reinforce one another with the initial impetus, most probably, stemming from attendance at worship services.

A GENERAL INDEX OF CHURCH INVOLVEMENT

The fact that ritual, organizational, and intellectual involvement in church life are highly interrelated justifies the additional construction of a more general index of church involvement. The use of such an index should not be taken to imply that scores on that index represent, strictly speaking, a single dimension of religious involvement. The primary purpose of such a general index is to simplify analysis in the remainder of the study. Thus, parishioners were assigned numerical scores commensurate with their involvement on each of the individual dimensions. The scores assigned were then combined to produce a composite score indicating overall commitment to the church. (A detailed description of the construction of this index may be found in Appendix B.) The range of composite scores runs from 5 (highest involvement) to 0 (lowest involvement), and the distribution of scores is presented in Table 7.

TABLE 7

DISTRIBUTION OF PARISHIONERS ON A COMPOSITE INDEX OF CHURCH INVOLVEMENT

	Composite Index of Involvement					
	High					Low
	5	4	3	2	1	0
Percentage of parishioners 100% = 1201[a]	8	14	23	22	19	14

[a] Since it was not possible to score all parishioners on the indices of organizational and intellectual involvement, it was consequently impossible to assign those parishioners C.I.I. scores. Thus, the reader will note a reduction in the number of cases shown in this table.

Relatively fewer parishioners fall into the two extreme categories than into the middle categories of the index. Only 8 percent show a "high" involvement whereas 14 percent exhibit virtually no involvement. Most parishioners accordingly are distributed between the two extremes with the shape of the frequency distribution being skewed somewhat in the direction of "low" involvement in church life as it is measured here.

In terms of the composite index, it seems reasonable to assume that the ideal type of parishioner, from the church's viewpoint, would be represented by a score of 5. These parishioners combine qualities on which the church could be expected to place a fairly high premium. They observe ritual regularly—an activity which the church consistently reaffirms as desirable. They are deeply devoted to the organizational life of the church; the very existence of church organizations is evidence enough that the church values participation therein. And they have a considerable intellectual involvement in the church. The church can hardly be expected to want it otherwise.

That the church would, in fact, value these characteristics in its parishioners will be a working assumption for the analysis. The issue will be reviewed once again after more has been

learned about the conditions contributing to differential involvement and about its consequences for other aspects of the parishioners' attitudes and behavior.[13]

INTERPRETATION AND VALIDATION
OF THE COMPOSITE INDEX OF INVOLVEMENT

The Composite Index of Involvement (C.I.I.) is intended to
represent the centrality of the church in the parishioner's life—to
distinguish, so to speak, those parishioners whose primary commitments in life are church-oriented from those who, while re-
taining their church membership, are primarily concerned with
"secular" matters.[14] The index gives greater weight to the proportion of the parishioner's total extra-curricular energies which
are devoted to the church than to the sheer amount of church
activity per se. Consequently, it is possible that two parishioners
may end up with different scores on the C.I.I., while being equally
observant ritually, belonging to the same number of church organizations, and reading the same church periodicals. The
parishioner who, in addition to his church activity, is also more
active in community organizations and who reads extensively in
the "secular" press would receive the lower C.I.I. score. He is,
in effect, devoting less of his available energies to the church.

Given the theoretical distinction between degree of involvement and level of activity, one might well ask if this distinction
is manifested in reality. If the concepts are empirically distinct,
shouldn't we also consider an index of activity as well as one of

[13] See Chapter 9.

[14] The reader must realize, of course, that this orientation is inferred
from the fact that such parishioners do not demonstrate any ritual, organizational or intellectual involvement in the church. It is possible that
some parishioners who have been scored "low" on the composite index
are deeply committed to the church or to religion more generally in ways
which cannot be measured in the present analysis. Nonetheless, it should
be clear that C.I.I. scores provide the best available guide to the saliency
of the church for parishioners in the present context. While some
parishioners may be wrongly judged by this procedure, the number of
errors should be minimized by the use of scores on the composite index.
This, then, is another working assumption of the analysis.

involvement? Or are they so highly interrelated that the C.I.I. may constitute an index of activity as well? To answer these questions, parishioners were first divided according to their scores on the C.I.I. For each group, the mean number of church organizations to which they belong and the mean number of church periodicals which they read were computed. As Table 8 shows, both of these measures of activity rise with increasing involvement. With these figures we can reasonably interpret the C.I.I. to represent not only involvement but church activity as well.

TABLE 8

MEAN NUMBER OF MEMBERSHIPS IN CHURCH ORGANIZATIONS AND MEAN
NUMBER OF CHURCH PERIODICALS READ ACCORDING TO PARISHIONERS'
SCORES ON THE COMPOSITE INDEX OF INVOLVEMENT

	Composite Index of Involvement					
	High					Low
	5	4	3	2	1	0
Mean number of church organizations belonged to	1.91 (97)	1.75 (167)	1.31 (272)	.92 (257)	.38 (227)	.00 (162)
Mean number of church periodicals read	1.24 (89)	.79 (164)	.38 (271)	.11 (257)	.03 (230)	.00 (162)

While this exercise has helped to clarify the meaning of the C.I.I., it does not constitute a validation of the index. For this purpose it is necessary to consider how satisfactorily the parishioner's C.I.I. score represents aspects of his commitment to the church other than those used in the construction of the index. The independent measures available for purposes of validation are:

1. Frequency of taking Holy Communion. (This measure, it will be recalled, was not used in the development of the C.I.I. although marginal tabulations of responses were presented earlier.)

2. Regularity of attendance at meetings of church organizations.

3. Whether or not the parishioner has ever held an office in a church organization.

4. The proportion of church organizations belonged to in which the parishioner has held office.

5. Whether or not the parishioner belongs to a Christian Social Relations group. (These are groups organized in some parishes for the purpose of carrying on discussion of current affairs from the perspective of Christian principles.)

6. Whether the parishioner is informed about the existence of a C.S.R. group in his parish (i.e., indicated negatively by the response "don't know").

7. Proportion of parishioners who would not turn to a religious source for advice on a difficult community problem.[15]

The first of these measures bears on ritual observance, the next four have to do with organizational commitment to the church, and the last one relates to what has been previously referred to as intellectual involvement, that is, the degree to which religious ideas are salient for the individual parishioner's secular life. Table 9 reports the parishioners' responses on each of these items according to their scores on the C.I.I.

Almost without exception, the higher the parishioner's C.I.I. score, the more he manifests church involvement on each of these independent measures. There is a positive relationship between the C.I.I. score and frequency of taking Holy Communion, regularity of attendance at meetings of church organizations, proportion of parishioners who now or in the past have been officers in church organizations, proportion of church organizations belonged to in which the parishioner has held office, and the proportion of parishioners who are members of a Christian Social Relations Group. In turn, as one would expect, there is a negative relationship between C.I.I. scores and the proportion of parishioners who do not know whether their parish has a

[15] It will be recalled that parishioners were asked: "If you wanted advice or information about a difficult community problem (not necessarily a family problem), would you do any of the following: go to your minister; read the Bible; pray; read a religious book, go to communion more often; none of these." The responses "read the Bible" and "read a religious book" were used in the construction of the intellectual involvement index. As a validating test, we may now compare the proportion of parishioners at each level of involvement (measured by the C.I.I.) who answered they would turn to none of the religious sources.

TABLE 9

The Greater the Parishioner's Score on the Composite Index of Involvement the Greater His Involvement in the Church in Other Ways as Well

| | Composite Index of Involvement | | | | | |
| | High | | | | | Low |
	5	4	3	2	1	0
Holy Communion						
1. Percentage taking Holy Communion once a week or more	34	23	15	10	7	0
Attendance at church meetings						
2. Percentage of members attending 50% of time or more (of those who belong to church organizations)	80	77	70	67	46	...ᵃ
Officer in church organizations						
3. Percentage holding office now or in the past	73	73	67	56	41	12
4. Percentage of present members who are officers in 50% or more of organizations belonged to (of those who belong to church organizations)	64	65	54	53	45	...ᵃ
C.S.R. group						
5. Percentage who are members in parishes having such groups	63	60	43	44	30	8
6. Percentage who don't know whether or not their parish church has a C.S.R. group	17	23	28	32	44	59
Advice on community problems						
7. Percentage who would turn to non-religious source for advice	3	8	12	23	25	41
Samples upon which percentages are based (100%):						
1. Total parishioners less no answers	99	169	275	256	217	135
2. Total parishioners who are members of organizations	102	171	245	187	78	0
3. Total parishioners less no answers	98	163	265	248	221	156
4. Total parishioners who are members of organizations	102	171	245	187	78	0
5. Total parishioners in churches having C.S.R. groups	54	70	100	93	57	36
6. Total parishioners less no answers	95	163	263	246	224	155
7. Total parishioners less no answers	102	171	276	259	230	163
Total number	102	171	276	259	230	163

ᵃ There are no parishioners in these cells.

Christian Social Relations Group and who would not turn to a religious source for advice on a difficult community problem.

The results presented in Table 9, therefore, function to validate the Composite Index of Involvement as a measure of the strength of parishioners' ties to their church. On a wide range of issues which might serve as additional indications of church involvement, the C.I.I. has been seen to predict clearly and consistently the distribution of responses. In the subsequent analysis, this composite index will be used as the basic measure of church involvement to facilitate the examination of the sources and consequences of parishioners' varying orientations to church life. Nonetheless, the conceptual independence of the three separate involvement indices—ritual, organizational and intellectual—must still be recognized and maintained. Therefore, while the bulk of the investigation will use the C.I.I., we shall also be interested in examining the three separate indices periodically throughout the analysis.

SUMMARY

In this chapter, we have focused attention on the difficult task of making meaningful "religious" distinctions among people. Because the 1,530 respondents in this study are all members of Episcopal parishes, and in light of the data available for examination, we have restricted the "religious" distinctions in this instance to the differential strengths of parishioners' ties to their churches. Three subsidiary measures of commitment—ritual, organizational and intellectual involvement—were found to be highly interrelated and were therefore combined to form a Composite Index of Involvement. This index, in turn, was found to predict the strength of parishioners' ties to their church on a variety of independent measures of involvement and activity.

The fact that parishioners are differentially involved in the church scarcely required documentation, of course. Having made the distinctions in a reasonably precise way, however, we are now in a position to consider two related questions concerning differential commitment. First, how can the differences be accounted for—what are the factors which lead some parishioners to a deeper attachment than others? Second, what are the effects of involvement—are the more committed led to act, think or behave differently as a consequence, and if so, in what ways? These questions provide the outline for the remainder of the inquiry.

Chapter 2

Sex, the Life Cycle and Church Involvement

In Chapter 1 it was evident that Episcopalians differ markedly in the closeness of their ties to the church. Some appeared highly committed to it ritually, organizationally and intellectually; some were only moderately committed, while still others, judging from the available indicators, seem to have made very little commitment beyond the fact of church membership. In this and the following three chapters, we shall be concerned with learning why these differences exist. A useful way to begin conceptualizing this problem is to distinguish first between those factors which facilitate active involvement in the church and those which motivate it.

Clearly, any complete understanding of involvement must begin by determining the extent to which a person's objective situation allows him to participate actively in the church. It cannot be taken for granted that every parishioner enjoys an equal opportunity in this respect. The salesman, for example, who spends half of his time away from home is obviously less able to involve himself deeply in the life of his church than the clerk whose occupational responsibilities are limited to working at a nearby office seven hours a day, five days a week. Similarly, a person who is physically handicapped is undoubtedly less capable of being active than his healthy counterpart. To some extent, therefore, differential church involvement should reflect the relative presence or absence of facilitating factors in the parishioner's environment.

Yet, the mere presence of facilitating factors is hardly sufficient to assure participation. A parishioner must be motivated to participate in the church as well. Motivation, of course, is a

38

complex concept which has received considerable attention from psychologists. Its forms and effects are manifold. For the purposes of the present examination, however, we shall consider as "motivating factors" those needs and desires which parishioners may experience, consciously or unconsciously, which church involvement seems either to satisfy or to sublimate. For example, if a lonely person turns to his church for the fellowship he desires, then loneliness will be viewed as a factor which motivates church involvement for that person.

There are two difficulties which will be experienced in this examination of motivating factors. First, the ultimate sources of a parishioner's needs and desires may vary considerably; they may derive from certain aspects of his personality, from his objective social situation, or, more likely, from some combination of both. For example, the desire for social status is not only a consequence of an individual's objective situation, but also reflects his perception of the social structure, and of his position within it. Since the data pertaining to the sample of Episcopalian parishioners offer no information regarding these subjective feelings, the investigation must be restricted to those objective factors about which data were collected.

Second, the church may function to resolve completely a salient need for one person, while proving totally irrelevant in resolving a similar need for another. Thus, one person may find that church involvement overcomes his feelings of loneliness while other lonely people may derive no satisfaction at all from being active in the church. Or, church involvement may provide the social status sought by one person, while offering no solution to a similar desire in another. In an analysis such as this, we can only hope to discover those motivating factors which most consistently lead many parishioners to intensify the level of their church involvement.

Such limitations notwithstanding, the intent of the study is to demonstrate that several determinable social situations generate needs or desires among parishioners which appear to be satisfied, or at least sublimated, through intense church participation. Furthermore, these social situations are not of a religious nature themselves but suggest, rather, the functions of religion in mediating certain problems experienced in secular society.

In their essentials, these remarks are as applicable to participation in secular voluntary associations as to church involvement. Commitment in either instance must be both facilitated and motivated. The factors facilitating involvement in one kind of organization are not likely to differ significantly from those facilitating commitment to another. In all cases, the member must be in an objective situation which allows him the time and opportunity to be highly active. Further, to the extent that secular and religious organizations function to alleviate the same kinds of needs, the motivating factors at work are likely to be the same. For the person who is primarily concerned with acquiring symbols of social status, becoming involved in the Episcopal Church may prove as functional as attaching himself actively to the Junior League. Similarly, for the lonely person, the church, the lodge and the lonely hearts club may be functionally equivalent. The differences which do exist probably derive from the unique functions served by different kinds of voluntary associations. The political club is not overtly capable of meeting the religious needs of its members. In turn, the church is not the most obvious vehicle for satisfying a desire for political participation. Since the present data deal primarily with involvement in the church, they do not permit further elaboration of these comparative notions. However, as shall be seen, differential commitment to the church cannot be wholly or even largely explained in terms of the unique, religious functions it is designed to serve.

Exploratory observations such as these should underscore the formidability of the task created by our initial question: what are the sources of differential church involvement? Quite clearly, we are not in a position to follow through fully on all the implications suggested above. The data at hand are primarily useful in drawing attention to some of the conditions in a parishioner's social situation which relate to the church ties he establishes. Some of these conditions may seem to fall into the general category of facilitating factors. Others, in turn, may be seen more logically in motivational terms. Very often, however, the distinctions will not be wholly clear, and we may not be able to determine the proper classification of some factors found to be related to church involvement.

This chapter deals primarily with the fluctuations in church involvement which appear over the course of the parishioner's life cycle. On the one hand, we suspect that opportunities for active participation will vary according to the parishioner's location in the cycle. Similarly, it is reasonable to assume the functions served by church involvement will not be consistent throughout life. Since men and women may differ in their opportunities as well as their motivations to associate closely with the church, the two sexes are considered separately, though comparatively. We now turn to some introductory observations on the overall patterning of church involvement among men and women.

SEX AND INVOLVEMENT

There is abundant evidence to the effect that the church is a more salient institution for women than for men. Church membership and attendance statistics support such a conclusion; similarly, this appears in the result of a number of attitudinal and behavioral studies on the topic.[1]

The general finding is also substantiated among Episcopalians. Episcopal women are more likely to attend church on Sundays and more likely to become deeply involved in the church's organizational life than are men. Correspondingly, the church and religion are more salient for Episcopal women intellectually. All this can be seen in Table 10 which reports for both men and

[1] Michael Argyle, in his *Religious Behavior* (Glencoe: The Free Press, 1959), examined data from the 1936 Census of Religious Bodies and found American women to outnumber men in church membership in all but the Eastern Orthodox Church. Female overrepresentation ranged from the ratio of 1.09 women to every man in the Roman Catholic Church all the way to a ratio of 3.19 among Christian Scientists. In 1954, George Gallup discovered 83 percent of his sample of American women claiming church membership, as contrasted with 75 percent of the men in his sample. (Reported in Leo Rosten, ed., *Religions of America*, New York: Simon and Schuster, 1955, p. 239.) Gallup arrived at comparable findings regarding church attendance; in a 1961 poll, 50 percent of his female sample reported attending church weekly as opposed to 43 percent of his men. (Reported in Rosten, *op. cit.*, 1963 edition, p. 247.) Similar differences are discovered with respect to belief in God and beliefs in an after-life as well as in the frequency of private prayers. (For a summary of these and other findings on this general topic, see Argyle, *op. cit.*, pp. 71–79.)

TABLE 10

WOMEN ARE MORE HIGHLY INVOLVED IN THE CHURCH THAN MEN

	Mean involvement scores	
Types of involvement	Men	Women
Ritual involvement	.64	.70
Organizational involvement	.31	.62
Intellectual involvement	.24	.36
Composite Index of Involvement	.35	.53
Number in sample	450	729

women the mean involvement scores on the sub-indices of involvement—ritual, organizational, and intellectual—as well as on the composite index. The range of mean involvement scores on each of these indices has been standardized to extend from a "low" of *0* to a "high" of *1.0*; the higher the score, the higher the involvement.[2]

[2] Standardized mean scores on involvement will be used frequently throughout the analysis to facilitate clarity in making group comparisons. In making the computation, the individual scores of parishioners in a given group are totalled and divided by the number of people in the group. This "average" score is then divided by the highest possible score on the index, thus placing the group score within the range from *0* to *1.0*. Hence in Table 10, the individual C.I.I. scores for the 450 men were added together and the total was divided by 450. Since the highest possible C.I.I. score was *5*, the average score for men was divided by *5*, producing a standardized mean involvement score of *.35* on a scale ranging from *0* to *1.0*.

It should be noted that such a procedure tells us nothing about the range of scores within any given group. For example, a mean score of *2.5* on the original C.I.I. index could have resulted from all the respondents scoring in the extreme categories; one-half scoring *5* and the other half scoring *0*. Or it could have resulted from only scores of *2* and *3*, equally divided among the respondents. As a safeguard against this, the standard deviations were computed for the C.I.I. scores of men and women; the results suggest that for each sex, the individual scores are generally clustered around the mean average for that group.

Additionally, to insure that the sex differences were not simply an artifact of mean score construction, the several indices of involvement were divided into low, medium and high, and the proportions of men and women falling into the "high" categories were compared. Various cutting

As will be seen shortly, the size of the differences between men and women also varies according to the point in the life cycle at which comparisons are made. However, except for those under twenty-one years of age (where both sexes are about equally involved), women are more active than men at every point. Why should the church and religion be more salient for women than for men?

The notion that the differences may be biologically determined enjoys, by now, very little currency. The most commonly expressed explanation draws upon the differential roles of men and women in American society. Although the differences in sex roles have decreased over the years, they have hardly disappeared. Upon reaching independent adulthood, women modally become wives and mothers. Men, while becoming husbands and fathers, also become breadwinners. So, it is frequently argued, the demands imposed by the family role of the mother and by the occupational role of the father have contrasting effects on church involvement. A more "natural" pathway to the church seems to exist for the wife and mother than for the breadwinner.

From an historical perspective, the relatively close ties between the church and the family have been amply documented. One observer, L. F. Wood, has suggested that the family and church have virtually identical value systems, share similar symbols, and appeal to the same sentiments. "The church has its roots in the family values. Witness such ideas as God our Father, love as the heart of religion, the brotherhood of man as a philosophy of social living, the bearing of one another's burdens, the forgiveness of offenses, doing to others as we would have them do to us, and sacrificial love as the means of helping those who most need help. All these are attitudes rooted in family living and central in religion." [3]

points were used in defining a "high" score, and in each instance, the findings were relatively the same as those presented in Table 10.

These same checks were used in all subsequent tabulations using mean scores. In every instance, the standard deviations indicate a clustering around the mean average. In addition, the results using mean scores corresponded with those obtained using a percentage.

[3] L. F. Wood, "Church Problems in Marriage Education," *The Annals of the American Academy of Political and Social Science*, 272 (November, 1950), p. 177.

While one may hesitate to accept Wood's contentions fully, his remarks are echoed in more moderate form by most church historians. Even today, with increasing secular attention being focused on the functions and needs of the family, the evidence is fairly clear that the church plays a relatively more important part in family life and exercises more influence over the structure of the family than over any other social institution. This is most evident in the major role which the church continues to play at the major rites of passage—birth, marriage and death. Moreover, with respect to the values of family life, the church is still influential in setting standards for sexual conduct, family planning, and the education of the young.

The church itself reaffirms its ties with the family in a variety of ways. Family life is frequently a topic for sermons. Much of the church's program is family-centered. And who can have missed the ubiquitous posters bearing the slogan: "The family that prays together stays together."

While the bonds linking family and church are still relatively strong today, those once connecting the church and economic life have weakened extensively over the years. A number of important historical investigations have pointed out the close relationship between religious values and the rise of capitalism.[4] While according to one recent study, this historical link has not been entirely severed, it seems patently clear that the contemporary church is more concerned with continuing to influence family values than with reasserting its historical authority in the economic realm.[5] As Helen Beem Gouldner comments: "The

[4] The classic statements of this thesis are to be found in Max Weber's *The Protestant Ethic and the Spirit of Capitalism,* trans. Talcott Parsons (New York: Charles Scribner's Sons, 1930) and in R. H. Tawney's *Religion and the Rise of Capitalism* (New York: Harcourt, Brace, 1926).

[5] In his examination of Detroiters, Gerhard Lenski (*The Religious Factor,* Garden City, N.Y.: Doubleday, 1955) was primarily interested in determining the possibly continuing effect of religion on economic values, particularly as it was discussed by Weber. Lenski himself admits that the results are inconclusive; the following summary demonstrates the inconsistencies of his findings.

"*As a general rule, commitment to the spirit of capitalism:*
(1) is especially frequent among white Protestants and Jews;
(2) is much less frequent among Catholics and Negro Protestants, even when position in the class system is held constant;

growth of industrial capitalism with its specialized skills, complex organization and dependence on an impersonal market has been accompanied by increasing autonomy of economic institutions: (1) the separation of economics and religion. . . ." [6]

Given the church's greater concern for family life, it might very well be concluded that the woman's more concentrated family role would be a factor motivating deeper church involvement than is apparent among men. Nonetheless, it cannot be overlooked that the woman's role also facilitates greater involvement. Women, as compared to men, simply have more time to devote to the church. This is borne out by the fact that the sex difference in involvement is more strikingly apparent in the organizational than in the ritual life of the church (recall Table 10). Clearly, organizational involvement requires a greater expenditure of time than ritual observance. The church's organizational program gives recognition to this difference, also. More of its activities are oriented toward women exclusively than toward men alone or toward the two sexes participating together.

It should be evident at this point that the parishioner's sex has at least a partial influence on the extent of his or her church involvement. But while differential sex roles may provide part of the explanation for the broad differences in involvement, other factors must be introduced to achieve a more refined understanding; one such factor is position in the life cycle.

CHURCH INVOLVEMENT AND
THE LIFE CYCLE: WOMEN

The view that religious interest varies over the course of the life cycle has been expressed by a number of observers. Moreover,

---

(3) is positively linked with regularity of church attendance among Protestants, both Negro and white;

(4) is negatively correlated with communal involvement both among white Protesants and Catholics;

(5) is linked with a high level of devotionalism in all three of the larger socio-religious groups: Catholic, white Protestant, and Negro Protestant;

(6) stands in no consistent relationship to degree of doctrinal orthodoxy." (Lenski, p. 115.)

[6] Helen Beem Gouldner, "Industrial Sociology," in *Sociology* by Leonard Broom and Philip Selznick (New York: Row, Peterson, 1958), p. 510.

there is a good deal of empirical evidence not only to document the variation, but also to suggest it follows a fairly consistent pattern. Religious interest is relatively high during adolescence, it declines during early adulthood, and slowly rises again throughout the remainder of life.[7] The present data permit us to determine whether the observed pattern also applies to Episcopalians. Moreover, we shall be able to make that determination with some refinements of previous research procedures which have relied exclusively on age to distinguish stages of life.

The journey through life is clearly more than the simple fact of growing older. It involves the assumption of different roles and responsibilities as one proceeds from infancy to adolescence, from courtship to marriage and further on to the stages of child-bearing, child-rearing, and finally, retirement. Much of what has already been said about the connections between religion and the family suggests that an analysis of religious involvement over the life cycle must be cognizant of a person's family role as well as his age. Thus the life cycle considered here, while it will distinguish three age categories, will dwell also on important events which take place within those age groups, namely marriage and the bearing and raising of children.

Ideally, of course, the relationship between life cycle and involvement should be examined by means of a longitudinal study; the involvement of given individuals would be measured periodically over the span of their lifetimes. Such a procedure is clearly impractical. Nonetheless, it is possible to approximate a longitudinal study through the use of cross-sectional data such as are available for the present analysis. By comparing—at a given time—the involvement of parishioners representing different stages in life, it is possible to infer the changes which would take place during the lifetimes of individual parishioners.

This inference is based on the implicit assumption that the profile of involvement across the life cycle of Episcopalians in

---

[7] The reader is particularly referred to the summary of findings presented in Argyle, *op. cit.*, chap. 6. Argyle compared five studies seeking to describe the profile of religious involvement over the life cycle, reflecting ritual participation, religious belief and private devotion. In each instance, the pattern of involvement was essentially the same as the one described above.

1952 would not differ significantly from the profile obtained from data collected at some other time. Therefore, if the older Episcopalians in the study are more involved than their younger counterparts, it will be inferred that parishioners generally increase their involvement as they grow older.[8] This basic assumption and the inferences derived from it would not be justified if some historical peculiarity led to a profile of involvement in 1952 which was not generally typical. Grounds for assuming such a peculiarity are not readily apparent, however, and we shall see shortly that the profile of involvement among Episcopalians in 1952 does not differ significantly from the findings collected by Argyle and others over the years.

In combining age, marriage and parenthood, however, we face an immediate difficulty. People do not all marry at the same time, nor do they produce children according to any specified schedule. Some never marry at all; still others never become parents. Nonetheless, it is possible to speak of a typical life cycle —one which is characterized by an unmarried adolescence and young adulthood, marriage some time during the late teens or the twenties, and the subsequent birth and growth of children. By establishing such a "normative" life cycle, it is possible to place the majority of respondents at more or less common stages of life. But, since there are no formal standards pertaining to the times for marriage and child-birth in American society, the categories used must be somewhat arbitrary and can only reflect the modal practices of contemporary Americans. For present purposes, Episcopalians were divided into the following "normal" stages of life:

1. Under thirty years of age and unmarried.

2. Under thirty years of age, married, but childless.

3. Under thirty years of age, married, with children twelve years old or younger.

[8] Strictly speaking, nonetheless, it should be pointed out that shifts in involvement, such as we shall infer from the data, must be taken to mean relative involvement, rather than specifying absolute levels. Therefore it is conceivable that in the face of a progressive decrease in church involvement throughout society, a given group of individuals might retain the same absolute level of involvement throughout their lives; we shall infer only that their relative level of involvement—compared with others around them—would increase.

4. Thirty to forty-nine years of age, married, with children twelve years old or younger.

5. Thirty to forty-nine years of age, married, with all children thirteen or older.

6. Fifty years of age or older, married, with all children thirteen or over.

Women who were thirty or older and still unmarried and/or childless will be omitted from the present analysis. These "deviants" from the normative life cycle will be considered in a separate, though comparative, analysis in the following chapter.

Table 11 reports the patterning of church involvement among women parishioners at each of the major stages of the life cycle; the figures represent the mean involvement scores of women at each stage, using the three sub-indices of involvement as well as the composite index. The table shows clearly that the ties of Episcopal women to their church vary as their life situations change. We shall turn now to a discussion of why these variations exist.

TABLE 11

WOMEN'S INVOLVEMENT IN THE CHURCH VARIES ACCORDING TO
THEIR LOCATION IN THE LIFE CYCLE

		Age and family status				
	29 or younger			30–49		50
	Un-married	Married, but childless	Children 12 and under	Children 12 and under	Children 13 and over	Children 13 and over
Mean involvement scores on:						
Ritual	.75	.60	.46	.58	.70	.72
Organizational	.48	.45	.44	.58	.66	.64
Intellectual	.29	.05	.19	.24	.37	.39
C.I.I.	.46	.32	.34	.45	.55	.55
Number in sample	65	10	40	113	133	101

Early Marital Life: The Weakening of Church Ties

The initial effect of marriage is to lessen the commitment of Episcopal women to their church. Whether judged on the basis of the Composite Index of Involvement or any of the sub-indices, women are less involved in the church at this point in the life cycle than are single women.

We can surmise that this is a period of major readjustment for the woman during which she will be preoccupied with her newly acquired responsibilities. Setting up house, establishing new routines, getting acquainted with new friends and relatives, and simply spending time with her husband are all likely to influence the amount of energy she can devote to the church. She is less likely to want to engage in organizational activities which will take her away from her husband. And, in some cases, at least, she may feel constrained to alter her own commitment to the church to mirror that of her husband.

As the "nuptial stage" of the life cycle gives way to the child-bearing period, a sharp decline is to be expected in ritual involvement. With the young child to care for, it is more difficult for both parents to attend worship services regularly. Organizational involvement scarcely changes at all from the previous stage, a somewhat surprising finding since care of the child would presumably have the effect of reducing opportunities for participation in this aspect of church life. Yet these women appear to maintain organizational ties to the church at about the same level as do the childless married women. Perhaps the availability of the husband to baby-sit might account for the absence of the expected change, but the data offer no means for testing this possibility. During the child-bearing period, there is a sharp recovery in intellectual involvement. This may represent a compensation for decreased ritual ties to the church, but it may also reflect a concern over the religious education of the children.

Viewing the involvement behavior of these women from the perspective of the entire life cycle, this is the period when most attention tends to be centered around the life and burdens of the family and when, consequently, opportunities for being active in the church are at about their lowest ebb.

The Renaissance of Interest in the Church

At the next stage of the life cycle, strong church ties tend to be reestablished. Women between the ages of thirty and forty-nine whose children are still under twelve years of age are appreciably more active in the church, in every way, than the younger mothers. In fact, they recover the ground lost when women leave their parental homes to get married. Note that the mean composite involvement score is *.45* at this stage, compared with *.46* for young, single women.

This renewal of interest in the church is not necessarily a function of these women being older, but rather, a result of their children growing up. The data do not tell us the exact ages of the children of parishioners; we only know whether they are under or over twelve years of age. Yet it is apparent that the children of the older women are much more likely to be of school age than the children whose mothers are younger than thirty. Common sense supports such a conclusion. So does other available information. Of the mothers aged thirty to forty-nine with young children, two-thirds belong to youth or school groups such as the P.T.A., while less than one-third of the younger mothers are members. Clearly, such interests arise only after the child enters the school system and are not prevalent among mothers with only preschoolers.

In this phase of the life cycle, then, a break occurs in the stress of caring for the child. A major share of the responsibility shifts from the mother to the school. Not only is the child enrolled in public school, but, very often, he is sent to Sunday School as well. The concomitant effect is to produce in the mother an interest in the institutions and agencies which assume the responsibility for her child's education. Thus, the interest in youth and school groups and the renewed interest in the church are, in effect, extensions of the mother's concern with the socialization and education of her children.

The Renaissance Continued

As the early child-rearing years pass and their children reach adolescence, Episcopalian women become more deeply involved in the church. Among women between ages thirty and forty-nine, those with older children score higher on every measure of involvement than their counterparts with younger children.

This increase in church involvement occurs despite the fact that these women are experiencing a major change in the direction and content of their interests and family responsibilities. No longer do their children dominate their leisure time and organizational life. Many lose interest in agencies of socialization. In ever greater numbers they give up membership in youth and school groups so that by the time they reach fifty years of age, less than one in eight retains affiliations (see Table 12).

TABLE 12

WOMEN LOSE INTEREST IN SCHOOL GROUPS BUT GAIN INTEREST
IN WELFARE GROUPS AS THEIR CHILDREN MATURE

	Age of children			
	12 years or younger		13 years or older	
	Age of mother			
	29 or younger	30–49	30–49	50+
Percentage of mothers who belong to youth or school groups	30	67	38	12
Percentage of mothers who belong to welfare groups	21	31	43	43
Number in sample	40	113	133	101

In the process, however, new interests develop—most frequently directed to humanitarian concerns. In Table 12 this is most clearly manifested by the sharp increase in the proportion of women who become members of groups whose programs are welfare-oriented.

This shift in interest as the woman is "emancipated" from domesticity has been commented upon by a number of observers, among them Talcott Parsons, who says: "[A] principal direction of emancipation [of the woman] from domesticity seems to lie in emphasis on what has been called the common humanistic element. This takes a variety of forms. . . . [One of these forms] consists in cultivation of serious interests and humanitarian obligations in community welfare situations and the like." [9]

In this restructuring and refocusing of interests, the church does not share the fate of the secular agencies of socialization, such as the P.T.A. It does not lose the loyalty of those whose

[9] Talcott Parsons, "Age and Sex in Social Structure of the United States," in *Essays in Sociological Theory* (Glencoe, Ill.: The Free Press, 1958), p. 97.

entry into church life was related to their concern with their children's religious education. On the contrary, as we have already observed, the church seems to retain the adherence of these women and even gains additional recruits, in the sense that more women become highly involved.

Unlike the secular agencies of socialization, the church's program is sufficiently ubiquitous to satisfy the interests of the "emancipated" woman, just as it served the familial interests of the mother. Women who are already highly involved in the church do not have to seek other outlets, if, for example, their interests have shifted from care of the young to care of the sick, the indigent, and the aged. At the same time, for some women who have not been highly involved at earlier stages, the church now offers an outlet for their newly developed humanitarian concerns as well. Some of them elect to satisfy these concerns through an increased involvement in the church rather than through secular welfare organizations.

This interpretation is supported by the finding (see Table 13) that women who are highly involved in the church and whose children have reached adolescence are less likely to belong to secular welfare groups than their counterparts who are less involved in the church. This suggests, though it clearly does not prove, that at this stage of the life cycle, being active in the

TABLE 13

CHURCH-INVOLVED WOMEN ARE LESS LIKELY
TO BELONG TO SECULAR WELFARE GROUPS

Women whose children are adolescents and whose own ages are:	Percentage who belong to secular welfare groups among those whose church involvement is:	
	High[a]	Low[b]
30 to 49	34	62
	(50)	(40)
50 or older	36	75
	(55)	(40)

[a] "High" involvement is defined as scores of 3 or higher on the Composite Index of Involvement.
[b] "Low" involvement is defined as scores of 2 or lower on the Composite Index of Involvement.

church may serve as a substitute for being active in secular welfare groups, and vice versa. Only a minority of women, as Table 13 shows, are active in both. The general propensity is for women to make a choice between the two.

The Time of "Final Decision"

As women reach the final phase of the life cycle, their concern for humanitarian-welfare pursuits seems even more intensified. This is particularly evident among those who are not deeply involved in the church. In Table 13, 62 percent of the women in this group who are between thirty and forty-nine years of age belong to secular welfare groups, as contrasted with 75 percent of those women fifty years old or older. It is reasonable to assume that this increased concern is typical of most women as they grow older, but that the channel through which they exercise their concern was established at an earlier age.

As seen in Table 11, there is no further increase in church involvement for the mother of adolescent children when she passes her fiftieth year. Thus, her "final decision" with reference to the church seems to occur when she is still relatively young —when she is in her thirties and forties and her children have reached adolescence. Either she has made the church a central part of her life by this time, seeking satisfaction of her interests through church involvement, or she depends on secular groups and activities to serve this function. Whatever her decision is at this point in her life, she tends to carry it through her old age provided her family remains intact.

MEN: THE LIFE CYCLE
AND CHURCH INVOLVEMENT

Earlier comparisons have shown that men are less prone to active participation in the church than women. However, the extent of the difference is not the same at all points in the life cycle, and the contrast also varies according to whether the composite index of involvement or the three sub-indices of involvement are used. Figure 1 shows the comparison between the sexes using the C.I.I.

The involvement of men diverges increasingly from that of

FIGURE 1

MEN'S INVOLVEMENT IN THE CHURCH DIVERGES MORE AND MORE
FROM THAT OF WOMEN AS THE LIFE CYCLE UNFOLDS

Mean involvement (*C.I.I.*)	Age and family status					
	29 or younger			30 to 49		50 or older
	Un-married	Married but childless	Children 12 and under	Children 12 and under	Children 13 and older	Children 13 and older

Mean involvement curve (C.I.I. scale from .00 to 1.00):

Men: .46 → .29 → .22 → .28 → .29 → .33
Women: .49 → .32 → .34 → .45 → .55 → .55

Number in sample:
Men: 46   13   11   99   59   75
Women: 65   10   40   113   133   103

Legend:
Men ————————
Women — — — — —

women as the life cycle unfolds. Both men and women are quite highly involved when they are young, unmarried, and still presumably under the influence of their parents. However, once they reach adulthood and embark on their own family and occupational careers, their levels of attachment to the church becomes increasingly dissimilar. Only at the final stage of the life cycle is there a slight reversal of the general trend toward increasing separation of the sexes.

Despite the growing divergence, however, there are similarities in the patterning of involvement over the life cycle. Though the turning points are not entirely parallel, the patterns tend toward a U-shaped curve in each instance—beginning with relatively high involvement, followed by a decline and then a recovery. It is primarily the difference in the extent of the recovery which accounts for the growing divergence between men and women.

The general propensity toward increasing differences in the behavior of the sexes is also evident when the comparisons are made using the sub-indices of involvement; it is most pronounced and unambiguous in the case of organizational involvement (see Table 14).

TABLE 14

MEN DIFFER LEAST FROM WOMEN IN RITUAL OBSERVANCE,
MOST IN ORGANIZATIONAL INVOLVEMENT

	Age and family status					
	29 or younger			30–49		50+
	Un-married	Married but childless	Children 12 and under	Children 12 and under	Children 13 and over	Children 13 and over
Mean involvement scores on:						
Ritual observance						
Women	.75	.60	.46	.58	.70	.72
Men	.80	.54	.55	.57	.57	.68
Difference	−.05	+.06	−.11	+.01	+.13	+.04
Organizational commitment						
Women	.48	.45	.44	.58	.66	.64
Men	.52	.31	.18	.25	.23	.27
Difference	−.04	+.14	+.26	+.33	+.43	+.37
Intellectual interest						
Women	.29	.05	.19	.24	.37	.39
Men	.23	.15	.09	.18	.21	.21
Difference	+.06	−.10	+.10	+.06	+.16	+.18
Number:						
Women	65	10	40	113	133	101
Men	46	13	11	99	59	75

Whatever index is used, the general pattern for both sexes is the same: a decline from the original level of involvement followed by a recovery which is more marked for women than for men. As a consequence, the difference between men and women tends to be greatest in the later phases of the life cycle.

But what accounts for these shifts and changes in the level of involvement among men? Why should it resemble the behavior of women at some stages of the life cycle and differ from it at others? The data themselves contribute very little to answering these questions. However, drawing on extant knowledge of the respective roles of the two sexes as the life cycle unfolds, speculative answers can be suggested.

The "Nuptial" and Early Child-Rearing Periods

During the "nuptial" and early child-rearing periods, men reduce their commitments to the church, just as women do. They differ from women primarily in the rate of reduction of their organizational involvement in the church.

Apparently the combination of occupational and family demands provides the impetus for both the general decline and, particularly, the marked decrease in participation in organizational life. This is clearly a period in his life when the man is preoccupied with finding a niche for himself in the occupational world. His new family responsibilities oblige him to take his role as breadwinner seriously. At the same time, his family situation does not function to reinforce his earlier inclinations to active church participation. His children are too young to evoke his interest in agencies of socialization outside the family. His wife is too busy in caring for the young and with household tasks to engage actively in extra-curricular activities. As a result, men, particularly if they themselves have assumed some of the responsibility for child care in addition to occupational responsibilities, are in a situation which restricts their opportunities for being active in the church. And since organizational involvement is the most time-consuming, it is this aspect of their church activity which suffers the most.

The Later Child-Rearing Period

At the next phase of the life cycle, when men are older (thirty to forty-nine) and their children are presumably of school age, the previously downward trend in their church involvement is halted and reversed. This is true for each aspect of their involvement, including organizational interests. There is a return to active participation in the church. From an overall view, mean involvement is *.28* at this stage, as contrasted with *.22* at the previous stage. This increase, while not as marked as it is for women over the same period, nevertheless represents the sharpest recovery in interest among men over the entire life cycle.

What accounts for this recovery among men? We have already suggested that the resurgence of interest among women is a consequence of their concern with the religious education of their children at a time when responsibility for the child is increasingly assumed by agencies outside the family. It seems reasonable to suppose that in a number of Episcopalian homes, both parents —not merely the mother—share a concern about the religious training of their child. This common concern is manifested by both of them becoming more active in the church. Church on Sunday becomes a family occasion. Father may teach Sunday School; mother may take part in young people's activities. In these families, then, the church plays an important part in the life of the total family, not merely in the lives of the mother and child.

In many Episcopalian homes, however, such total family involvement does not apparently occur. The mother increases her church activity while her husband does not.

The Later Phases of the Life Cycle

As the male parishioner's children grow older and he himself approaches, and then passes, his fiftieth year, the level of his church involvement remains about the same as in the previous stage when he and his children were younger. There is a slight increase in participation, but by the time he is fifty, the male parishioner is still considerably less involved, on the average, than was true of his unmarried youth. Women, on the other hand, reach and maintain a level of involvement during these stages which is substantially greater than that achieved at any earlier period of their lives.

Why should this be so? It seems evident from the foregoing that the children's growth into adolescence effects a more marked change in the role of the mother than of the father. The mother's familial responsibilities gradually lessen, giving her increased leisure time. Her interests, as we have previously seen, also shift from primary preoccupation with the child to broader humanitarian and welfare concerns. Her changed situation as well as her changing interests mutually encourage closer ties to the church.

To a lesser extent, the man is also likely to experience some sense of greater freedom from family responsibilities. However, his occupational responsibilities continue much as they had in the past, and his opportunities for increasing his activity in the church are not appreciably enhanced. To the extent that they are, it would appear that the organizational program of the church is not as attractive to him as it is to the woman. Generally speaking, the church's program is more oriented to the interests of women of this age than the interests of men. This situation is undoubtedly a result, in part, of the man's having less time for participation in the first place—creating a self-perpetuating pattern. Men do, however, exhibit somewhat increased intellectual involvement in the church, and, as they near or reach retirement, their ritual observance tends also to increase.

SUMMARY

This chapter began with a question: What leads Episcopalians to make differential commitments to their church? It was found, at the outset, that the parishioner's sex bears some relationship to his involvement. On the whole, women are more involved in the church—ritually, organizationally, and intellectually—than men. This gross difference was interpreted as a function of the different roles which women and men still play in our society. Both the finding and the interpretation conform to those previously made by earlier investigators, and constitute a discovery only in the sense that we are able to talk specifically about Episcopalians.

Some newer insights have been gained in regard to the patterning of church involvement over the life cycle. The parishioner's church ties are closely related to his particular life situation. Speaking generally, it should be noted that involvement (1) is relatively high in the premarital years, (2) declines sharply with marriage and the birth of children, and (3) recovers as the children reach school age. For women, involvement continues to increase as they and their children grow older, while for men it remains relatively static.

For a woman, the shifts coincide with changes in the kinds of responsibilities she assumes for her children. These are greatest when the children are young, and at this time her involvement in the church suffers most. As the children grow older, and as her interests shift from problems of child-rearing to more generally humanitarian concerns, her interest in the church is concomitantly revived and strengthened. Men also are affected by their family responsibilities but while these change over time, occupational responsibilities basically do not. As a consequence, the sharp recovery of interest in the church manifested by women is not mirrored among men.

However, the data and existing knowledge only allow us to go a short distance in explaining the variations observed. While it is possible to point to some of the conditions which may have led to a shift upward or downward, these conditions are not sufficient to explain why many Episcopalians deviate from the modal patterns of involvement. For example, why do some Episcopalians continue to be highly involved in the church during a period such as the child-rearing phase when most parishioners are reducing their church activity? Why do some men continue to increase their involvement throughout their lives, while most level off by the time their children reach adolescence? In the ensuing chapters, more factors conditioning involvement will be examined, and the answers to these and the more general questions will begin to emerge.

Chapter 3

The Church as a Family Surrogate

In Chapter 2, parishioners who could be classified in terms of a "normative" life cycle were examined. In that discussion, the term "normative" was used primarily to mean "typical." As will be seen, however, the term can also carry the connotation of "preferred" or "expected." In this latter sense, the typical life cycle in American society is also the expected one. Hence, those who deviate from it do so in more than a statistical sense; to some extent, variations from the "normative" life cycle represent a failure to measure up to implicit expectations and standards of society.

The historical link between church and family has been previously commented upon. At least in American society, the link may be seen in a primary commitment by the church to a particular kind of family, comprised of father, mother, son(s) and daughter(s)—the so-called "nuclear family." The church's commitment to this type of family is constantly reinforced in its literature, in sermons, in church programs, and in the religious education of the young. The Christian family is constantly cited as the basic building block of a Christian society. Although procreation is more explicitly a religious duty for Roman Catholics, it is implicitly accepted as such by most Protestants as well.

The church hardly stands alone in its endorsement of the nuclear family. Just as the church sees the family as central to Christian training, American society generally sees it as having a responsibility for training in democracy and good citizenship. Much of the secular society is organized around the family unit. Not surprisingly, the consumer economy is geared to housing, feeding, transporting and entertaining the nuclear family. A vast advertising industry reflects the importance of this image in both its packaging and merchandizing. "Family size," "family plan," and "fun for the whole family" all spring from the glossary of what is considered ideal in American society.

The normative life cycle, examined in the previous chapter, describes the typical and expected process for creating and living within such a nuclear family. Thus, to the extent that persons deviate from this, they are flying in the face of the prescribed patterns of family life, endorsed by both the church and the secular society.

Naturally enough, the idealization of the nuclear family is accompanied by an implicit, and sometimes explicit, devaluation of those family situations which do not conform to the norm. Except when one is young, even the slightest deviation may be perceived as somehow dysfunctional to the well-being of the personality, the society and the church. However, not all deviations from the pattern are viewed as equally dysfunctional. The person who remains single throughout life is perceived as constituting less of a threat to the norm than the one who is married and then divorced. This is evident in the common responses to the two deviations. The single person evokes sympathy and pity. The divorcée is more likely to arouse disapprobation; and where children are involved, the degree of disapprobation is generally even greater.

What does this suggest in regard to church involvement? It seems probable that certain consequences would follow from the church's giving implicit, and, in the case of divorce, explicit recognition to these values. Logically, the first consequence might be an overrepresentation among church members of persons with complete family ties. Such persons, more than the unmarried, the childless or the widowed, might be expected to feel a sense of identity with an institution whose values mirror their own situations. However logical this may be, it is obvious that the effect is at most only a partial one. Clearly, not all church members belong to complete nuclear families. Family deviants of all types —even the divorced—are present among the members of the nation's churches.

There is a second possible consequence. Since family deviants are present among church members, it is reasonable to expect that they might be less highly involved in church life than parishioners with complete family ties. Hearing sermons on family life, being excluded from family-centered church organizations and reading church literature extolling family virtues seems unlikely to evoke commitment from parishioners whose incomplete family ties are already experienced as a form of deprivation. So, if the church's position on family life does, in fact, have an effect, we should expect to find evidence of that effect in the recruitment of members, and also in the involvement of church members.

The Episcopal data available for the present study offer no insights into the recruitment hypothesis. In fact, there is very little evidence to be found elsewhere which deals with this problem. In a study of married Protestants in Indianapolis, Indiana, Gerhard Lenski reported a greater interest in religion among respondents with children than among those without.[1] While this would tend to support the above proposition, it should be noted that Lenski's data do not consider church membership as such, but measure religious "interest" among a group comprised, supposedly, of both church members and non-members.

Bernard Lazerwitz, in his examination of a national sample of nearly six thousand respondents, drew a profile of religious preference across stages of the life cycle.[2] Although Lazerwitz did not consider church membership as such, one of the categories for his denominational comparison was "no religion." Between 1.3 percent and 2.7 percent of the respondents at each stage of the life cycle reported they had no religious preference— with one exception. Among single respondents under thirty-five years of age, 4.6 percent gave this answer. This observation is at variance with the consistent finding that young people, prior to marriage, are modally high on involvement within the church. Conceivably Lazerwitz's finding indicates a somewhat greater disaffiliation with religion among the famililess, since the group in question is the only one strictly limited to single respondents.

[1] Gerhard E. Lenski, "Social Correlates of Religious Interest," *American Sociological Review* (October, 1953), pp. 533–544.

[2] Bernard Lazerwitz, "A Comparison of Major United States Religious Groups," *Journal of the American Statistical Association,* 56, no. 295 (September, 1961), pp. 568–579.

Since the upper age limit of the group (thirty-five) extends somewhat beyond the normal age of marriage, one might speculate that the lack of religious affiliation is greatest among those who have failed to comply with the expected pattern of family life. Nonetheless, the argument is conjectural and hardly sufficient to test the recruitment hypothesis.

There is even less empirical evidence available for testing the second proposition—that church members with complete nuclear families will be more highly involved than those with incomplete families. In fact, the authors were unable to find any research which satisfactorily dealt with the issue—directly or indirectly. However, the data on Episcopal parishioners allow an exploration of this proposition in some depth. The following discussion will examine church involvement in terms of the effect of deviation from the standard family pattern. Parishioners under thirty years of age will not be considered in this examination, since the implications of family status for involvement do not apply to them.

FAMILY STATUS AND INVOLVEMENT—
AN OVERVIEW

Table 15 presents the church involvement of all parishioners over thirty, comparing those with complete, partial and no family ties. The hypothesis that family deviants would be alienated from the church appears not only unfounded, but is actually contradicted by the data. Rather than being less involved, parishioners with incomplete families are more involved, and substantially so. The table also shows that the nature of incompleteness makes a dif-

TABLE 15

PARISHIONERS WHOSE FAMILY TIES ARE INCOMPLETE OR
ABSENT ARE MORE INVOLVED IN THE CHURCH

	Marital and family status			
	Spouseless		Has spouse	
	Childless	Has children	Childless	Has children
Mean involvement scores				
(C.I.I.)	.62	.57	.51	.43
	(75)	(84)	(103)	(593)

ference as well. Parishioners who lack both a spouse and children are the most involved. Furthermore, it appears that lacking a spouse is more conducive to active church participation than not having children. (This last relationship virtually disappears when age and sex are controlled, however, as will be shown later.)

Essentially the same relationship appears when the comparison is made using the three sub-indices of involvement instead of the composite index (see Table 16). Those with complete family

TABLE 16

PARISHIONERS WHOSE FAMILY TIES ARE INCOMPLETE OR ABSENT ARE MORE RITUALLY OBSERVANT, ORGANIZATIONALLY COMMITTED AND INTELLECTUALLY INVOLVED

	Marital and family status			
	Spouseless		Has spouse	
	Childless	Has children	Childless	Has children
Mean involvement scores on:				
Ritual observance	.81	.71	.70	.64
Organizational commitment	.63	.66	.49	.48
Intellectual interest	.51	.40	.40	.28
Number in sample	75	84	103	593

ties are least ritually observant, organizationally committed and intellectually interested; those with no family ties are the most involved. Those with partial families fall between the two extremes; missing a spouse or missing children makes no difference for ritual observance and intellectual interest. Those without a spouse, however, are more organizationally committed than those without children.

The facts, then, not only disconfirm the original expectation, but force a retreat from the logic underlying it as well. While the findings confirm the general observation of a close connection between church and family, it is necessary to reinterpret the significance of this connection with regard to church involvement. It should be remembered that the data say nothing about the likelihood of church membership, but only concern the intensity of involvement among church members. The problem, therefore, is to explain why one kind of family situation leads to greater involvement than another among people who share their church membership in common.

In part, the answer undoubtedly lies in the fact that the several family situations differ in the degrees to which they facilitate church involvement. The complete absence of family ties means fewer family responsibilities and hence, more time to be active; having both a spouse and children, presumably, are more demanding on one's time and energies. In turn, having one but not the other family component creates demands which lie somewhere between the two extremes.

On the motivational side, the most persuasive explanation suggests that the church provides those who lack complete families with an opportunity to derive compensatory or substitutive gratifications. For some, the identification with an institution whose value system is rooted in the family, whose symbolism, imagery and programs are closely associated with the family enables them to experience, vicariously, the family life they either miss or find incomplete. For most of these parishioners, we suspect, the church provides an alternative for satisfying the basic needs of companionship. It develops a sense of belonging, of identification with an association which has a purposeful existence. Through the church, they obtain emotional and psychological supports missing in their lives. One question remains open. Even assuming the validity of what has been said, why do they choose the church and not some secular substitute? It was suggested at the outset that certain secular activities might also function to resolve many of the needs discussed above. This is obviously a significant point to which attention must be given before the analysis is complete. Since it is more appropriately discussed in the context of additional evidence, further consideration will be delayed until the relevant data have been presented and examined.

As previously indicated, these generalizations can be refined somewhat when sex and age are introduced as relevant factors. Although the differences between the two extreme types remain pretty much the same, this is not the case for the two semi-familied groups—the spouseless and the childless. To examine this, we shall turn first to the woman parishioner, her family ties and her church involvement.

WOMEN: FAMILY TIES AND INVOLVEMENT

The relationship between the woman's family situation and her church involvement is shown in Table 17. The vertical columns of the table show that, irrespective of family situation, the older women are more involved than the younger. The shift is relatively slight for women in the two extreme groups but rather marked for those in the two intermediate family situations.

TABLE 17

The Effect of Family Ties on a Woman's Church
Involvement Varies with Her Age

| | Marital and family status | | | |
| | Spouseless | | Has spouse | |
	Childless	Has children	Childless	Has children
Mean involvement (C.I.I.)				
score among women aged:				
30–49	.56	.49	.50	.50
	(25)	(28)	(32)	(246)
50 or over	.65	.67	.66	.55
	(40)	(45)	(30)	(103)
Difference in involvement				
scores of two age groups	.09	.18	.16	.05

The horizontal rows of the table, in turn, indicate that among the younger respondents, both types of semi-familied women resemble the familied women in their level of involvement. All three groups are notably less involved than the famililess. Among the older respondents, an interesting shift occurs. The semi-familied women now resemble the famililess in involvement rather than those with complete family ties.

It will be recalled from Table 15, when all parishioners were examined together, the spouseless exhibited a higher level of involvement than the childless. This difference turns out to have been a function of differences in the sex and age composition of the two types. When these effects are controlled, the differences, for women at least, largely disappear. It appears, therefore, that the critical factor is the number of family components, rather than the type.

Equally interesting is the new information regarding the sharp change in the involvement of the two semi-familied groups from one age level to another. How is the change to be accounted for? Why do the semi-familied women increase their involvement so much more than the extreme groups? And in turn, why do they both resemble one extreme as younger women, and the other extreme when they are older?

The data suggest that something happens to the semi-familied women at about the time they reach fifty; something which happened to the famililess women at an earlier age, and which, evidently, never happens to women who achieve and retain complete families. This something, we believe, is a change in the self-perception of their family status—an acceptance of the incomplete family. While she is still relatively young, a woman with a partial family is not inclined to see herself as appreciably different from the woman who has both a husband and children. She is obviously aware of the missing component, but views the incompleteness of her family as a temporary aberration which time will correct. A child for the childless is still a possibility. So is another husband for the woman with children only. On the other hand, the woman who has not married by the time she is thirty, and consequently has no children, is less likely to see her family situation in such optimistic terms.

After fifty, however, even the semi-familied woman must ultimately reassess her situation. When she gives up hope of ever completing her family circle, she must redefine her status as more resembling the famililess. Thus, if her response to the church resembles that of the familied women when she is younger, and that of the famililess in later years, it is because she perceives herself as first one and then the other. Such an explanation would seem to carry a good deal of logical validity as well as organizing the peculiarities of the data. Nonetheless, the observations require further examination and replication before the explanation can be accepted with confidence.

The data suggest an explanation to another aspect of the behavior of the semi-familied and famililess women. This has to do with the significant degree of intensification in their church involvement—famililess women at an early age and semi-familied women later on.[3] In the earlier discussion, it was suggested that intensified church involvement might function as a family surrogate—that is, as a substitute for the void experienced in the lives of the unmarried, the divorced, the widowed and the childless. The data certainly support such an interpretation, but one might still wonder why the church is chosen to fill this void rather than some secular activity. Not everyone lacking a spouse and/or children is a church member. Yet, presumably, all such people share the same needs for family ties. If the hypothesis is correct, then the non-church members either have found alternative means to satisfy these needs or the needs remain unsatisfied. While this study of Episcopal parishioners cannot be used to examine church recruitment, the data do suggest that involvement in secular groups, for some parishioners, may be an acceptable substitute for intense involvement in the church (recall Table 13).

It seems evident that the propensity toward greater church involvement is accentuated for the woman who is both famililess (or semi-familied) and has failed to establish roots in the secular community. This "double deprivation," so to speak, intensifies the need for some kind of identification. This line of reasoning is supported by corollary information collected from the parishioners. To introduce this information, it will be necessary to digress for a moment from the main theme of the analysis.

In recent years, increasing attention has been given to the concept of "anomie," or normlessness. The notion underlying this research is that people differ in the degree to which they are integrated into their society or into some primary group—the extent to which they share its values and secure a sense of meaning in their lives by that participation. Anomie, then, is the quality attributed to persons who, rather than being well-integrated into the society, feel alienated from it, and do not perceive themselves as "fitting in." Investigators have been chiefly concerned with

---

[3] Actually, Table 17 does not report the church involvement of famililess women under 30. It will be recalled from Table 16, however, that the mean involvement score of this group was .46. This is significantly lower than the scores of famililess women at ages 30–49 and for those 50 and over. The scores in these cases are, respectively, .56 and .65, as Table 17 shows.

studying the personality effects of the urbanization process, through which small tightly-knit communities become complex, impersonal metropolises. Although this research is by no means complete, a number of recent studies have employed an anomie scale developed by sociologist Leo Srole.[4] Five items from that scale were included in the Episcopal study. Parishioners were asked to accept or reject the following five statements; the more statements accepted, the greater degree of anomie attributed to the parishioner.

Item 1. Nowadays a person has to live pretty much for today and let tomorrow take care of itself.

Item 2. These days a person doesn't really know on whom he can count.

Item 3. It is hardly fair to bring children into the world the way things look for the future.

Item 4. In spite of what some people say, the lot of the average man is getting worse, not better.

Item 5. There's no use writing to public officials because they are not really interested in the problems of the average man.

It was expected that among women over fifty years of age, those with complete families would exhibit less anomie than those who were missing one or both family components. It was also presumed that irrespective of their family situations, women who were highly committed to the church and/or secular affiliations would be less anomic than those who did not avail themselves of either outlet. In short, anomie was postulated as an outcome of these unresolved needs which the family, church and secular activities would normally relieve. The indicators are admittedly crude, but the findings, as Table 18 shows, generally confirm these expectations. (See Appendix B for a description of the "anomie" index construction.)

The important finding is that, among the famililess women over fifty, those with limited church involvement and no secular activities are the most likely to experience anomie as it was measured by the five statements. In one respect, the table does

[4] See Leo Srole, "Anomie, Authoritarianism and Prejudice," *American Journal of Sociology,* 62 (July, 1956), pp. 63–67, and "Social Integration and Certain Corollaries: An Exploratory Study," *American Sociological Review,* 21 (December, 1956), pp. 709–716.

TABLE 18

FAMILILESS WOMEN WITHOUT "HIGH" CHURCH INVOLVEMENT OR SECULAR
PRIMARY GROUP TIES SCORE HIGHEST ON ANOMIE SCALE

| | Percentage who score "high"[c] on Anomie Scale among women 50 years of age or older who: | |
	Have a husband and children	Do not have a husband and/or children
"High" church involvement[a] and/or secular primary group ties[b]	25 (80)	30 (110)
"Low" church involvement[a] and no secular primary group ties[b]	23 (22)	48 (19)

[a] Parishioners who scored *3* or higher on the C.I.I. are designated as having "high" church involvement in this table; those scoring *2* or lower are designated as "low."

[b] Secular primary group ties are defined here as membership in a recreational or social organization.

[c] See the methodological notes (Appendix B) for the definition of "high" anomie.

not conform to expectation—the familied women who have such ties score slightly higher than their counterparts who lack religious and secular group ties. But whether there is a slight difference, or none at all, it would appear that the identification with a family tends to provide the woman with basic insurance against uncertainty and malaise. When complete family ties exist, women seem to gain little additional protection from anomie by being active members of the church or secular primary groups.

MEN: FAMILY TIES AND INVOLVEMENT

As already noted, men, on the whole, are less active in church life than women. The extent of their activity, however, is also highly related to their family situation, although because of the small number of men with less than complete family ties, the relation and the interpretations which follow must be considered tentative. Table 19 shows that at each age level, the church involvement of men is sensitive to the relative completeness of their family circles. Men who are without any immediate family ties are the most involved; those with complete families, the least. Men with partial families occupy an intermediate position be-

TABLE 19

The Church Involvement of Men, Like Women, Is Also Related
to the Relative Completeness of Their Family Unit

| | Marital and family status | | | |
| | Spouseless | | Has spouse | |
	Childless	Has children	Childless	Has children
Mean involvement score among men aged:				
30–49	*.73*	*.33*	*.38*	*.29*
	(3)[a]	(6)[a]	(19)	(158)
50 or over	*.57*	*.44*	*.40*	*.33*
	(7)[a]	(5)[a]	(22)	(86)

[a] The small number of cases upon which scores have been computed should be noted.

tween the two extremes. The level of involvement is slightly higher among the older than among the younger group.

In some respects, then, the relationship between men's church involvement and their family situations is similar to that of women. This is most evident in the figures for the extreme groups: the familied and the famililess. The famililess are notably more involved at both age levels. Also, spouselessness is related to involvement in about the same way as childlessness—another similarity between men and women parishioners.

Aside from the generally higher involvement of women, however, the sexes differ in two other respects. The state of his family situation has more of an effect of the involvement behavior of a man than was the case for women. Note, for example, that at the thirty to forty-nine age level, men who are famililess have an involvement score of *.73* as compared to *.29* for the familied, a difference of *.44*. The corresponding scores for women were *.56* and *.50*, a difference of *.06*. Essentially the same pattern appears at the older age level.

Men and women also differ with respect to the involvement behavior of the semi-familied. It will be recalled that the semi-familied women behaved like the familied women among the younger group, and like the famililess women among the older group. Semi-familied men, however, retain an intermediate position between the two extremes at both age levels. It must be noted that the observed differences are based on the relatively few spouseless men available for analysis. Still, the comparison between men and women deserves at least speculative consideration.

Why do these differences exist? The first difference suggests that men experience a relatively greater deprivation through the absence of one or both family components than is experienced by women. This is surprising in view of the central importance of the family in women's lives. However, the difference might be explained by the fact that a man's preoccupation with economic pursuits leaves him fewer opportunities, compared with women, for resolving his deprivation through participation in primary groups outside the family. As a consequence, the woman's role in our society affords a greater capacity for adjusting to a family deprived situation, and she is less likely to be forced into finding a substitute within the church.

As to the more circumscribed differences bearing on men and women with partial families, the data themselves offer some clues as to why this should occur. Semi-familied men between the ages of thirty and forty-nine differ from their female counterparts in having a higher level of involvement than those with complete families. This is not a consequence, however, of the semi-familied men having increased their ties to the church from those prevailing at an earlier age. If we look at married men under thirty who are childless (Figure 1)—at a phase in the family cycle when it is relatively normal to be childless—we find that the level of their involvement is virtually identical with that found among semi-familied men between thirty and forty-nine. Men with partial families, then, retain their relationships to the church as they grow into middle age, whereas men with families drift away from church involvement during this period.

SUMMARY

In the previous chapter, the analysis focused on parishioners as they progressed through the normative life cycle which represents a standard endorsed by both the church and the secular society. In this chapter, we have examined those parishioners who fail to conform to the prescribed pattern. It was impossible to determine whether these family deviants are more or less attracted to church membership, although the scanty data available suggest that perhaps the church is less attractive to them.

The data do provide an insight into their participation within the church. Contrary to expectations, the family deviants display a higher level of involvement than those parishioners whose family situations reflect the normative life cycle. It was suggested that this results from the church's functioning as a family surrogate for the parishioners who find themselves lacking in this respect. With minor differences, the finding holds for both men and women.

While famililess women parishioners were consistently higher in involvement than those with complete family ties, the behavior of the semi-familied women parishioners presented a peculiar shift. When they are younger (thirty to forty-nine years of age) these women more closely resemble their counterparts with complete families. It would appear that this is due to the self-perception of their deprived family situations as only temporary. The childless wife still hopes for a child, and the widow or divorcée still feels that a new husband is in store for her. Women in the older age group (beyond their fiftieth year) revise their hopes for the future, and with them, the self-perception of their present family statuses. Accepting the fact that they have not met the expectations of normative family status, they come more closely to resemble their famililess counterparts in terms of church involvement. Pursuing this notion a little further, it was hypothesized that if the church (and secular organizations) provides a means of integration into the society, those famililess and semi-familied women who are neither active in the church nor in secular organizations will demonstrate a higher degree of anomie, or normlessness. This was discovered to be the case. And church involvement had little or no effect on the anomic scores of those women who enjoy complete family ties—further indicating that the church and the family both fulfill the same function in this regard.

In turning to the male respondents, the same general patterns were discovered. Although they are modally less involved in the church than women, men still reflect the same effects of family status on church involvement. Once again, the famililess are consistently more involved than those with complete families—the effect of family status in this instance is greater than the corresponding effect for women. And the semi-familied male parishioners display a level of involvement which lies between the two extremes. Unlike women, however, this intermediate position is maintained by semi-familied men at both age levels. It was suggested that, at the earlier stages in the life cycle, men are less able, due to economic preoccupations, to seek non-church resolutions to their incomplete families. Unlike the semi-familied women at this point, men maintain their previous level of involvement. Hence, when a man passes his fiftieth year, he is not faced with the need to revise his orientation toward the church.

Finally, by controlling for the independent effects of sex and age, it was determined that the effects of family deprivation do not depend on the type of family component which is missing, but only on the number. The effects of childlessness and spouselessness are the same.

Chapter 4

Social Class and Involvement

The relationship between social class and religious behavior has received somewhat more attention in the literature than has been accorded some of the preceding topics. Existing research in this area has examined the effects of social class on such religious dimensions as church membership, ritual attendance and religious beliefs. It will soon be evident, however, that the existing data are not altogether consistent. We shall begin by reviewing some of the previous research on this topic, and then turn to the present data on Episcopalian parishioners in an attempt to understand the implications of one's standing in the secular community for involvement in the church.

Even prior to the rigorous collection and examination of empirical data, a body of impressionistic evidence and speculation suggested that social class and church involvement were related. Working class Americans were believed to be largely indifferent or even hostile to religion—a survival, in part, from church opposition to unionism at the turn of the century. Moreover, the Marxian element in working class radicalism fostered the view that the churches were controlled and used by the "ruling class." The upper class has also been seen as generally weak in religious involvement, although their orientation to religion has been regarded more as one of complacency than of antagonism. The postulated lack of religiosity on the part of the working and upper classes has been supported by the observation that organized religion has been challenged most often by groups and individuals representing the labor and intellectual communities.

On the whole, observers past and present have viewed organized religion in America as primarily the domain of the middle class. This viewpoint is clearly expressed by the church's contemporary critics who assert that institutional religion has become mired in the middle class values which constitute the secular status quo. The "comfortable pew" of which Berton speaks is comfortable only to those who are committed to middle class values such as respectability and domestic tranquility. When Gibson Winter suggests the churches have been captured by suburbia, he is speaking of a predominantly middle class suburbia.

This view of religion in America was generated and sustained by the impressions of concerned observers spanning several decades. Until the late thirties, however, there were no national statistics on the religious practices of different classes and occupational groups with which to either refute or confirm these notions.

In terms of church membership, the "community studies" of the thirties and forties tended to confirm the observers' impressions of religion in America, at least in part. Even as the first measures of social class were being constructed, the lower class was found consistently underrepresented among church members. This was partially explained by the workers' general failure to join voluntary associations, either secular or religious. On the other hand, the findings in regard to the relative positions of the middle and upper classes were hardly consistent—the relative degrees of church membership for these classes varied from study to study.

More recent empirical evidence tends to confirm the earlier conclusions regarding the lower classes and church membership. The American Institute of Public Opinion (July 20, 1954) found 79 percent of its cross-sectional national sample claiming to be church members.[1] Among professional and business respondents, 83 percent claimed membership, as contrasted with 77 percent of those classified as manual workers. On the other hand, 83 percent of the college educated reported they were members, com-

[1] Since this figure is somewhat higher than the membership rolls of the nation's churches at that time, it is possible that many respondents mistook church membership to mean traditional association with a particular denomination.

pared with 81 percent of the high school educated and 73 percent of those with only grade school educations. In terms of occupational and educational status, then, it would appear that lower or working class Americans are less likely to belong to a church than are the middle and upper classes. Nonetheless, the percentage differences are very small and hardly conclusive. Furthermore, with only these crude indicators of social class, it is impossible to make any meaningful distinction between the upper and middle classes, so this puzzle must remain unresolved for the moment.

Looking beyond mere church membership, several of the community studies also found the lower class to be the poorest church attenders. As in the case of membership, though, the studies do not resolve the relative positions of the middle and upper classes.

Bultena, in a study limited to the population of Madison, Wisconsin, found very little difference in the church-going practices of different classes.[2] Nonetheless, the working class respondents seemed to be slightly less active than either the middle or upper classes. Among professional persons in his sample, 68.8 percent were affiliated with a church. The parallel figure for businessmen was 70.9 percent, for clerical workers, 72.2 percent, and for workers, 67.5 percent. In his study of Elmtown's Youth, Hollingshead found an inverse relationship between church attachments and rising class.[3] His data, however, were based on a sample of adolescents rather than on the entire population of the midwestern community studied.

A poll conducted by the Catholic Digest in 1951 produced a linear relationship between social class and ritual attendance. Sixty-two percent of the lower class reported attending church at least once a month, in contrast with 69 percent of the middle class and 75 percent of the upper class. Only the relative position of the lower class is maintained when we turn to the findings of a national poll by the American Institute of Public Opinion in 1955. Manual workers were the least likely (44 percent) to have

[2] Louis Bultena, "Church Membership and Church Attendance in Madison, Wisconsin," American Sociological Review (June, 1949).

[3] August Hollingshead, Elmtown's Youth (New Haven: Yale University Press, 1949).

attended church during the four weeks prior to the poll. However, those with professional and business occupations were less likely to have attended than were white collar workers, 48 percent and 50 percent respectively, reversing this portion of the *Catholic Digest* findings—although, once again, the indicators of social class are less than ideal for distinguishing the middle from the upper class.

When religious belief is taken as a measure of involvement, even the heretofore consistent finding with regard to the lesser commitment of the lower class is overturned. In their study of Middletown, the Lynds noted that the lower class—the least likely to belong to a church or to attend services—were the most likely to hold traditional religious beliefs.[4] This observation has been replicated in numerous studies since. Among his Detroiters, Lenski found doctrinal orthodoxy to decrease with an increase in education.[5] Similarly, Yoshio Fukuyama found an inverse relationship between religious belief and social class in his examination of Congregational parishioners.[6]

Such disparate findings as these can only lead the investigator to a feeling of uneasiness with regard to the general relationship between religious involvement and social class, each variously defined. Taken alone, or together, the studies noted above scarcely constitute a conclusive statement on this subject. The fact that only marginal data are presented leaves open the question as to whether social class may be related differently to church involvement among persons who differ in other respects.

One body of theory suggests that social class may relate more closely to the type of religious involvement than to the degree. H. Richard Niebuhr advanced the thesis that social class played an important part in the development of American denominations.[7] He noted that the economically deprived were more likely to form or join fundamentalist, rather than liberal, religious

[4] Robert and Helen Lynd, *Middletown* (New York: Harcourt, Brace, 1929).

[5] Gerhard Lenski, *The Religious Factor* (Garden City, N.Y.: Doubleday, 1955).

[6] Yoshio Fukuyama, "The Major Dimensions of Church Membership," *Review of Religious Research* (Spring, 1951).

[7] H. Richard Niebuhr, *The Social Sources of Denominationalism* (New York: Henry Holt, 1929).

groups. This tendency was attributed to a greater need for experiencing religion emotionally, than simply observing it ritually. Niebuhr further suggested that the ethics of hard work and ascetism commonly found among the fundamentalist sects had the effect of ultimately resolving the economic hardships of their followers. As members of the sects followed the injunctions to work and save, they became more prosperous, and the sects came to take on a more church-like, ritualistic character.

Russell Dynes has suggested that this conception of church and sect may be used to reconcile some of the inconsistencies regarding the effect of social class on religious involvement.[8] Following the earlier discussions of the nature of sects and churches, Dynes created a number of statements which might be used to distinguish individual orientations toward either a church-like or a sect-like religious outlook. His initial findings pointed out that lower class individuals tended to exhibit a preference for the sect-like orientation, as opposed to the church-like orientation of those higher in socio-economic status.

In a more recent examination, N. J. Demerath applied Dynes' framework, first to a sample of Lutheran parishioners, and then to several other denominational groups.[9] Using several indicators of social status, the earlier findings were replicated in each instance. As Demerath suggests, the use of the church-sect dichotomy in this sense may provide one means for accommodating the different dimensions of religiosity such as those mentioned earlier in this study.

In similar terms, it has been widely accepted that such differences are reflected in the socioeconomic cross-section of the various denominational groups. However, the statistics only relatively confirm such beliefs. Denominations do tend to appeal more to one social class than another, but no denomination draws its membership exclusively from one social class. In fact, the heterogeneity in the social class composition of individual American denominations is at least as striking as the modal differences which exist among them.

[8] Russell Dynes, "Church-sect Typology and Socio-Economic Status," *American Sociological Review* (October, 1955).

[9] N. J. Demerath, III, *Social Class in American Protestantism* (Chicago: Rand McNally, 1965).

The most comprehensive statistics on this subject are relatively old, dating back to 1946–1947, and it seems reasonable to suppose that the situation has changed somewhat since that time, particularly with respect to the social class composition of the Roman Catholic Church. However, the statistics provide an approximation which, in all probability, is still applicable to the present situation. From a report published on these data, Table 20 abstracts the figures on the social class composition of America's seven largest denominations.

TABLE 20

DISTRIBUTION OF RELIGIOUS GROUPS BY "CLASS" [a]

Denomination	Social class position			Total	Number of cases
	Upper	Middle	Lower		
Episcopal	24.1%	33.7	42.2	100.0	599
Congregational	23.9%	42.6	33.5	100.0	376
Presbyterian	21.9%	40.0	38.1	100.0	961
Methodist	12.7%	35.6	51.7	100.0	2,100
Lutheran	10.9%	36.1	53.0	100.0	723
Roman Catholic	8.7%	24.7	66.6	100.0	2,390
Baptist	8.0%	24.0	68.0	100.0	1,381

[a] Source: Anonymous, "Socio-Economic Status and Outlook of Religious Groups in America," Information Service, XXVII, no. 20, part 2, May 15, 1948. In this study, the economic categories "upper," "middle," and "lower," represent groupings in which respondents are placed by interviewers after a careful appraisal of the respondent's dress, home and its neighborhood and furnishings, ownership of phone and automobile, occupation, use of luxury items, possession of comforts as opposed to necessities, etc.

Viewed in terms of their relative appeal to the upper class, the Episcopal, Congregational and Presbyterian churches score about the same and clearly rank above the other denominations. The Methodist and Lutheran churches appeal much less to this class but are ranked slightly above the Roman Catholic and Baptist churches which have the least appeal to the upper class.

However, it is misleading to place too much emphasis on these rank differences, given the general propensity of all denominations to have a heterogeneous class membership. From the viewpoint of our particular interest in the Protestant Episcopal Church, this church, relatively speaking, enjoys a high social status. Compared to the Lutheran, Methodist, Roman Catholic or Baptist churches, it attracts a membership which is modally of a higher class. However, the statistics do not support the popular stereotype that Episcopalians are predominantly upper class. As a group, they may be more well-to-do than Lutherans, but the average Episcopalian can scarcely be described as wealthy.

To set these statistics in proper context, three observations should be made in passing. First, it cannot be inferred that, all other things being equal, a person holding upper class status will be more prone to join the Episcopal than, say, the Methodist Church. Denominational affiliations are primarily based on inheritance rather than individual choice. The differences observed here clearly have been conditioned by factors associated with the history of these denominations, particularly with respect to the periods in which the denominations' major ethnic groups migrated to the United States. While it has been supposed that status considerations affect what migration goes on from one denomination to another—the notion, for example, that upwardly mobile Lutherans will be more prone to become Episcopalians or Congregationalists than Methodists—the evidence to this effect is more anecdotal than precise.

Second, in suggesting a fairly high degree of heterogeneity in the social class composition of different denominations, the statistics obscure the fact that local congregations in each denomination may be much more homogeneous in class makeup. A number of community studies suggest that this is indeed the case. Goldschmidt,[10] in a study of churches in rural California, found that less than 2 percent of the membership of a Congregational Church came from the ranks of unskilled workers, whereas in a Pentecostal Church in the same community, 82 percent of the members were unskilled workers. Hollingshead and Redlich, in describing the religious affiliations of the upper class (what they call Class I) residents of New Haven, Connecticut, comment:

> Within the Protestant group, 61 per cent of the families are Congregationalist, 17 per cent are Episcopalians, 7 per cent

[10] Walter R. Goldschmidt, "Social Structure of a California Rural Community" (an unpublished doctoral dissertation in anthropology at the University of California, Berkeley, 1942).

are Lutherans, 5 per cent are Baptists, 2 per cent are Methodists and other denominations comprise the remaining 7 per cent.

. . . .

> In each religion . . . the [upper class] membership is concentrated in a small number of congregations. For example, there are 24 Congregational churches in the community, but over 93 per cent of the core group members belong to three of these churches.[11]

On the whole, however, we are inclined to agree with Bultena in commenting on his Madison, Wisconsin, data: "Though it is clearly evident that church people tend to group themselves in churches and denominations according to social class, it is probable that we find more heterogeneity in class status in the average church than in any other average social grouping." [12]

Finally, it is necessary to enter one further caveat about these statistics. They are not confined to bona fide church members but are based on how respondents to public opinion polls classify themselves when asked their religious denominations. Thus, the statistics undoubtedly include many respondents who are nominally identified with a denomination but maintain no formal connection with it as a church member. It is difficult to know how much the statistics might be changed if only bona fide church members were polled. Our own data do not permit an exact comparison with the figures on the social composition of Episcopalians reported in Table 20 above. In terms of income distribution, though, the Episcopalian parishioners in our sample closely resemble those described in the poll. Note, for example, that 40.0 percent of our sample report incomes of $4,000 or less as compared to 42.2 percent reported as lower class in Table 20. And, 22.4 percent of our sample earn $7,500 per annum or more, a figure roughly comparable to the 24.1 percent reported as being in the upper class among Episcopalians in Table 20. However tenuous these comparisons, the two bodies of data do document the fact that the average Episcopalian is far from being wealthy and confirm the general pattern by which Episcopalians are distributed across the class structure.

[11] August B. Hollingshead and Fredrick C. Redlich, *Social Class and Mental Illness* (New York: John Wiley, 1958) p. 73.
[12] Bultena, *op. cit.*, p. 387.

Given the relative inconsistency and superficiality of the available data on social class and religious affiliations, and the fact that it has essentially no bearing on the strength of church attachments, there seems to be little solid information upon which to ground the present examination. In fact, the existing research findings would allow two observers to arrive at diametrically opposed expectations, each supported by logical arguments and empirical data.

TABLE 21

DISTRIBUTION OF EPISCOPALIAN PARISHIONERS
BY ANNUAL FAMILY INCOME

$4,000 or less	40.0%
$4,001–$6,000	26.8
$6,001–$7,500	9.9
$7,501–$10,000	9.6
$10,000 or more	12.8
100% =	1318
No answer	212
Total cases	1530

In terms of facilitating factors, it might be expected that the upper class, with their generally greater involvement in the organizational life of their communities, would have less time to devote to the church. However, the life style of the upper class might just as logically give them greater leisure time in which to establish closer ties with their churches. Empirical data could be found to confirm either explanation.

On the motivational side as well, theoretical notions might lead to contradictory expectations. Given the popular stereotype of the Episcopal Church as having a high status, it might be expected that the upper class Episcopal parishioner might desire being seen as an active church member, reinforcing his status. It is also conceivable that in an institution having a basically upper class orientation, class barriers might arise which would limit the access of lower class members, at least in the church's organizational life.

If organizational membership does, in fact, serve status functions, however, we might logically expect just the opposite behavior on the part of the upper class Episcopalians. For such persons, being an active Episcopalian is only one of several ways to manifest their generally high status. With many and varied opportunities to participate in activities which convey status qualifications, the upper class parishioners are less dependent on the church for this purpose than are their less well-off counterparts. For the lower classes—presuming they have aspirations for improving their social position—the church might be perceived as a vehicle for doing so and consequently, it is they who would most desire being known as active Episcopalians.

Returning for a moment to the distinction between church and sect, the Episcopal Church tends toward those characteristics which have been postulated as closer to the religious inclinations of the upper rather than the lower class members of society. Its theology can scarcely be described as fundamentalist, its ritual is highly formalized, allowing for very little, if any, spontaneity in religious fervor. Its formal prescriptions bear more on what one does than on how one should feel religiously, and its attitude toward the existing world leans more toward compromise and identification than rejection or aloofness. Assuming these characteristics, it would not seem at all surprising that they lead to greater involvement on the part of wealthier parishioners who theoretically, at any rate, have been thought to have religious inclinations along these lines.[13]

To determine the effects of social class on church involvement among Episcopalians, a composite index was created from parishioners' education and annual family income. On education, those reporting less than a high school diploma were scored 0; those with a high school education and/or some college were scored 1; parishioners who reported they had received a college degree and/or post-college education were scored 2. In terms of annual family income, those reporting less than $4,000 per year

---

[13] Of course, if this were the only consideration, one would expect the Roman Catholic Church to attract an even higher status membership. But, as was suggested earlier, perhaps the primary cause of denominational class differentials is to be found in the migration dates of their major ethnic groups, and the tendency for membership by inheritance rather than conversion. It is reasonable to assume, however, that within the framework of membership, the formality of the religious rituals might be more conductive to participation by upper class members.

were scored *0*; parishioners with family incomes between $4,000 and $10,000 were scored *1*; and those with annual family incomes in excess of $10,000 received a score of *2*. The composite index, then, ran from a "low" of *0* to a "high" of *4*. (A more detailed description of the construction and validation of the social class index is presented in Appendix B.)

WOMEN: CLASS AND INVOLVEMENT

The relationship between social class and church involvement among the women parishioners in the sample is presented in Table 22.

TABLE 22

SOCIAL CLASS IS NEGATIVELY ASSOCIATED WITH CHURCH INVOLVEMENT

| | Index of social class | | | | |
| | Low | | | | High |
	0	1	2	3	4
Mean score on the Composite Index of Involvement	*.63*	*.58*	*.49*	*.48*	*.45*
	(69)	(183)	(225)	(131)	(29)

When the Composite Index of Involvement is used, it is apparent that the higher a parishioner's social class, the lower her involvement is. Those women scored lowest on the social class index have a mean C.I.I. score of *.63,* as contrasted with *.45* for those with the highest social class score.

This initial finding, then, seems to confirm the hypothesis that involvement in the Episcopal Church is seen as a means of achieving high social status among those women who do not enjoy that status in secular society. By definition, those women scored highest on the index of social class already enjoy the status commensurate with education and income. Presumably that high status also affords them access to a wide range of prestigious organizations and activities in the secular community. For them, involvement in the Episcopal Church would be only one of several ways of consolidating their high social status. Table 22 shows that they are relatively uninvolved.

On the other hand, women scored low on the social class index enjoy less status to begin with, and presumably are not in as good a position to achieve a higher status by participating in prestigious secular organizations. For them, the Episcopal Church would seem a more important institution, and as Table 22 indicates, they are more involved in it.

It will be recalled that an alternative hypothesis was discussed earlier. Parishioners of a generally lower social status might feel somewhat uncomfortable participating in a church which is commonly regarded as upper class. The status barriers which prevent lower class parishioners from participating in prestigious secular organizations might also be felt in regard to involvement in the Episcopal Church. Table 23 indicates that this alternative hypothesis may also be true, at least in part.

TABLE 23

WOMEN'S SOCIAL CLASS IS NEGATIVELY RELATED TO EACH OF THE SUB-INDICES OF INVOLVEMENT, BUT THE RELATIONSHIP IS STRONGEST WITH REGARD TO INTELLECTUAL INVOLVEMENT

| | Index of social class | | | | |
| | Low | | | | High |
	0	1	2	3	4
Mean scores on:					
Ritual involvement	.77	.69	.62	.66	.66
	(94)	(229)	(253)	(134)	(29)
Organizational involvement	.63	.66	.58	.60	.52
	(71)	(196)	(232)	(133)	(29)
Intellectual involvement	.51	.38	.31	.27	.28
	(92)	(219)	(252)	(134)	(29)

If status barriers exist with regard to participation in the Episcopal Church, they should be most evident in those aspects of involvement which require the closest social interaction among church members. It will be noted in Table 23 that the clearest association between class and involvement appears in the case of intellectual involvement. Reading religious literature, turning to religious sources for advice and being influenced by the church require little if any contact with other church members. In this aspect of church involvement, lower status women are much more committed than their higher status counterparts.

In matters of ritual and organizational involvement—requiring more social interaction—lower status women are still more involved than those of higher status. The effect of class is weaker and more ambiguous, however. This fact suggests, then, that lower status women may feel somewhat restricted from full participation due to the greater prestige enjoyed by their coreligionists. For the time being, there seem adequate grounds for accepting both of these somewhat contradictory hypotheses.

The overall relationship between social class and church involvement appears to hold for women of all ages (see Table 24). Among the young, middle-aged, and older women, church

TABLE 24

AT ALL AGE LEVELS, INVOLVEMENT GENERALLY DECLINES WITH INCREASING
SOCIAL STATUS AMONG WOMEN PARISHIONERS

| | Index of social class | | | | |
| | Low | | | | High |
	0	1	2	3	4
Mean scores on C.I.I. for women aged:					
Under 30	.64	.46	.34	.27	.40
	(5)ᵃ	(32)	(29)	(17)	(2)ᵃ
30–49	.57	.56	.48	.49	.44
	(18)	(79)	(141)	(75)	(20)
50 and over	.65	.65	.59	.55	.49
	(46)	(71)	(55)	(39)	(7)ᵃ

ᵃ Note the small number of cases upon which the mean scores are based.

involvement decreases with increasing social status. The effect is clearest among the youngest groups, even when the extreme cells (based on small numbers of cases) are discounted. And with the exception of one small cell in the table, the data confirm the earlier observation that involvement increases with age. Whatever their social status, older women are more involved than are the young.

When the individual sub-indices of involvement are substituted for the composite measure, essentially the same pattern emerges. For each age group, social class has a greater effect on intellectual involvement than on ritual or organizational, and involvement on each of the three dimensions increases with age. (The tables showing the joint effects of age and class on the sub-indices of involvement are presented in Appendix B.)

The data presented thus far have been used to substantiate the hypothesis that lower status women turn to the Episcopal Church as a means of achieving the status they do not enjoy in the secular society. There are two parts to this hypothesis. First, it is assumed that women lacking education and high income cannot command the status enjoyed by those who possess both. This part of the hypothesis is largely a matter of definition. The second part suggests that women who are lower in social class to begin with will not be afforded access to those organizations and activities which might otherwise enhance their social standing. The lower class woman is not likely to be found in any abundance in the Junior League, D.A.R. or the elite country club. Women who are denied access to a broad range of prestigious activities for status gratification might understandably turn to that institution which is most accessible to them—the Episcopal Church to which they belong.

The available data permit three tests of the second part of the hypothesis. If lower status women are involved in the church because they are unable to participate fully in the secular community, the observed relationship between class and involvement should be most noticeable among those women who do not in fact participate. First, the data report the total number of organizational memberships for each respondent. If a lower status woman belongs to many organizations, it seems safe to assume that her life is not quite as restricted as has been pictured above. Therefore, among women with many organizational memberships, it should be expected that the relationship between class and involvement would be less striking than among those with only a few memberships. Table 25 somewhat confirms this expectation.

Among women reporting one to three memberships, the relationship between social class and involvement is strong and consistent. Among those with four or more memberships, the effect is much more ambiguous. Moreover, in looking down the columns in the table, we note that for upper status women, membership in a large number of organizations is positively associated with church involvement, while for those scored lowest on social

TABLE 25

Women's Social Class Has a Greater Effect on Involvement among
Those Reporting Few Organizational Memberships

| | Index of social class | | | | |
| | Low | | | | High |
	0	1	2	3	4
Mean involvement scores for *women with:*					
1 to 3 memberships	*.60*	*.57*	*.56*	*.39*	*.33*
	(32)	(82)	(57)	(29)	(6)[a]
4 or more memberships	*.53*	*.65*	*.53*	*.48*	*.46*
	(17)	(65)	(92)	(70)	(24)

[a] Note the small number of cases upon which score is based.

class, the reverse is true. This would suggest that church involvement for the upper status woman is part and parcel of general community activity; involvement in the Episcopal Church does not differ significantly from her participation in secular organizations. For the lower status woman, however, high church involvement seems to result in part from an inability to participate in other organizations.

When an upper status woman reports few organizational memberships, it seems fairly safe to assume that this represents a matter of personal choice. The college-educated woman of reasonably high financial means is barred from few clubs. And we have seen in Table 25 her involvement in the Episcopal Church tends to reflect her general participation in organizations.

While community activity is more a matter of choice for the upper status woman, there is no denying that overall she is more active than her less fortunate counterparts. Women scored *4* on the index of social class report an average of 4.03 secular organizational memberships; the average number of secular organizations for women scored *0* on social class is 1.21. Similarly, when respondents were asked to evaluate their overall participation in the life of their community, upper status women were much more likely to report active participation (see Table 26).

Despite the strong relationship between social class and perceived community activity, we note that over one-fourth of the women scored lowest on status report they are at least fairly

TABLE 26

UPPER STATUS WOMEN ARE FAR MORE LIKELY TO FEEL THEY PARTICIPATE
ACTIVELY IN THE LIFE OF THEIR COMMUNITIES

"How actively do you feel you participate in the life of the community?"	Index of social class				
	Low				High
	0	1	2	3	4
Very actively	4%	7%	10%	14%	21%
Fairly actively	25	40	42	45	54
To some extent	37	34	32	33	25
Hardly at all	34	19	17	9	0
100% =	95	227	246	129	28

active in the life of the community. It is a fair assumption that such women, again, do not feel as restricted in access to community activities as has been suggested earlier. If the hypothesis is true, then, the relationship between social class and involvement should not be as strong among women active in the community as it is among the inactive. Table 27 suggests that this is the case.

Lower status women are more involved than upper status women in both groups, but the size and consistency of the effect is greater among those who do not feel they participate actively in the life of the community. This difference is due largely to the previously observed relationship between church involvement and general activity among upper status women.

TABLE 27

CLASS AFFECTS CHURCH INVOLVEMENT MORE AMONG WOMEN WHO DO NOT FEEL
THEY PARTICIPATE ACTIVELY IN THE LIFE OF THE COMMUNITY

	Index of social class				
	Low				High
	0	1	2	3	4
Mean involvement among women whose community participation is:					
Very or fairly active	.64	.59	.51	.53	.49
	(24)	(96)	(119)	(74)	(21)
To some extent or hardly at all	.63	.55	.46	.41	.37
	(42)	(81)	(95)	(51)	(7)[a]

[a] Note the small number of cases on which score is based.

Community participation has virtually no effect on church involvement for those women scored lowest on social class. But as we move up the status ladder, the effect of community participation on involvement increases steadily. This would seem to confirm the view that church involvement for upper status women is simply part of the general milieu of community activity, while for lower status women the church may be an alternative to participation in secular organizations which are effectively not open to them.

In terms of sheer activity, then, the hypothesis has been substantiated by two tests. The relationship between social class and involvement is weakest among women who belong to many organizations and among those who feel they participate actively in the life of the community. Unfortunately, the data examined thus far cannot adequately indicate the prestige quality of women's participation. If lower status women turn to the church primarily when they are unable to derive status gratification from secular organizations, it would be important to note the status of the organizations to which they belong. Given the variety of organizations reported by the respondents, however, this would be impossible, especially in the case of local organizations and activities.

The status and prestige attendant on organizational membership may be measured indirectly, however. While a woman may derive prestige from simply belonging to an important organization, a far greater status is achieved from serving as an officer. Moreover, it is quite possible that being an officer in a relatively low status organization in the community would carry a good deal of status gratification for the lower status woman. In the questionnaire, respondents were asked to indicate whether they had ever served as officers in any of the organizations to which they belonged. It is possible, therefore, to examine the proportion of women who have served as officers in their secular organizations. As might be imagined, holding an office is highly related to social class (see Table 28).

If holding an office in a secular organization is actually a source of status, then we should expect that the relationship between social class and involvement would be reduced among women who report holding an office. Table 29 confirms this

TABLE 28

UPPER STATUS WOMEN ARE MORE LIKELY TO HAVE SERVED AS OFFICERS IN THE
SECULAR ORGANIZATIONS TO WHICH THEY BELONG

	Index of social class			
	Low			High
	0	1	2	3	4
Percentage of those belonging to secular organizations who have held office	46 (52)	57 (154)	54 (212)	60 (122)	83 (29)

expectation. Among those women who have not enjoyed the status to be derived from office-holding, lower status women are more likely to be involved in the church than their upper status counterparts. Yet among those women who have held office in a secular organization, there is virtually no relationship between class and involvement.

In summary, the analysis has shown that lower status church-women are generally more involved than those who enjoy a higher social status. The relationship between class and involvement is less striking along those dimensions which require social interaction among members, suggesting that lower status women may feel somewhat restricted from participation in a prestigious church. Nevertheless, lower status women are more involved

TABLE 29

WOMEN'S SOCIAL STATUS HAS NO EFFECT ON CHURCH INVOLVEMENT AMONG THOSE
WHO HAVE HELD OFFICE IN SECULAR ORGANIZATIONS

	Index of social class			
	Low			High
	0	1	2	3	4
Mean involvement among women who belong to secular organizations and who:					
Have held office	.46 (24)	.53 (81)	.46 (110)	.46 (72)	.46 (24)
Have not held office	.62 (26)	.55 (62)	.47 (94)	.46 (48)	.40 (5)ᵃ

ᵃ Note the small number of cases on which score is based.

along each of the three dimensions: ritual, organizational and intellectual.

The most recent evidence presented indicates that church involvement among upper status women is an integral part of community activity in general. The involvement of upper class women tends to increase with increasing secular activity. Among lower status women, the reverse is true. Church involvement for them is an alternative to participation in secular activities which might provide status rewards. The lower status woman who is denied access to status gratification in the secular society turns to the church as an alternative source of gratification. This conclusion was substantiated by the observation that class has no effect on involvement among women who appear to have enjoyed some degree of status in the secular community. Among women who have held office in secular organizations, the lower status women are no more or less involved in the church than are those higher in social class.

The preceding analysis should provide the beginning of an insight into the status implications of church involvement. Clearly it does not present the whole picture. We shall reexamine these conclusions when we turn to social class and involvement among men and will reexamine the whole issue in Chapter 5.

MEN: CLASS AND INVOLVEMENT

The relationship between social class and church involvement is neither as strong nor as consistent among men as it was among women. Nevertheless, the effect is essentially in the same direction, as Table 30 shows; the mean scores of women are presented here for comparative purposes.

Part of the reason for the weaker effect of class on involvement among men is due to the fact that men are less involved than women generally. We note that lower status men—most involved among men—are less involved than even the highest status women. In comparing men and women at each class level, women are the more involved in every instance. The difference is greatest among those of lower status and is the least among those in the middle.

As among women, social class has its strongest effect on the

TABLE 30

LOWER STATUS MEN ARE MORE INVOLVED IN THE
CHURCH THAN UPPER STATUS MEN

	Index of social class				
	Low				High
	0	1	2	3	4
Mean involvement scores on the C.I.I. among:					
Men	.39	.34	.37	.31	.25
	(36)	(88)	(127)	(112)	(44)
Women	.63	.58	.49	.48	.45
	(69)	(183)	(225)	(131)	(29)

intellectual involvement of men, and the weakest effect appears on the organizational dimension. The relationship between social class and the sub-indices of involvement is presented in Table 31.

The consistency of the effect of social class on ritual involvement is broken only by the high degree of participation among those men scored 2 on the index. These men at the middle of the status ladder are the most observant of ritual among men, and their mean score even exceeds that of their female counterparts (recall Table 23). Overall, the effect of class on ritual involvement among men is greater than was observed earlier among women.

It will be recalled from Chapter 3 that men and women dif-

TABLE 31

SOCIAL CLASS HAS ITS GREATEST EFFECT ON THE INTELLECTUAL
INVOLVEMENT OF MEN

	Index of social class				
	Low				High
	0	1	2	3	4
Mean scores of men on:					
Ritual involvement	.61	.59	.71	.56	.40
	(56)	(128)	(160)	(136)	(52)
Organizational involvement	.37	.22	.31	.28	.30
	(41)	(104)	(135)	(116)	(44)
Intellectual involvement	.50	.27	.27	.19	.11
	(48)	(110)	(153)	(135)	(53)

fered more on organizational involvement than on either of the other dimensions. This was attributed in part to the greater occupational concerns of men and to the commensurate overrepresentation of women's organization in the church's program. It is hardly surprising, then, to note that social class has virtually no effect on the organizational involvement of men, although there is again a slight tendency for lower status men to be more involved than those of higher status.

In terms of intellectual involvement, the effect of class is strong and clear. The strength of the relationship depends largely on the very high level of intellectual involvement among those men scored lowest (0) on social class. A similar pattern was observed among women, though, as will be recalled from Table 23. Comparatively, men and women at the lowest level of status have virtually the same level of intellectual involvement. But among men, involvement on this dimension decreases more rapidly with increasing class, and the overall effect is greater among men than among women.

When age is introduced as a control variable, the relationship between class and involvement becomes more inconsistent than among women (see Table 32).

Among men under thirty years of age, the negative association between class and involvement is generally maintained, although this observation must be based on relatively few cases. By con-

TABLE 32

SOCIAL CLASS HAS A LESS CONSISTENT EFFECT ON MEN'S INVOLVEMENT
WHEN AGE IS CONSIDERED

| | Index of social class | | | | |
| | Low | | | | High |
	0	1	2	3	4
Mean involvement (C.I.I.) scores among men aged:					
Under 30	.50	.36	.40	.29	.00
	(6)[a]	(21)	(21)	(7)[a]	(1)[a]
30 to 49	.25	.32	.35	.30	.25
	(15)	(38)	(71)	(63)	(22)
50 and over	.49	.35	.40	.32	.25
	(15)	(29)	(35)	(42)	(21)

[a] Note the small number of cases on which scores are based.

trast, the effect is curvilinear among middle-aged men. Involvement increases from the lower end of the class index to the middle category, and then decreases again as we move to the highest score. Men highest (4) and lowest (0) on social class have the same involvement level. Among the older men, the original effect of class on involvement is regained, although it is not completely consistent.

The effect of age on involvement is also inconsistent. We recall from the examination of women parishioners that involvement increased with age at each class level. A corresponding effect is found only among men of fairly high social status (scores of 3 and 4). Among men with low or moderate social status, involvement declines as they enter their middle years, and as they pass their fiftieth year, it returns to a level virtually the same as that of their youth. The observed decline and recovery might also be explained in terms of occupational activities. As a man enters his primary breadwinning years, it is conceivable that he is unable to devote as much attention to religious matters as was possible during his youth and will be possible later in his retirement years.

Among women, involvement in the Episcopal Church appeared to function as an alternative source of gratification for those women denied access to other prestigious organizations and activities in the secular community. While the effect of social class is not as strong among men, a similar conclusion may be reached. As Table 33 shows, upper status men are much more likely to have held offices in secular organizations than is true of those men with lower scores on the social class index.

When holding secular office is introduced to the examination

TABLE 33

UPPER STATUS MEN ARE MORE LIKELY TO HAVE HELD
OFFICE IN SECULAR ORGANIZATIONS

| | Index of social class | | | | |
| | Low | | | | High |
	0	1	2	3	4
Percentage of men belonging to secular organizations who have held office:	32 (37)	39 (100)	48 (122)	59 (112)	68 (41)

of social class and involvement among men, a finding similar to that discovered among women appears. While the effect of social class is not completely erased among men who have held office in secular organizations, the effect is nonetheless weaker and less consistent than is true among men who have not held such offices (see Table 34).

TABLE 34

SOCIAL CLASS HAS LESS EFFECT ON CHURCH INVOLVEMENT AMONG
MEN WHO HAVE HELD OFFICE IN SECULAR ORGANIZATIONS

| | Index of social class | | | | |
| | Low | | | | High |
	0	1	2	3	4
Mean involvement (C.I.I.) scores among men who:					
Have held office	.33	.30	.35	.23	.26
	(12)	(35)	(57)	(64)	(28)
Have not held office	.39	.34	.32	.36	.20
	(20)	(50)	(59)	(44)	(13)

The contention that church involvement serves as an alternative to status gratification in the secular society cannot be made as strongly among men as was justified in the case of women. In Table 34 it will be noted that social class is related to church involvement even among those men who have held secular offices, and among those who have not, the relationship is not altogether consistent. Still there are grounds for concluding that a similar process takes place among men as was observed among women.

SUMMARY AND CONCLUSIONS

Among church members, lower status parishioners appear consistently more involved in the church than is true of those who enjoy a higher social status. This was observed in terms of the composite measure of involvement. Along the individual dimensions, the effect is more noticeable in intellectual involvement than in ritual or organizational participation in the church. It seems quite likely that lower status parishioners feel somewhat uneasy about participating in a church commonly regarded as upper class. This would account for the lessening of the relationship in those aspects of involvement which call for close social interaction among members.

In the light of the data examined thus far, a case may be made for the hypothesis that involvement in a prestigious church such as the Protestant Episcopal may serve to alleviate the unfulfilled status needs of lower class members. It does not appear that upper status parishioners turn to the church to consolidate their social standing. Among women, at least, church involvement seems only part of a general orientation toward community activity. If an upper status woman is active generally, this is reflected in her church involvement; if she is inactive generally, this, too, is reflected in her church ties.

These conclusions should ring a familiar bell. In the immediately preceding chapter, it was suggested that the church may serve as a family surrogate for the families. Evidently, the church may serve as an alternative gratification for those deprived of social status just as it serves those deprived of family ties. This issue will be examined in more depth in the following chapter.

Before turning to it, however, there is a need to compare these findings for Episcopalians with the research on social class and religion cited earlier. Previous research is far from being consistent, particularly when different measures are used to define religion. It has been rather consistently found, however, that the lower class is the most resistant to church membership per se. While our own data have nothing to say on this matter, they do show that among church members, parishioners of lower status are the most likely to be deeply involved. This suggests, as a possible clue to the discrepant findings, that they may be a function of the different populations studied. While the church underattracts the less privileged population generally, it obtains greatest allegiance from those it does attract.

Chapter 5

A Theory of Involvement

The preceding analysis has aimed at the elaboration and evaluation of previous speculations and empirical research on the subject of religious involvement. These have been tested in the light of the present data on Episcopal parishioners' religious behavior. In this endeavor, we have sought to ferret out the persistent correlates of religious involvement. While some of the prior findings and expectations have been generally confirmed, some have found little support, and others have been contradicted.

Such an eclectic approach has generated two problems which require some resolution if the analysis is to progress further. One problem is methodological. Since sex, age, family, and socioeconomic status each have an independent effect on involvement, these effects should be controlled as the analysis continues. However, controlling for all of them simultaneously would have the consequence, given the size of the sample, of reducing the number of cases in each cell of future tables to statistically unstable sizes. Some way must be found, therefore, to introduce the necessary controls in a more simplified, but still effective form, enabling the analysis to proceed meaningfully but with a minimum of confusion.

The second problem is of theoretical import. Some recognition of the significant relationships between several independent variables and church involvement has been achieved. The question now arises as to whether these may be ordered within some more general proposition concerning the nature of involvement. Why should being female, older, famililess, and lower class more readily predispose parishioners to church involvement than the opposites of these characteristics?

AN INDEX OF PREDISPOSITION TO INVOLVEMENT

In the interest of resolving both problems, a composite index was constructed which simultaneously reflected all four of the characteristics found to have independent effects on involvement. The procedure followed was a relatively simple one. Each parishioner was assigned a score commensurate with his possession of those attributes which were associated with involvement. On the basis of sex, women received a score of *2* and men a score of *0*. To this was added a score based on age: *2* for parishioners over fifty years of age, *1* for those between thirty and fifty, and *0* for those under thirty. This combined score was further modified by a score for family status: parishioners who were both childless and spouseless received an additional *2*; *1* was given to those with either a spouse or child, and *0* to those having both a spouse and a child. Finally, a score based on socioeconomic status was added: a score of *2* was given to all parishioners low (*0* or *1*) on the index of social class, *1* for those scored *2* or *3* on class, and *0* for those designated as highest (*4*) on class. (A more detailed discussion of the predisposition index is presented in Appendix B.)

Scores on the composite predisposition index ranged from *0* to *8*. In terms of the scoring procedure, parishioners scored *0* on the index would be *young, upper-status men* with *complete families*. Those scored *8* would be *lower status, elderly women* with *neither spouse nor children*. The higher the score, the more the number of attributes possessed by the parishioner which are predisposing to high involvement. As it turns out, no one in the sample was scored at the lowest end (*0*), but some parishioners were scored at each of the other levels of predisposition to involvement.

The scoring of individual parishioners, it is to be recognized, did not take into account their actual involvement in the church. For example, all women were scored *2* on the basis of sex regardless of whether or not they were deeply involved in the church. All men received *0*, even deeply involved men. In each instance, scoring was based on the overall relationship between a given attribute (such as sex) and involvement.

Observations from earlier chapters suggest that the combination of these attributes has a cumulative effect on involvement. For example, sex and social class were seen to affect church involvement jointly. Similarly, missing both family components was reflected in a greater involvement than missing only one. The construction of the composite predisposition index is based on the assumption that a combination of all the attributes should produce an even stronger effect on parishioners' involvement. Parishioners scored 8 on the predisposition index should be the most involved, those scored 1 should be the least involved. Furthermore, involvement should increase steadily with the number of predisposing attributes which parishioners possess. Table 35 tests this basic assumption and strongly supports it.

TABLE 35

CHURCH INVOLVEMENT INCREASES WITH INCREASING PREDISPOSITION SCORES

| | Index of predisposition to involvement | | | | | | | |
| | Low | | | | | | | High |
	1ᵃ	2	3	4	5	6	7	8
Mean involvement scores on C.I.I.	.23	.31	.36	.45	.51	.60	.62	.72
	(23)	(155)	(205)	(312)	(246)	(136)	(91)	(33)

ᵃ Recall that no parishioner was scored *0* on the index.

Parishioners scored lowest on the predisposition index show a mean involvement score of *.23*. With each successive rise in predisposition score, there is a corresponding increase in mean involvement. Where it was discovered earlier that one might speak of a person being predisposed to church involvement by virtue of sex, social class, age or family status, it is now evident that parishioners may be classified as more or less predisposed in terms of the number of predisposing attributes they possess. The effects of the several factors are clearly additive.

With few exceptions, the same pattern emerges when the subindices of involvement are considered. Minor fluctuations will be noted in regard to ritual involvement, but the overall relationship is still clear. And predisposition scores provide a powerful predictor of parishioners' organizational and intellectual involvement in their church (see Table 36).

TABLE 36

RITUAL, ORGANIZATIONAL AND INTELLECTUAL INVOLVEMENT
ALL INCREASE WITH INCREASING PREDISPOSITION SCORES

| | Index of predisposition to involvement | | | | | | | |
| | Low | | | | | | | High |
	1	2	3	4	5	6	7	8
Mean scores on:								
Ritual								
involvement	.43	.60	.60	.64	.67	.71	.79	.77
	(30)	(185)	(258)	(380)	(300)	(185)	(107)	(48)
Organizational								
involvement	.24	.32	.34	.50	.54	.66	.66	.71
	(23)	(160)	(219)	(333)	(262)	(153)	(95)	(36)
Intellectual								
involvement	.13	.17	.24	.27	.38	.41	.49	.60
	(31)	(178)	(242)	(363)	(284)	(177)	(100)	(46)

The findings of Tables 35 and 36 provide assurance that the predisposition index will satisfy the need for simultaneously controlling for the several attributes as the analysis proceeds. The problem now is to understand why the several attributes, individually and in concert, have the observed effect on parishioners' church involvement.

THE SITUATIONAL BASES OF INVOLVEMENT

At this point, it is important to remember the earlier distinction between factors facilitating and motivating involvement. Facilitating factors, it will be recalled, refer to the degree to which the parishioner's objective situation allows his involvement; motivating factors bear on his desire to be involved.

It is quite conceivable that the relationships discovered thus far are merely examples of the former—differences in opportunities for involvement generated by parishioners' social circumstances. Involvement, at least as it has been measured here, requires an investment of the parishioner's time—time to attend worship services, to participate in organizational meetings, and to read religious literature and periodicals. Such free time, quite possibly, is more readily available to women, to older persons, and to people without family ties, contrasted with men, the young, and those who are bound up in the responsibilities of family life.

A man's occupation generally commands the better part of his day and perhaps invades his leisure as well. While the woman's daily commitments may be no less demanding, they are, at any rate, normally more flexible. In understanding the effect of family status, the responsibilities of caring for children may often preclude participation in church activities. Regarding age differences, young people are more likely to be preoccupied with the multifarious activities vaguely included in the process of "shaping a future"; older people, on the other hand, have arrived at their "futures," many have retired, and they are generally afforded a greater leisure.

If the concept of leisure is modified to consider those requirements imposed by cultural mores regarding life-styles, social status differentials may also be understood as exemplifying a set of facilitating factors. While the upper-status parishioners may be freed from the mundane drudgeries of life, they are expected to participate in a broader spectrum of secular activities—service, civic and social. Those with lower social status, on the other hand, may actually be barred from some of these activities, and certainly such participation is not expected of them. Leisure time, so modified, would appear to represent a scarcer commodity for the upper class than for those whose class status places no such demands for secular participation.

The effect of facilitating factors, of course, is cumulative—that is, demands on free time increase with the number of "time-consuming" attributes a person possesses. Hence, while women may have more free time than men, childless women have more than mothers. Taking this into account strengthens the contention that existential differences in opportunities for church involvement contribute to explaining the results reported in Tables 35 and 36. However, this is clearly not the whole explanation.

The nature of the involvement indices themselves precludes this possibility. The indices measure not only how active people are in the church; they also reflect the proportion of a parishioner's total energies which is devoted to it. In particular, the measures of organizational and intellectual involvement, it will be recalled, are indicators of involvement as well as activity. Moreover, intellectual involvement is not a function of available time as much as it reflects the saliency of religion for the individual. If the amount of available time stood alone in differentiating involvement, the relationship between scores on the predisposition index and intellectual involvement should not have appeared.

The explanation in terms of facilitating factors, while making common sense, is not sufficient to incorporate all the various relationships which exist. Hence, while the facilitating effects of these attributes may determine much of one's church involvement, it seems likely that there may be some other dynamic operating with regard to the relationships. But what is that dynamic? What theoretical reconciliation is possible among such diverse attributes?

SOCIETAL VALUES AND INVOLVEMENT

The beginning of an answer has already appeared. Chapter 4 closed with the observation of a similarity in the effects of family status and social class on church involvement. In both instances, the church appeared to serve as an alternative source of gratification for parishioners who were missing something in their secular lives. The church was characterized as a family surrogate for the famililess and as a source of status for those denied it in the secular community. Church involvement was seen as a response to deprivations experienced by parishioners.

In a sense, each of the attributes associated with church involvement represents a departure from the implicit and explicit ideals of American society. First, with regard to sex, there appears little doubt that our society remains, even to this day, a male-dominated one. Despite the extensive inroads into the social, political and occupational structures gained by women since the passage of the Nineteenth Amendment in 1920, equality of the sexes can scarcely be called a reality even today. Women still fight for equal employment opportunities, are denied serious consideration for many professions, and are still shackled by traditional images concerning the role of the "decent" woman in society. Especially with regard to those functions which are most highly valued by the society, judged by the responsibility and respect involved, it is the service of males which is called for in nearly all instances. Child-rearing is perhaps the single exception to this generalization, insomuch as it is considered a crucial function for the survival and growth of the society. Few if any males, however, exhibit any desire to have child-rearing made their responsibility. On the other hand, many women aspire to positions and occupations now dominated by men.

With respect to age, the flood of adolescent entertainers and the few, conspicuous elder statesmen appear to be exceptions to a general value placed on responsible youth in America. And while even adolescents are expected to grow into mature young adults, the elderly are especially devalued by the norms of contemporary American society. Witness the increasing concern with geriatrics as an effort to prevent old people from becoming a burden on society. While the call for employment of senior citizens may frequently stress the economic value of this important resource, it seldom fails to mention the importance of restoring a sense of meaning to the lives of the elderly. The list of such examples might be continued at length without altering the conclusion that the young, rather than the old, are closer to the mainstream of American values.

The stature of the family as a sacred institution in American society has already been discussed in Chapter 2. Deviations from the normative family pattern evoke feelings of sympathy or rebuke. While the deviant may be pitied for his deprivation in this regard, there is also the implicit feeling that an important norm has been violated, and the deviant is regarded as something of a threat to society. A partial break with the normative pattern seems less critical than a total break. Even if one has no children, it is somehow better to be married than to be single. The most highly valued situation, however, is to have both a spouse and children.

Finally, Americans value, in deeds if not always in words, material wealth and high social status. The theme of upward mobility underlies the American dream. It is central to much of our educational system. Certainly, while few are able to achieve high status and wealth, such are the goals to which most Americans aspire.

It would appear then that those characteristics which are most closely associated with more intense church involvement are, at the same time, least valued by the general society. The data, of course, describe only Episcopalian parishioners. Nonetheless, it seems likely that the same variables would influence church involvement in other denominations as well, although perhaps to different degrees.

It does not necessarily follow that these variables would have the same cumulative effect on influencing church membership per se. As seen in the preceding chapter, the lower and working classes are less likely to provide church members than are the middle and upper classes. Similarly, we suspect that persons deprived of complete families are less likely to be church members than those who are not deprived in this way. The fact that the church and the family are so closely connected is probably a bar to membership on the part of those without families. The church, of course, is only one institution which can help alleviate social deprivation. Lower status and famililess people may turn to other institutions for relief more readily than they turn to the church. The important point is that among people who are attracted to membership, the church wins a greater commitment from those whose attributes are less highly esteemed by the general society.

As far as the data examined thus far in the analysis apply, there should be little doubt that those characteristics which are devalued by the secular society and by the church, are positively related to high church involvement—this is a matter of fact. More interesting is the question of why this should be true. Is there some reason to expect that other devalued characteristics would have the same effect, or is the devalued nature of these particular attributes simply a matter of chance? It has already been suggested that the answer to this puzzle may lie in the gratifications derived from participation in the larger society.

Talcott Parsons laid the groundwork for such an explanation when he chose to approach the broad problem of stratification in terms of moral evaluation.

Stratification *in its valuational aspect* then is the ranking of units in a social system in accordance with the standards of the common value system.[1]

.   .   .   .

Specific judgments of evaluation are not applied to the system unit as such—except in a limiting case—but to particular properties of that unit—always by comparison with others in the system. These properties may be classificatory, in the sense of characterizing the unit independently of its relations to other objects in a system as in the case of sex, age or specific abilities, or they may be relational, characterizing the way in which it is related to other entities as in the case of membership in a kinship unit.[2]

The attributes which a society values most it is also more likely to reward. Such rewards appear in different forms: money, power, status, attention, a sense of belonging, and so forth. People who lack the valued attributes, are to some extent, deprived of the concomitant rewards. The church, then, becomes an alternative source of rewards for those who cannot fully enjoy the fruits of secular society. Parishioners who feel outside the mainstream of society by virtue of being famililess find a surrogate family in the church. Elderly parishioners who may feel cast out of the youth-oriented secular society find acceptance within the church. Lower class parishioners are taught that secular status is ultimately irrelevant. Women who are denied serious consideration for the responsible positions in secular society find they can be very important to the life of the church. In sum, the church offers a refuge for those who are denied access to valued achievements and rewards in everyday American life.

This *Comfort Hypothesis* would help explain the observed effects of sex, age, family status and social class on church involvement. Parishioners whose life situations most deprive them

---

[1] Talcott Parsons, "A Revised Analytical Approach to the Theory of Social Stratification," in *Essays in Sociological Theory* (Glencoe, Ill.: The Free Press, 1954), p. 388. (Emphasis in the original.) An earlier statement of this position may be found in Parsons' 1940 essay: "An Analytical Approach to the Theory of Social Stratification," reprinted in the same volume.

[2] *Ibid.*, p. 389.

of satisfaction and fulfillment in the secular society turn to the church for comfort and substitute rewards. This is most clearly seen in the case of the two extreme types on the predisposition index. On the one hand, the upper class young father is the darling of our society. His life situation represents much that is considered ideal. He is afforded access to valued achievements and, in turn, is granted greater rewards. As Tables 35 and 36 show, he is hardly involved in the church at all. At the other extreme, the older lower class spinster enjoys little that would be considered ideal in terms of predominant secular values. Her inability to participate fully and meaningfully in the secular society results in a far greater involvement in church life.

However correct this interpretation may be, it does not encompass the behavior of all parishioners. There remains a minority of members whose social attributes would presumably predispose them away from the church but who are nevertheless highly involved in it. At the other extreme, there are those who have all the characteristics associated with deep involvement, but who are relative apostates. And at every point between these extremes are instances in which the various attributes do not have the expected effects.

These seeming disconfirmations might be accommodated within the general theory in a number of ways. It is possible that the effects of some of these attributes are conditioned by other aspects of the parishioner's total life situation. For example, among women who report holding office in secular organizations, social class does not affect church involvement. While the lack of education and income would normally be felt as a deprivation, the feeling of devaluation is evidently alleviated through the acquisition of status by other means. The church is one but not the only source of comfort for the socially deprived.

Furthermore, no claim is made that the attributes examined in this study are the only factors determining a person's subjective status within the society. Many people are deprived of secular rewards by virtue of their race. National origins prevent others from fully participating in American social life. Similarly, certain bizarre physical deformities deprive people of participation to a greater extent than would be warranted by their physical limitations. There are theoretical grounds for expecting that these forms of deprivation would affect the extent of church involvement, although the present data do not permit an empirical test of the expectation.

If it were possible to exhaust the indicators of social deprivation, it is still unlikely that a complete understanding of church involvement would be forthcoming. The phenomenon is clearly more complex than that. Nevertheless, it should be evident that the *Comfort Hypothesis* provides one important avenue toward the explanation of religious differences.

SUMMARY AND CONCLUSIONS

This short chapter has represented an attempt to synthesize what had been observed earlier and to establish a more general theoretical framework for understanding religious involvement. The result has been the discovery of a very strong cumulative relationship between the possession of four attributes and extensive participation in church life. Parishioners whose life situations most deprive them of prestige and gratification in the secular society are the most involved in the church. The church, then, was characterized as an alternative source of rewards for the socially deprived.

This interpretation would seem to be in harmony with the observations of contemporary critics of the church. However, before considering that issue, as well as the more general question of this study's implications for the church's role in society, it seems wise to examine the church's effectiveness in challenging its parishioners. If the church is found to perform both a comforting *and* challenging role, the implications will be different than if we learn that it serves a comforting function only. Whether parishioners are challenged by their commitment to adopt values promulgated by the church is the subject of Part Two of the book.

THE CONSEQUENCES
OF CHURCH INVOLVEMENT

Chapter 6

The "Political" Role of the Church

The preceding chapters have dealt with the social sources of church involvement and have sought to explain why some parishioners become more deeply committed than others. In Part Two, constituting the remainder of the book, we shall be concerned with investigating the consequences of differential involvement: What differences does it make that some people are more religious than others?

There is a wealth of anecdotal material on this topic. The biographies of saints and of church leaders as well as prominent laymen all testify to the power of religion to change individual lives. Such examples say little, however, about the effect of religion on ordinary laymen.

This subject has received some scientific attention, though not very much and the results have not been highly conclusive. The earliest studies perhaps are those conducted by Hartshorne and May in the late twenties and early thirties.[1] They were interested in assessing the effects of attendance at worship services and participation in Sunday Schools on ethical behavior such as being honest and kind to others. By and large, the investigators found very little evidence of a religious effect. Given the limited range of the effects studied and the nonrepresentativeness of the samples, however, their research cannot be said to resolve the problem.

Later in the thirties, Thorndike, in one of his studies of cities,[2]

[1] Hugh Hartshorne and Mark A. May, *Studies in the Nature of Character* (New York: Macmillan, 1928). See especially volume I, *Studies in Deceit.*

[2] Edward L. Thorndike, *Your City* (New York: Harcourt, Brace, 1939).

found that where a high proportion of an urban population are church members, the city's morals (measured in terms of crime, juvenile delinquency, and other forms of deviant behavior) are somewhat lower than where the proportion of church members is smaller. But, once again, the study design tends to weaken the conclusiveness of the finding and indeed, does not warrant the inference that church membership causes immorality.

On a somewhat different topic, more recent evidence suggests that churchgoers tend to be somewhat more conservative in their social attitudes than non-churchgoers. In his *Communism, Conformity and Civil Liberties*,[3] Stouffer finds that churchgoers generally, and active ones in particular, are less civil libertarian than are non-churchgoers. Even in Stouffer's study, however, only a correlation between the two relevant variables is available, and there is no evidence that the church experience per se produced the anti-civil libertarian attitudes.

Lenski attempts to deal with civil libertarianism in his study of Detroiters, and some of his data suggest that the effect of religiosity differs among Catholics as contrasted with Protestants. Lenski's Catholic sample seems to confirm Stouffer's findings, while high religiosity among Protestants appears to result in more civil libertarianism. However, Lenski frequently changes his measures of religious involvement and it is difficult to judge the continuity and consistency of his findings.

The fact that so little of what might be called scientific research has appeared in this area deserves an explanation—one which might also preface the following examination of Episcopalians. The existing deficiency seems to issue from two major problems. The first of these is the difficulty of making meaningful measurements of religiosity. As was discussed at length in Chapter 1, the churches have generally failed to elaborate specific definitions of what constitutes a "religious man." The second major problem concerns the lack of firm expectations as to the behavior appropriate for a conscientious parishioner. While the churches have constantly attempted to lay down general guidelines for social behavior, they have hesitated in most instances to demand specific behavior from their members. Moreover, it

[3] Samuel A. Stouffer, *Communism, Conformity and Civil Liberties* (Garden City, N.Y.: Doubleday, 1955).

has seldom been possible to evaluate the effectiveness of these general attempts to inform church members.

What can we hope to learn ultimately from the data now available? It is first evident that no comparison can be forth-coming which would evaluate the effect of church membership as such, for all the subjects in this study are Episcopalian parish-ioners. However, in dealing with the first problem mentioned above, some effort has already gone into the measurement of differential degrees of involvement reflected in parishioners' re-ligious behavior. Hence, it is possible to determine the effects, if any, of deep church involvement as contrasted with nominal or weak involvement.

In terms of the second problem, the effects of church involve-ment might take a variety of forms. An individual might be moved to restructure his life's goals. His view of society might be affected, and his conception of the church's role in society modi-fied. His involvement in the church might bring about a state of calm and serenity, or a sense of frustration and despair. These are but a few of the effects attributed to the religious commit-ment of specific individuals in the past. What indicators do the data provide? For present purposes, there is information on two broad areas which one might reasonably expect to be affected by church involvement. These are:

(1) Parishioners were asked a number of questions regarding the propriety of the Protestant Episcopal Church and clergy be-coming involved in the social and political issues of the day. It is possible, therefore, to assess the effect of church involvement on parishioners' perceptions of the Church's legitimate responsibili-ties in the realm of public affairs.

(2) At the same time, parishioners were asked for their own personal opinions on several current issues, most of which had been the subjects of Church policy statements. We may deter-mine if deep church involvement has the effect of bringing parishioners into agreement with the Church on such issues.

When the analysis turns to questions of this nature, a meth-odological problem is introduced which was of no practical con-sequence for the preceding discussion. In determining the sources of involvement, there was no question as to the direction of the observed relationships. To the extent that women were more deeply involved than men, it was reasonable to infer that being female predisposed women parishioners to higher degrees of involvement than was the case for men. Sex, like the other variables considered, was clearly prior in time to the variable of church involvement. In the present instance, however, such an inference is not necessarily warranted. If it were discovered, for example, that church involvement and honesty were highly related to one another, two explanations might be logically supported. First, it might be contended that church involvement had the effect of instilling the virtue of honesty in its members. On the other hand, however, it could just as logically be contended that honest parishioners value the church experience more than the dishonest. This problem cannot, of course, be avoided in a situation where there is no definite time dimension. The only means for resolving such a problem would be to conduct a longitudinal study over a period of time whereby the temporal appearance of the relevant variables could be observed.

This difficulty notwithstanding, it is still possible to establish the degree of association between church involvement and parishioners' orientations to a number of important social and political matters. Even if there can be no final conclusion as to the direction of the relationships, it is still of significant value to know whether the relationships exist at all. In the very least, such discoveries provide a departure point for subsequent research on the interplay between church involvement and ideology. And in those instances where a relationship might be reasonably expected, and none exists, we have added that much more to our understanding of church involvement.

The present chapter will examine the extent to which involvement is related to parishioners' attitudes toward the Protestant Episcopal Church's participation in the political life of the secular society. Chapter 7 will focus on the relationship between involvement and agreement with the Church's actual positions on social, economic and political issues.

THE HISTORICAL ROLE OF THE CHURCH IN SOCIETY

As is suggested by contemporary criticism of the church, one of the more controversial and still unresolved questions in American religious and political life revolves around the appropriate role of the church in public affairs. The range of opinions on this issue is exemplified by statements such as "the church should stick to religion and stay out of politics," and "everything in the sight of God is the responsibility of the church."

At one time or another throughout American history, the church's actual role has reflected many points along the continuum between these two extremes. In prerevolutionary America, the idea that the church had both authority and competence in the political realm was accepted and practiced in some of the colonies—Massachusetts for example. In others, notably those in which the Church of England was predominant, the doctrine of the separation of church and state was already realized in practice. With the establishment of the Republic and the formal adoption of the First Amendment to the Constitution, the church's potential for influence in public affairs was markedly circumscribed. The question of the church's role in government was seemingly settled; still at issue was its role in dealing with social problems and questions of morality.

Through the late nineteenth century, the prevailing position of the churches was one of relative aloofness from social problems. The legitimate path for the church to follow was to win individuals to Christ, not to try to Christianize a still unredeemed society. This emphasis on individual responsibility was reflected, of course, in the general temper of much of the nineteenth century, secular as well as religious.

The late nineteenth and early twentieth centuries saw the introduction of "social gospel" theology and with it, the church's social responsibility again became a salient issue. The traditional posture of aloofness came under increasing attack. For a time, it was widely believed that secular society itself could be Christianized without the conversion of its secular members. The extent of change required in the system was an open issue, however, and "social gospelers" differed in their appraisals of this requirement. Nonetheless, there was substantial agreement that capitalism in its existing form constituted a formidable obstacle to the advent of the Kingdom of God on earth.

It should be noted that social gospel ideology, even at its height, never became the predominant view of American denominations, their clergy, or their parishioners. Nevertheless, it had an effect, which, despite a subsequent decline, has continued to exert some influence on American Protestantism even today.

In the Protestant Episcopal Church, the social gospel movement was not without influence. In fact, a number of Episcopalian clergymen were among its pioneers. Two unofficial church bodies—the Church Association for the Advancement of the Interests of Labor, and the Society of Companions of the Holy Cross—were among the first organized groups to champion the movement's cause and ideals. Sparked by the "social gospelers," demands that the Church assume some official responsibility for dealing with social issues and problems grew to such an extent that in 1901, the General Convention of the Church officially acknowledged this responsibility. It passed a resolution establishing a commission to deal with relations between capital and labor. In the preamble to the resolution, the Convention set forth its conviction that the Church has a legitimate role to play in the economic and political life of society.

Once the initial step was taken in 1901, consideration of resolutions on social issues became an accepted practice of the General Convention. This active social role was legitimated as the Church's moral and religious duty growing out of its commitment to the brotherhood of man. This is clearly reflected in the following resolution passed in 1937:

> The Church must not sit quietly by when the world faces acute social and political problems. It is intensely concerned with those crises that bring misery and need to God's children. Hunger, persecution, exploitation and injustice, all the ills that beset man and hinder the development of free personality, are its responsibility. Our hearts must be stirred in such a way that it will be our desire and passion to find jobs for the jobless, to carry hope to the hopeless, to assure relief to the oppressed, and in the words of the Oxford Conference on Life and Work, "To secure the best possible social and economic structure in so far as such structures and institutions are determined by human decisions."

Though the Protestant Episcopal Church has officially acknowledged social and political responsibilities for itself, the basic question of the legitimacy of its participation in the social order is by no means a closed issue. The topic is continually recurrent, leading Weston to call it an "endless debate." [4]

At the present time, the Church recognizes a responsibility to express its point of view on important questions of social, economic, and political policy. While it is not committed to an aggressive program of social action, neither does it advocate a posture of aloofness from the social world. In effect, while accepting the basic premises of the American political, economic, and social structures, the Church is concerned that its views on important issues be considered in the marketplace of ideas.[5]

CONTEMPORARY ATTITUDES CONCERNING THE SOCIAL ROLE OF THE CHURCH

The preceding observations represent the official Protestant Episcopal Church position. The analytic question we now wish to pursue is an assessment of the association between parishioners' involvement and their perceptions of the Church's proper role in society.[6] Are the more involved more likely to accept the Church's position? Before turning to this issue, however, it seems of descriptive interest to learn how parishioner sentiment compares with the views of bishops and priests.[7]

[4] M. Moran Weston, "Social Policy of the Episcopal Church in the Twentieth Century" (unpublished Ph.D. dissertation, Joint Committee on Graduate Instruction of Columbia University, 1953).

[5] Because the data were collected in 1952, and are being reported on in 1966, the literary question arises as to what tense to use in describing the results. We have opted for the present tense because what we shall be saying about the Protestant Episcopal Church is generally as true today as it was fourteen years ago. Use of the past tense would inadvertently create the mistaken impression that basic changes have occurred since 1952, as for example saying "the Church was concerned that its views on important issues. . . ." To be consistent, we shall also use the present tense in reporting on the data though, here, of course, changes in parishioner attitudes may very well have occurred since 1952.

[6] At issue here is the basic question of the Church's right to take an active role in public affairs. The particular positions considered appropriate for the church to adopt are discussed in Chapter 7.

[7] It will be recalled that the study collected data from clergy—bishops and priests—as well as parishioners. Heretofore, it has not been relevant to report on the data from clergy since the question of relative involvement in the Church is not an issue for them.

TABLE 37

Most Episcopalians Disagree That "Aside from Preaching, There Is
Little the Church Can Do about Social and Economic Problems"

	Bishops	Priests	Parishioners
Agree	1%	3%	10%
Disagree	96	96	86
Uncertain	3	1	4
100% =	94	250	1479
No answer	6	9	51
Total number	100	259	1530

Most Episcopalians agree that the Church has a worthwhile
contribution to make in the realm of public affairs and that it
should be concerned about making its position known. Fewer
than five percent of the clergy and just ten percent of the laity
subscribe to the proposition that "aside from preaching, there
is little that the Church can do about social and economic problems" (Table 37). And, there is scarcely greater support for
the proposal that "the Church should stick to religion and not
concern itself with social and economic problems" (Table 38).

This substantial agreement in principle, however, is not maintained when the question is raised as to how the Church is to
implement its concern with public affairs. In contrast to the
more than 90 percent of the clergy who felt that the Church
should concern itself with social and economic problems, about
70 percent agree that "it is proper for the Church to state its

TABLE 38

Most Episcopalians Disagree That "The Church Should
Stick to Religion and Stay out of Politics"

	Bishops	Priests	Parishioners
Agree	2%	1%	16%
Disagree	94	97	78
Uncertain	4	2	6
100% =	95	249	1478
No answer	5	10	52
Total number	100	259	1530

position on practical political issues to the local, state, or national government." The disparity is substantially greater among parishioners with 78 percent approving of the principle and 46 percent the practice (Table 39). While these figures exemplify

TABLE 39

PARISHIONERS MORE THAN CLERGY ARE IN DISAGREEMENT AS TO WHETHER "IT IS PROPER FOR THE CHURCH TO STATE ITS POSITION ON POLITICAL ISSUES TO THE LOCAL, STATE, AND NATIONAL GOVERNMENT"

	Bishops	Priests	Parishioners
Agree	72%	70%	46%
Disagree	16	20	42
Uncertain	12	10	12
100% =	92	248	1471
No answer	8	11	59
Total number	100	259	1530

the existence of the disparity, its character is more fully revealed in the responses to several more specific questions designed to establish the limits of acceptable behavior on the part of the Church and of its clergy within the realm of public affairs. Table 40 reports the proportion of clergy and parishioners consenting to the idea of the clergy speaking out on each of six current social issues.

Looking first at the responses of parishioners, they are most willing to accept the idea of the clergy speaking out on an issue of immediate and direct concern to the Church—*prayers in school*. They are least likely to approve of the clergy expressing their opinion on issues which are both controversial and involved in the economic structure of society—*labor legislation like the Taft-Hartley Law* and the issue of labor-management relations. Parishioners' resistance exhibits itself in most cases even though the questions are worded in a nonpartisan form.

The other three issues—political corruption, anti-Semitism, and birth control—share the qualities of not being highly controversial, and of being moral rather than economic in content. The majority of parishioners consider these issues as suitable subjects on which clergymen might voice their opinions though they are considered less appropriate than *prayers in schools*.

TABLE 40

EPISCOPALIANS ARE MORE INCLINED TO CONSIDER IT ALL RIGHT
FOR THE CLERGY TO SPEAK OUT ON SOME ISSUES THAN ON OTHERS

Issues	Percentage saying it is all right for clergy to speak out		
	Bishops	Priests	Parishioners
Prayers in schools	91	95	88
Political corruption	96	96	75
Anti-Semitism	87	95	69
Birth control	78	80	64
Labor relations like the Taft-Hartley Law	62	63	35
100% =	92	257	1473
No answer	8	2	57
Total number	100	259	1530

	Percentage disagreeing with the statement: "The Church has *no* responsibility to try to bring about more active cooperation between management and labor."		
	Bishops	Priests	Parishioners
	92	94	55
100% =	96	250	1466
No answer	4	9	64
Total number	100	259	1530

Judging from this evidence, it would appear that the Church can expect the most support from its members when it deals with issues which are manifestly the business of the Church. Somewhat less, though still substantial support is forthcoming to uphold the Church's right in dealing with moral issues, particularly those on which there is consensus regarding the correct stand to be taken. The figures indicate that the Church can expect considerably less support when it ventures into the economic realm. Such support is weak even when the issues are broached in nonpartisan terms. If a partisan position were taken by the Church, it seems likely that support would be even weaker, since parishioners whose own economic positions might be threatened would be unlikely to concur.

The clergy, bishops and priests both, are more likely than are parishioners to define all of these activities as being legitimate functions of the Church. And, insofar as they make distinctions, the clergy do not necessarily reflect the distinctions made by parishioners. Parishioners, for example, are more likely to support the clergy speaking out on an issue such as *prayers in schools* than on *political corruption* and *anti-Semitism;* the clergy perceive all as about equally legitimate. There is a suggestion here that clergy may be less inclined than the laity to make a distinction between religious and moral issues. However, this may be related to the controversiality of the moral issue. While one can expect a high consensus that political corruption is bad, the clergy exhibit less willingness to speak out on *birth control,* about which there remains some controversy in the Church as well as in the general community.[8]

Like parishioners, the clergy express most resistance to taking a stand on labor legislation such as the Taft-Hartley law. Comparatively, however, we note a majority of the clergy still approve of even this activity whereas such approval is forthcoming from only a minority of laymen. The extent of the clergy's resistance to speaking out on labor legislation is still considerably greater than their opposition to having the Church assume a responsibility for bringing about more active cooperation between management and labor. Here, in fact, only a very small minority of clergy are opposed. The very strong support of the clergy, as compared with the mild support of the parishioners, must be attributed to the clergy's greater awareness of the existence of an active program along these lines already conducted by the National Church. Under the circumstances, the clergy are perhaps less inclined than the laity to perceive the issue as one requiring a partisan stance on the Church's part.

A related but distinct component of the general debate about the church's proper role in public affairs has to do with the clergy's participation in politics. To what extent are Episcopalians willing to permit the parish priest to engage in political

---

[8] It should be noted that birth control and related issues have received somewhat more attention in the years subsequent to the survey of Episcopalians.

activity? Some insight into an answer is provided by the responses to a series of questions concerning acceptable ministerial behavior during an election campaign (Table 41).

TABLE 41

EPISCOPALIANS WOULD GRANT ONLY LIMITED APPROVAL
TO THE CLERGY'S PARTICIPATION IN POLITICS

Type of participation	Percentage saying it is all right for parish clergy to participate in politics		
	Bishops	Priests	Parishioners
Urge citizens to vote	95	97	89
Encourage its members to study political issues and candidates	91	92	76
Have some effort on the Sunday before election to get out the vote	71	70	50
Permit candidates to speak at the parish house	38	44	21
Endorse candidates for office	4	6	9
100% =	96	257	1519
No answer	4	2	11
Total number	100	259	1530

Nine out of ten parishioners agree that it is proper for the parish priest to urge his parishioners to vote. Seventy-six percent would have him encourage the membership of his church to study political issues and candidates. However, the more that the priest's activity would thrust him and his parish into the political arena as an active participant, the more reluctant are parishioners to voice approval. Only half approve his making some effort on the Sunday before election to get out the vote. Less than one-fourth think it proper to permit candidates to speak in the parish house, and only one parishioner in eleven would approve of the priest endorsing candidates for office.

The parishioners are exhibiting here the same attitude-set revealed in their responses to the more general questions regarding the church's participation in political, social and economic affairs. There is almost unanimity that the clergy should not completely divorce themselves from politics but no authority is given them save that of treading most softly in the political arena. Any suggestion of partisanship is clearly rejected. It is to be recognized, of course, that the data say nothing directly about the minister's right to engage in partisan politics as a private citizen. In his official role, however, parishioners are overwhelmingly reluctant to grant him this privilege.

Comparatively, the responses of the clergy—bishops and priests alike—parallel those of the laity; that is, they tend to rank the acceptability of the different activities in the same order. However, with one exception, the clergy are consistently more inclined than the laity to consider each activity acceptable as ministerial behavior. The sole exception—their greater disinclination to approve of the clergy endorsing candidates for office—is significant in its revelation that the clergy do not wish to use their official position for partisan political activity even as much as parishioners might allow. This cannot be interpreted to mean that the clergy are generally more resistant than the laity to having the Church take a partisan stand on public issues, however. Evidence to be presented later will show that they are much more disposed than parishioners to support partisan activity on the Church's part, at least in social and economic affairs. On the specific issue of partisan participation in politics, though, the finding reported may be reasonably generalized to include any sort of activity which would identify the minister publicly with the cause of one political party over another. But as the figures indicate, this is true for the vast majority of parishioners as well.

INVOLVEMENT AND POLITICAL PERMISSIVENESS

What bearing, if any, does the degree of the parishioner's involvement have on the kind of "political" role he envisions for the Church? Before turning to the data, it might be wise to consider the possibilities. Basically, there are three possible but conflicting outcomes.

First, the more deeply involved parishioners might be the most likely to favor an active role for the Church in secular affairs. This could be called the *Church Hypothesis*. Implicit in the Church's programs and preaching is the belief that involvement should have some effect on men's lives. If such were not the case, its intensive proselytizing would constitute something of an extreme anachronism. Those parishioners who become deeply involved in church life, then, should be expected to conform to the Church's desire to have its teachings inform the larger society.

Such an expectation, however, does not jibe necessarily with what we already know about the nature of involvement. It will be recalled that the highly involved were found to be the most in need of compensation for the deprivations experienced in their everyday lives. This, at least, is the implication of the data showing that those whose social characteristics are least valued in the general community are most active in church participation. What the earlier analysis did not indicate was whether church involvement under these circumstances reflected a wish to escape from the world or an attempt to live comfortably within it. These alternative interpretations suggest quite different relationships between involvement and permissiveness.

If deep church involvement reflects a sense of alienation from the world and a desire to escape from it through attachment to the church, the involved parishioner can hardly be expected to want his church to participate actively in the world he rejects. On the contrary, he is likely to want the church to escape from the world with him. Such an expectation might be called the *Marxian Hypothesis* in light of Marx's well known dictum that "religion is the opiate of the masses." In accord with this hypothesis, we should anticipate a negative relationship between involvement and permissiveness.

Finally, it is possible that parishioners deeply committed to the church because of felt deprivations might not exhibit a concommitant alienation from the secular world. The kinds of gratifications derived from church involvement may serve as adequate substitutes for what parishioners are denied in their secular lives. In this sense, church involvement may help the deprived to cope with the world rather than to escape from it. If the *Comfort Hypothesis* discussed earlier is correct, it would be reasonable to expect that church involvement would not be associated with political permissiveness one way or the other.

In summary, then, it is conceivable that differential church involvement and political permissiveness may be positively related, negatively related, or not related at all. What evidence may be introduced to test these alternatives? There is no difficulty in distinguishing parishioners according to the degree of their church involvement; we have recourse to either the Composite Index of Involvement or any of the three sub-indices—ritual, organizational, and intellectual. A measure of permissiveness is lacking, however. While parishioners' attitudes toward the Church's political role might be measured by responses to the individual questions examined earlier in the chapter, it seems wiser to consider the development of a single measure of permissiveness. Such a composite measure should reflect several responses, thus increasing confidence in its validity.

A SCALE OF POLITICAL PERMISSIVENESS

It will be recalled that parishioners were asked to indicate whether they would approve or disapprove of the clergy's participation in five political activities: urging citizens to vote, encouraging parishioners to study political issues and candidates, making some effort on the Sunday before election to get out the vote, permitting candidates to speak at the parish house, and endorsing candidates for office. Parishioners' responses to these questions followed a consistent pattern so that the number a parishioner endorsed was generally sufficient to predict which activities met his approval. If a parishioner approved of two activities, for example, he almost invariably endorsed "urging citizens to vote" and "encouraging parishioners to study political issues and candidates." If he approved four, the one activity he failed to approve was "endorsement of candidates for office." Given this pattern of response, it was possible to rank parishioners on a six-point ordinal scale, using Guttman's scaling technique. Table 42 reports the distribution of parishioners on this scale of political permissiveness.

As the overall responses to the five items would suggest, few parishioners are located on either extreme of the scale. Only 6 percent (scale type 5) would permit the minister to go so far as endorsing candidates for office. At the other extreme, only 8 percent (scale type 0) would deny their minister even the mildest forms of political activity. The distribution of parishioners along the scale represents a curve slightly skewed in the direc-

TABLE 42

DISTRIBUTION OF PARISHIONERS ON POLITICAL PERMISSIVENESS SCALE

	Scale Types					
	Most permissive					Least permissive
	5	4	3	2	1	0
Percentage of parishioners 100% = 1509ᵃ	6	16	34	27	9	8

ᵃ Twenty-one parishioners did not provide sufficient information to be scored on this scale.

tion of moderately active ministerial participation in the political realm.

Manifestly, this scale describes only one aspect of the more general conceptions parishioners have of the appropriate political role of the Church. However, a parishioner's position on the composite scale is predictive of his responses to other questions on the same general topic. For example, Table 43 reports the proportion of parishioners of each scale type who felt that the "Church should concern itself with social and economic problems and not stick to religion only," and who replied "it is proper for the Church to state its position on practical political issues to the local, state, or national governments."

TABLE 43

ATTITUDES TOWARD ROLE OF CHURCH IN PUBLIC LIFE ARE CORRELATED WITH PARISHIONERS' POSITIONS ON THE POLITICAL PERMISSIVENESS SCALE

	Percentage who agree					
Statements	Most permissive					Least permissive
	5	4	3	2	1	0
Church should concern itself with social and economic problems and not stick to religion only	88 (91)	85 (237)	81 (495)	80 (397)	57 (127)	56 (115)
It is proper for the Church to state its position on practical political issues to the local, state, or national governments	75 (90)	60 (236)	45 (497)	44 (393)	23 (126)	26 (113)

The higher a parishioner's score on the political permissiveness scale, the greater his willingness to have the Church concern itself generally with political and economic problems. Similarly, the more permissive parishioners expressed a greater acceptance of the Church's informing local, state and national governments of its position on practical political issues. While there is a relatively strong relationship between the parishioners' scale scores and their responses to both questions, the stronger relationship is that between the scale score and the second question, proposing that the Church take a specific kind of action. This second question presumably provides a slightly better indication of how parishioners might respond to actions by the Church as opposed to simply endorsing the general principle of political participation. The close correspondence between the scale score and the responses to both questions, however, lends support to the scale's validity as a measure of parishioners' basic sentiments regarding the political role of the Church.

The scale's validity is even more strongly supported when parishioners of each scale type are compared in their responses to the set of questions which asked whether it was proper for the clergy to speak out on a number of specific social and political issues (Table 44).

Once again, the predictive power of the scale is demonstrated and its validity as a measure of political permissiveness is sup-

TABLE 44

SUPPORT OF THE CLERGY'S SPEAKING OUT ON ISSUES IS HIGHLY
CORRELATED WITH POSITION ON THE POLITICAL PERMISSIVENESS SCALE

Issues	Percentage who agree that it is all right for clergy to speak out					
	Most permissive					Least permissive
	5	4	3	2	1	0
Prayers in school	89	89	87	85	81	71
Political corruption	86	85	79	69	49	36
Anti-Semitism in community	76	78	71	59	42	40
Birth control	68	66	55	46	35	30
Labor relations like the Taft-Hartley Law	71	53	33	27	6	11
Total number	94	242	510	411	132	119

ported. The most permissive parishioners (scale type 5) exhibit the greatest willingness to grant clergy the right to speak on each of the issues. Support declines as the scale score decreases; the least permissive (scale type 0) show the most resistance to the clergy speaking out on any issue. In fact, on only one issue—prayers in schools—do the majority of the least permissive parishioners agree the clergy should seek an informing role. This, of course, is the one issue of the five which bears directly on the Church's own interest and welfare.

Those who are most permissive, then, are willing to have the Church discuss both economic and non-economic issues, both Church-related and non-Church-related issues. Those who are least permissive hesitate to permit the Church to speak out on any issues, save those with a direct and traditional religious content. One set of issues, however, does not fit this pattern: those involving church-state relations. In this instance, even the more politically permissive are cautious about violating the traditional boundaries between church and state. On two questions dealing explicitly with church-state relations, there is little difference in the attitudes of the more and the less permissive parishioners: a substantial majority of each scale type take a position which would preserve the traditional separation (Table 45).

Both permissive and non-permissive parishioners agree, by and large, that religious instruction in public schools should not

TABLE 45

ATTITUDES TOWARD CHURCH-STATE RELATIONS ARE NOT CORRELATED
WITH POSITION ON THE POLITICAL PERMISSIVENESS SCALE

| | Percentage who agree | | | | | |
| Attitudes | Most permissive | | | | | Least permissive |
	5	4	3	2	1	0
Religious instruction in public schools should *not* be compulsory	69	87	83	76	77	82
	(90)	(240)	(501)	(403)	(131)	(115)
Government funds should *not* be used for support of parochial or religious schools	65	83	82	78	77	79
	(91)	(237)	(495)	(400)	(127)	(114)

be compulsory. When asked: "Should government funds be used for support of parochial schools?" most parishioners answer the question negatively, and the degree of permissiveness once again has little relationship to this response. In other words, permissive parishioners, it would seem, are as committed as the nonpermissive to the traditional norms of church-state separation.

It is evident from the data that the most permissive parishioners are not advocating that the Church become deeply embroiled in issuing pronouncements on the state of the social order. Certainly, they would not go so far as to abolish the limiting boundaries between church and state. At the same time, they are concerned that the Church not bury its head in the sand but, rather, express its positions on the important issues of the day. The least permissive parishioners take no such view. They adhere quite closely to the dictum that the "Church should stick to religion and stay out of politics." These varying definitions of what the Church may properly do in the realm of public affairs have been effectively reflected in the composite scale of political permissiveness.

INVOLVEMENT AND PERMISSIVENESS

The construction of the scale of political permissiveness now permits an examination of the relationship between involvement and permissiveness. To this end, parishioners were first grouped according to their scores on the Composite Index of Involvement. This index, it will be recalled, ranked parishioners according to the overall degree of their involvement. The scores range from 0 to 5, with a score of 5 signifying the greatest involvement and a score of 0 the least involvement. The next step is to compare the six involvement groups in terms of their political permissiveness. In making the comparison, mean permissiveness scores have been computed in the same fashion as mean involvement scores were computed earlier, ranging from a low of 0.0 to a high of 1.0. Table 46 reports the mean permissiveness scores of parishioners at each level of involvement.

Table 46 shows no consistent relationship in either direction between involvement and permissiveness. The amount of permissiveness neither rises nor declines in any regular pattern with

TABLE 46

THERE IS NO RELATIONSHIP BETWEEN CHURCH INVOLVEMENT AND PERMISSIVENESS

| | Composite Index of Involvement | | | | | |
| | High | | | | | Low |
	5	4	3	2	1	0
Mean score on political permissiveness scale	.48 (100)	.53 (171)	.52 (272)	.58 (256)	.53 (229)	.53 (163)

respect to changes in the degree of involvement. The most involved are slightly less inclined to be permissive than any of the other involvement groups. However, the fact that the mean permissiveness score for involvement group 2 differs almost as sharply from the general norm as does the score for involvement group 5 suggests that the differences are not meaningful.

It should be recognized that procedures such as the one adopted for computing mean permissiveness scores necessarily introduce an element of arbitrariness. As a result, they may inadvertently obscure existing relationships between the variables being examined. To guard against this possibility, a Pearson r correlation was computed for the association between involvement and permissiveness basing the computation on the data in their original form. Unlike mean scores, the correlation coefficient has a range from -1.0 to $+1.0$. A correlation equal to $+1.0$ would mean that there is a perfect, positive relationship between involvement and permissiveness. A correlation equal to -1.0 would indicate a perfect, negative relationship, and a correlation of 0 means there is no relationship in either direction. In this instance, the correlation computed was $-.04$, confirming the conclusion of Table 46 that involvement and permissiveness are irrelevant to each other.

Before drawing any more general conclusions from these results, however, it is wise to consider the possibility that involvement has a different meaning for some parishioners than for others. In the analysis reported in Chapter 5, it will be recalled, certain social characteristics were found to predispose parishioners to deep involvement while the counterparts of these characteristics had the opposite effect. However, neither effect was complete. While a group of parishioners might share social attributes which predispose them to a certain level of involvement, some deviated from the norm in their attachments to the church.

To determine the effect of such considerations on the findings just reported, Table 46 was recomputed with parishioners grouped according to their scores on the index of predisposition to involvement—the index which distinguishes parishioners according to the number of social attributes they possess which are predisposing to involvement. Table 47 shows that whether

TABLE 47

At Each Level of Predisposition, Involvement
Is Unrelated to Political Permissiveness

| | Composite Index of Involvement | | | | | | |
| | High | | | | | Low | |
	5	4	3	2	1	0	Pearsonian r
Mean permissiveness scores among the:							
Highly predisposed	.51	.49	.47	.49	.52	.46	−.027
	(46)	(57)	(76)	(44)	(21)	(13)	
Moderately predisposed	.45	.54	.53	.53	.52	.50	−.004
	(52)	(101)	(168)	(179)	(155)	(103)	
Undisposed	.80	.60	.59	.59	.57	.60	.025
	(2)*	(13)	(28)	(33)	(53)	(47)	

* Note the small number of cases upon which the mean score is based.

parishioners are highly predisposed (scores of 6 to 8 on the predisposition index), moderately predisposed (scores of 3 to 5) or undisposed (scores of 1 or 2), their actual level of involvement is irrelevant to their attitudes toward a political role for the Church. The lack of relationship between involvement and permissiveness is further indicated by the Pearson r correlation coefficients which are presented in the table.

Reading down the columns of the table an interesting relationship between predisposition to involvement and permissiveness is apparent. Parishioners who are denied prestige in the secular community (highly predisposed) are generally less approving of a political role for the Church. This would seem a partial confirmation of the *Marxian Hypothesis* which was discussed above. The more down-trodden parishioners exhibit a greater tendency to want the Church to escape from the secular society. However, in contradiction to the *Marxian Hypothesis,* deep commitment to the Church does not enhance this orientation. Nor, does it decrease the desire to have the Church withdraw from society. While involvement in the church clearly serves to comfort the sufferings of its members, such involvement is simply irrelevant to attitudes toward Church participation in the political sphere.

To insure that the findings were not an artifact of the Composite Index of Involvement, Tables 46 and 47 were recomputed, substituting the indices of ritual, organizational, and intellectual involvement in place of the composite index. For each index, the results were substantially the same. Also introduced was a measure of the parishioner's political sophistication, in case the implications of involvement for permissiveness differed among the politically sophisticated and among the unsophisticated. Politically sophisticated parishioners were found to be more permissive toward the Church's political role than were their unsophisticated counterparts. But, neither among the politically sophisticated nor among the unsophisticated was there a consistent relationship between involvement and permissiveness.

Judging from the effect of the predispositional index, it appears that parishioners' views on the political role appropriate for the Church are somewhat informed by their position in the secular culture. However, their location in the life of the parish has no effect. Thus, parishioners may bring to the church a desire to escape from the world or a desire for the church to change the world. Their involvement in the church, though, does not basically affect these wishes one way or the other: it neither increases their desire for withdrawal from the world nor encourages them to view the church as an instrument of social change. In sum, the two—involvement and political permissiveness—are essentially irrelevant to one another.

That this should be the case confirms the proposition expressed earlier that the extent to which a parishioner experiences gratifications from his everyday life in the secular world will influence his involvement in the church. The greater his gratifications within secular society, the less likely he is to become deeply involved in the church. In turn, those who are denied the rewards of the secular world are more prone to involve themselves deeply in the church. Whatever their attachments to the church, however, those deprived of status are less permissive than other parishioners. Involvement simply has no effect on this tendency.

SUMMARY

The foregoing analysis has contributed some information on the position which Episcopalians as a whole adopt toward the Church's involvement in public affairs. The predominant preference is to have the Church and its clergy steer a middle course between "sticking to religion," narrowly defined, and having it become embroiled in the controversial issues of the day. However, the more extreme positions at both ends of the continuum are maintained by a minority of both clergy and laity.

With one exception—partisan participation in political activity—the clergy are relatively more supportive of the principle that the Church has a responsibility for the secular society of which it is a part. They are also more inclined to have this principle realized in practice, though within relatively the same limits imposed by parishioners. Bishops and priests are remarkably alike in their points of view on this issue with the priests exhibiting a slightly more permissive attitude. The priest, of course, is under a great cross-pressure as he tries to resolve his own point of view, faced as he is with differences of opinion between his bishop and his parishioners. It is of more than passing interest that generally speaking, the priest tends more toward the views of the former than the latter.

Finally, a political permissiveness scale was constructed so that we might determine the effect of involvement on parishioners' attitudes toward the church's political role. No relationship was discovered, even when predisposition to involvement and political sophistication were held constant. The latter two factors, though, did affect the permissiveness of parishioners. The conclusion to be drawn from these findings is that church involvement does not basically alter the orientation toward the secular world which the parishioner brings with him to the church. Therefore, the mere fact of being deeply involved in the church gives no indication of one's attitude toward the church's participation in the political realm.

Given these findings, one might speculate as to the effects of a shift by the Church from the moderate policy of political action it now pursues. If the Church elected to get out of "politics" altogether and stick to religion as a minority of its members would advocate, the result undoubtedly would be the disenchantment of those who hold a more permissive view. Their disenchantment, however, would not be informed so much by degree of involvement as by other factors operating to influence the parishioners' attitudes. Should the Church move to the opposite extreme and become actively engaged in public affairs in a highly partisan way the disenchantment would come from those holding a non-permissive view, but no more so from involved parishioners than from the uninvolved. In sum, it is unlikely that the net balance of involvement among parishioners would be altered by a shift on the part of the Church toward either political activity or inactivity, although the level of involvement of individual parishioners might well change.

Chapter 7

Social Ideology and Involvement

Episcopalian parishioners, modally, do not want their Church to withdraw totally from the world. Yet, neither do they wish to see the Church thrust wholeheartedly into the task of reshaping the secular order. Chapter 6 indicated that most parishioners subscribe to a position somewhere between the two extremes. While the Church is conceded a moral responsibility for influencing society in the direction of Christian ideals, the extent of that responsibility and the methods appropriate to it represent an issue which has plagued clergy and laity since the time of Christ. The equivocation of Episcopalian parishioners on this issue is matched by the history of religious institutions in the United States.

The sects which have stressed either extreme withdrawal or extreme social regeneration have never had a serious impact on the mainstream of American Christianity. The experiments in utopian society generated by idealized conceptions of the Christian society have largely disappeared, leaving behind only bare remnants to mark their fate. Contemporary sects which emphasize moral regeneration of society as well as of the individual have influenced only the fringes of society. Moral Rearmament is typical of these. Others which view society as inherently sinful to be saved only by the second coming of Christ (e.g., the Jehovah's Witnesses) have been equally limited in their appeal. Theological discussion regarding Christian responsibility, while rampant at times, has neither involved laymen to any major extent, nor has it influenced the parish ministry in any important way. The theology of the social gospel might represent an exception to this generalization. However, while it has certainly influenced Christian social thought in America, no single group or denomination has embraced it to any large extent. And the average lay Christian today is probably unaware of the issues raised by the social gospel movement half a century ago.

Among the major Protestant denominations in contemporary America, the prevailing attitudes represent a middle ground between the extreme positions which, at one time or another, have enjoyed some currency. The basic economic and social premises of American society are accepted in principle. There is no call among the major denominations for a militant restructuring of society along some utopian Christian lines. On the other hand, complete disregard for the state of society is neither encouraged nor condoned. The Christian is expected to concern himself with the state of society and to feel a responsibility for working towards the elimination of social ills. What he actually thinks and what he does, however, are largely for him to derive from the dictates of his own conscience.

Increasingly, though, churches have begun introducing social issues into debate at denominational meetings and passing resolutions which express an official point of view. Most American denominations of any size have, by now, taken stands on such diverse issues as racial integration, civil liberties, alcoholism, conscientious objectors, immigration policy, and the like. Some have even adopted policy statements on American foreign policy. In general, there has been a tendency for churches to avoid economic issues and issues which bear on the basic structure of the society. Similarly, they have tended to skirt those issues on which American opinion is sharply divided and which have a high saliency for the persons concerned. Wherever such issues are considered, policy statements are likely to be equivocal rather than partisan. Thus a church may adopt a resolution endorsing the desirability of labor and management working together harmoniously. And, in at least one instance, a denomination has passed a resolution to the effect that capitalism was not necessarily the only economic philosophy acceptable to Christians. But, stronger statements than these are not likely to appear and, for the most part, issues of this kind tend to be avoided altogether. It seems fair to say that the social action pattern of American Protestantism has generally adapted to the society, rather than been the advocate of basic structural changes. Nonetheless, there is some semblance of a regenerative spirit with respect to issues primarily ethical or ideological in content. Here, even in the face of divided parishioner sentiments, the churches have frequently adopted stands of a clearly partisan nature.

To varying degrees, denominations attempt to communicate to their clergy and membership the resolutions on social issues which are passed at denominational meetings. The Protestant Episcopal Church has established a Department of Christian Social Relations to perform this function and to carry on a general program of education in responsible Christian citizenship. However, the clergy and membership are under no constraint to accept or comply with any position advocated by the Church. This is true of the social pronouncements of the Episcopal Church and of other major Protestant denominations as well. The guiding principle generally accepted in such matters is that the ultimate responsibility must rest with the individual clergyman and parishioner.

The fact of church membership and the degree of involvement therein may or may not be relevant for a parishioner's social ideology. The influence of church membership per se lies beyond the scope of this analysis, as discussed above. While the data provide a record of the apparently prevailing social ideology of Episcopalians in 1952 (the time at which our data were collected), there is no way to form a comparison with non-Episcopalians, or non-church members generally.

Within the framework of Episcopalian church membership, however, it is possible to determine the effect of parishioners' church involvement on their social ideologies. It is already known from findings reported earlier that the more involved parishioners acknowledge a greater church influence on their opinions (see Table 9). One might expect to find, therefore, a positive relationship between involvement and the extent to which the parishioner's social ideology conforms to that advocated by the Church. This proposition can be directly tested, however, only with respect to those issues on which the Church has adopted an official position. On other issues, it is more difficult to decide how such a test should be conducted, since the authors do not wish to act on behalf of the Church in distinguishing the "right" position from the "wrong" one. There is, perhaps, a possible resolution to this difficulty which would be to reformulate the expectation of parishioners' attitudes as follows. For issues on which there is no official Church policy, one should expect a positive relationship between deep church involvement and the degree to which parishioners adopt a point of view based on general rather than personal advantage. In other words, the hypothesis is that altruism will motivate the involved parishioner more than it does the uninvolved. This seems a reasonable expectation since it reflects the most general Christian teachings, and provides the common theme running throughout the official positions actually taken by the church.

The particular issues available for consideration are dictated, of course, by the content of the questionnaire. From the possible choices, we have elected to focus on six. The issues and the range of the attitudes expressed are:

1. *The United Nations*–the acceptability of the United Nations as an agency of international cooperation. Attitudes range from support of the United Nations to opposition to it.

2. *Immigration policy*–the acceptability of the current immigration policy of the United States government. Attitudes range from support for a liberal policy to support for a more restrictive one.

3. *Conscientious objectors*–the right of conscientious objectors to refuse to bear arms. Attitudes range from complete endorsement of this right to outright refusal to grant it.

4. *Civil liberties*–the fundamental freedoms of the individual at home and abroad. Responses range from acute concern that basic human rights be defended to indifference towards the problem.

5. *Labor*–the rights of labor in a free society. Attitudes range from partisanship towards labor in its relations with management to rejection of labor's right to organize.

6. *Government control*–the desirability of government control of business. Attitudes range from approval of increased governmental regulation of private industry to rejection of any form of government control, even in wartime.

These issues share two relevant characteristics. First, they deal with matters of social policy on which clearly differentiated points of view are possible. Second, the issues are by no means the exclusive concern of the Church but are of considerable relevance to the general community. While similar in these regards, the issues differ in a number of important respects. The first two —the United Nations and immigration policy—deal with international affairs; the last four with domestic affairs. In turn, the first four are primarily ideological rather than economic in nature while the last two clearly have a primarily economic quality. The Church has adopted a statement of policy on five of the six issues; government control representing the exception.[1] On four of the issues, the Church's stand is firm and the resolutions are explicit, signifying unqualified endorsement of a given position. For example, the Church has taken an extremely strong supportive stand on the United Nations. Similarly, it has adopted a firm and unequivocal commitment to a liberal immigration policy, the rights of conscientious objectors to refuse to bear arms, and the sanctity of human rights and fundamental freedoms. While recognizing the basic rights of labor, however, the Church avoids taking any position which could be interpreted as strictly partisan.

The attitude which a parishioner adopts on these six issues clearly does not add up to a comprehensive account of his social ideology. However, they touch on his ideology at a number of points where the influence of the Church should be at its height. Hence, to the degree that there is a relationship between involvement and social ideology, it should be apparent on these issues.

THE SOCIAL IDEOLOGY OF EPISCOPALIANS: CLERICAL AND LAY

Before turning to the specific analysis of the effect of involvement on the parishioner's social ideology, we might first orient ourselves by noting briefly how Episcopalians as a whole feel about the set of issues to be examined. As previously indicated,

---

[1] The discussion of these issues, it should be noted, is restricted to official church positions in existence at the time our data were collected. Since we shall analyze the effect of church policy on parishioner attitudes, subsequent policy statements are, of course, irrelevant for our purposes.

this will not permit any conclusions as to whether the simple fact of church membership influences such attitudes. However, it will afford an opportunity to judge the degree to which the social values advocated by the Church have received general acceptance by parishioners.

In the process of doing this, we shall again compare the attitudes of the laity with those of the bishops of the Church and its priests. Of course, attitudes of the clergy cannot readily be related to their church involvement. Their position in the Church presumes involvement therein. However, it is of ancillary interest to learn how the parishioners and clergy compare in their social attitudes, particularly in the case of those issues on which the Church-at-large has adopted an official position.

In proceeding, it is necessary to understand and appreciate the manner in which resolutions of the Protestant Episcopal Church on social issues come into being. For a resolution to be adopted as official policy, it must be passed by both the House of Bishops and the House of Delegates. Membership in the former is restricted to Bishops of the Church while the latter is composed equally of clergy and laity, four clergymen and four lay members representing each diocese. All bishops are automatically members of the House of Bishops. Representatives to the House of Delegates are elected at Diocesan Conventions by vote of the clerical and lay delegates there. Given the character of the adoption procedure, we should expect some correspondence between the attitudes of the clergy and the membership-at-large on particular social issues and the form and content of the resolutions passed by the General Convention. However, since the laity are least represented of the three groups, it is reasonable to expect that parishioners will be less likely to agree with the official positions taken by the Church, than are the clergy. And the bishops, having relatively the greatest responsibility for the formulation of policy, should be the most likely to support the official positions.

The United Nations

More than other denominations of European origins, the Episcopal Church has retained relatively strong, though informal, ties with its mother church, the Church of England. This greater continuity with historical origins has contributed, among other things, to an international-mindedness on the part of the Episcopal Church which is unique in American religion. The Church's international orientation is exemplified by many actions taken throughout its history. Just prior to the study, the orientation was best illustrated perhaps by the very strong support which the Church had given to the United Nations. Resolutions to this effect were passed at both the 1949 and 1952 triennial meetings, the 1952 resolution reading as follows:

> *Whereas,* earlier world conditions, such as made for national isolation and the promotion of selfish national interests in many parts of the world, have now been eclipsed by new conditions resulting from modern commerce, revolutionized facilities for transportation and communication, and world-scale military activities, so that the most acute present-day economic and social problems are worldwide in their impact and require solution on an international scale; and
> *Whereas,* under existing present-day conditions the only possible pathway to world peace lies through collective security; and
> *Whereas,* the United Nations system offers the only organized machinery in existence for the practical attainment of collective world security; therefore, be it
> *Resolved,* that we, seeing in the developing and strengthening of the United Nations the best political hope of mankind, pledge our support to the United Nations organization. We urge that the charter be revised and strengthened in accordance with Article 109:3, looking towards its future development into a world organization open to all peoples with defined and limited power, adequate to preserve peace and to prevent aggression through the encouragement and enforcement of World Law.

This statement, along with the earlier one adopted in 1949, constitutes a steadfast affirmation of the Church's belief in the United Nations as an agency for international cooperation. Its position on the eventual transformation of the United Nations into a world government of some kind is rather obscure, but there is a clear implication that under certain conditions the Church would lend its support to such a move.

In this policy statement, the Church adopted a firm and partisan position. Moreover, the Church has devoted considerable energy to communicating this position to both clergy and membership. Several pamphlets have been issued on the United Nations, clergymen have been urged to make it a topic for their sermons, and also encouraged to organize discussion groups on the subject. How, then, do clergy and laity react to this particular action of the national Church?

Parishioners, as it turns out, are largely unaware that the Church has even taken a stand. The bishops and the parish ministry are substantially better informed than the membership, but even a sizeable minority of the Church leaders are unaware of the Church's position.[2] In fact, more of the clergy than the membership express the opinion that the Church has not taken a stand on the United Nations. The evidence to this effect is reported in Table 48 which shows the distribution of responses to the statement, "The Church nationally has taken a strong stand in support of the United Nations—Yes, No, Don't Know."

TABLE 48

The Degree of Awareness among Clergy and Parishioners of the Stand in Support of the United Nations Adopted by the National Church

"The Church nationally has taken a strong stand in support of the United Nations."	Bishops	Priests	Parishioners
Yes	62%	66%	36%
No	26	20	8
Don't know	12	14	56
100% =	90	251	1454
No answer	10	8	76
Total number	100	259	1530

This relative lack of knowledge of the Church's action does not imply, necessarily, resistance to such a stand being taken. Earlier in the questionnaire, respondents were asked whether or

[2] The slightly larger proportion of informed priests than bishops is perhaps explained by the fact that retired bishops were included among those to whom the questionnaires were sent. Presumably, they are less likely to keep up to date with current church affairs than the active clergy.

TABLE 49

CLERGY AND PARISHIONER SENTIMENT ON THE CHURCH ENCOURAGING
ITS MEMBERS TO SUPPORT THE UNITED NATIONS

"The Church should actively encourage its members to support the UN."	Bishops	Priests	Parishioners
Agree	94%	86%	64%
Disagree	4	6	22
Uncertain	2	8	14
100% =	96	251	1472
No answer	4	8	58
Total number	100	259	1530

not they favored having the Church encourage its members to support the United Nations (Table 49).

Bishops and priests overwhelmingly subscribe to the proposition. A somewhat smaller proportion of the laity, but nevertheless a majority, concur. Parishioners who are aware of the Church's official position are more likely to endorse the proposal than those who are misinformed or uninformed. The uninformed exhibit the greatest uncertainty as to the desirability of the proposal (Table 50).

In answering this latter question, however, respondents may

TABLE 50

PARISHIONERS WHO ARE INFORMED THAT THE CHURCH HAS ADOPTED A STRONG
STAND IN SUPPORT OF THE UNITED NATIONS ARE MORE LIKELY THAN THE
MISINFORMED OR UNINFORMED TO ENDORSE THE ADOPTION OF SUCH A STAND

"The Church should actively encourage its members to support the UN."	"The Church nationally has taken a strong stand in support of the United Nations."		
	Yes	No	Don't Know
Agree	78%	53%	57%
Disagree	14	36	25
Uncertain	8	10	18
100% =	509	107	785
No answer	12	1	38
Total number	521	108	823

conceivably be approving of the Church's right to take such a stand rather than expressing their sentiments about the United Nations per se. That this is probably not the case, however, is suggested by responses to two other questions asking for more direct attitudes about the United Nations (Table 51). Clergy

TABLE 51

CLERGY IN PARTICULAR BUT A MAJORITY OF PARISHIONERS AS WELL
ARE BASICALLY APPROVING OF THE UNITED NATIONS

"The United Nations is not worth the money we in the United States have spent on it."	Bishops	Priests	Parishioners
Agree	2%	9%	25%
Disagree	90	83	60
Uncertain	8	8	15
100% =	100	259	1512
No answer	. . .	. . .	18
Total number	100	259	1530

"It is all right for United States troops to serve under officers of another country appointed by the United Nations."	Bishops	Priests	Parishioners
Agree	93%	88%	64%
Disagree	5	8	28
Uncertain	2	4	8
100% =	98	259	1507
No answer	2	. . .	23
Total number	100	259	1530

and parishioners show about the same propensity to a favorable response on these questions as on the earlier one (Table 49).

Judging from the response to all of these questions, well over 80 percent of bishops and priests are consistently favorable to the United Nations as compared with about 60 percent of the membership. On the one hand, the more favorable view of the clergy undoubtedly reflects their greater awareness that the Church has, in fact, expressed strong support for the United Nations. On the other hand, it also reflects the fact that their representatives had more influence in formulating the Church's position in the first place.

The generally favorable attitude toward the United Nations is not maintained in equal support for the implication in the Church's position that it might be desirable for a world government to some day supplant the United Nations. Nevertheless, a surprising proportion of respondents express support of such a proposal, the clergy, once again, being more supportive than the parishioners (Table 52).

TABLE 52

FEWER CLERGY AND PARISHIONERS SUBSCRIBE TO THE DESIRABILITY OF THE UNITED NATIONS SOME DAY BEING SUPPLANTED BY A WORLD GOVERNMENT THAN SUPPORTED THE UNITED NATIONS ITSELF

"It would be a good thing if the U.N. were some day replaced by some kind of world government."	Bishops	Priests	Parishioners
Agree	60%	60%	47%
Disagree	15	22	33
Uncertain	26	18	20
100% =	97	259	1512
No answer	3	. . .	18
Total number	100	259	1530

Immigration Policy

In accord with its generally liberal policy on international affairs, the Church has also been a leading advocate of liberalizing American immigration policy. Its stand on this issue is not as forthright as the one just reported on the United Nations; nevertheless, basic dissatisfaction with the existing American policy is clearly implied. The resolution, passed at the 1952 triennial meeting, called for a review of existing immigration policy and its assumptions and recommended temporary provisions "to meet adequately the complex emergency problem of uprooted and homeless people compelled to live outside of their own countries." As this last phrase implies, the Church is seriously concerned with the problem of displaced persons and has carried on an active and well-regarded refugee aid program.

In this connection, a resolution passed at the 1949 General Convention reads in part,

> Resolved, That this fifty-sixth General Convention of the Protestant Episcopal Church join its forces with those of other religious and general community groups in urging the eighty-first Congress of the United States to extend the provisions of administrative requirements, delete any discriminatory aspects related to race, religion, or nationality, and provide the necessary funds to expedite America's full share in the resettlement of these people.

The questionnaire did not determine how familiar clergy and laity are with Church policy on immigration. As to their attitudes, the clergy appear to make a distinction between the refugee problem and the need for basic revisions in America's

TABLE 53

THE CLERGY EXPRESS MORE CONCERN THAT REFUGEES CONTINUE TO HAVE ACCESS TO THE UNITED STATES THAN THAT UNITED STATES IMMIGRATION LAWS BE CHANGED. PARISHIONERS MAKE NO SUCH DISTINCTION AND ARE SHARPLY DIVIDED ON BOTH QUESTIONS

"The United States has already admitted too many refugees since the end of World War II."	Bishops	Priests	Parishioners
Agree	3%	8%	37%
Disagree	85	77	44
Uncertain	12	15	19
100% =	96	256	1476
No answer	4	3	54
Total number	100	259	1530

"The immigration laws should be changed so that the quota system does not favor certain nations as opposed to others."	Bishops	Priests	Parishioners
Agree	51%	60%	37%
Disagree	26	23	42
Uncertain	23	16	21
100% =	94	256	1471
No answer	6	3	59
Total number	100	259	1530

immigration law. They are more concerned with the United States keeping its door open to refugees than with the need for a revision of immigration laws. To a degree, this reflects the relative emphasis which the national Church has given to the two aspects of the problem. Parishioners make no such distinction. They are as likely to uphold the one as the other. However, they express much less consensus in their attitudes on immigration laws than was true of their views on the United Nations (Table 53). Given the somewhat different quality of the questions asked about the immigration policy as over against the United Nations, no definitive comparison of attitudes on the two issues is possible. The apparently more liberal view adopted by both clergy and laity with regard to the United Nations is, in a sense, reflected in the more forthright and unambiguous stand of the Church on this issue. Once again, however, the greater correspondence between Church policy and the attitudes of the clergy may also reflect their greater influence in its formulation.

Conscientious Objectors

At the General Convention of 1943 (at the height of World War II), a joint committee on conscientious objectors was created. Its task was, among other things, "to assure the members of the Church who by reason of religious training and belief are conscientiously opposed to participation in war of the continuing fellowship of the Church with them and care for them." By this action, the national Church gave recognition to a long standing sympathy for the problems of conscientious objectors and affirmed its commitment to give them wholehearted support in defending their decision.

The clergy on the whole are in substantial agreement with the principle underlying the Church's stand; the laity, however, are not (Table 54). Over 90 percent of both bishops and priests are in agreement that "Episcopalians should recognize the right of conscientious objectors to refuse to bear arms." Fifty-three percent of the parishioners concur but a substantial minority— 34 percent—do not. That so many parishioners disagree undoubtedly is related to the fact that the questionnaires were administered while the Korean war was in progress. But, this finding is significant in suggesting that under cross-pressure situa-

TABLE 54

CLERGY ARE MORE SUPPORTIVE OF CONSCIENTIOUS OBJECTORS
THAN ARE PARISHIONERS

"Episcopalians should recognize the right of conscientious objectors to refuse to bear arms."	Bishops	Priests	Parishioners
Agree	95%	93%	53%
Disagree	4	6	34
Uncertain	1	1	13
100% =	95	256	1478
No answer	5	3	52
Total number	100	259	1530

tions, the values of the Church are much less likely to be affirmed by the membership.

A distinction should be made between the degree to which a principle is supported and the actions considered appropriate in defending it. Episcopalians, clergy and laity alike, express much greater resistance to the proposal that "Episcopalians have a moral obligation to give financial and other assistance to conscientious objectors" than they did to the idea that "Episcopalians should recognize the right of conscientious objectors to refuse to bear arms." Among the clergy, something over 90

TABLE 55

ONLY A MINORITY OF PARISHIONERS FEEL OBLIGATED
TO AID CONSCIENTIOUS OBJECTORS

"Episcopalians have a moral obligation to give financial and other assistance to conscientious objectors."	Bishops	Priests	Parishioners
Agree	60%	60%	26%
Disagree	29	24	56
Uncertain	11	16	18
100% =	94	255	1478
No answer	6	4	52
Total number	100	259	1530

percent were willing to defend the principle, as contrasted with 60 percent supporting this particular proposal for action. The corresponding figures for laymen are 53 percent and 26 percent (Table 55).

Disagreement in this instance may not constitute a conscious rejection of the Church's stand. Nevertheless, in view of the responses to both questions, it is evident that the Church has not succeeded in making its own view on this issue the overwhelming moral guide for its parishioners.

Human Rights

In almost all of the recent resolutions on social issues which the national Church has adopted, a pervading concern with human rights and fundamental freedoms can be discerned. The matter also received explicit attention, most notably perhaps, in the following resolution passed at the 1952 General Convention.

> *Whereas,* we believe that the nature and destiny of man by virtue of his creation, redemption, and calling, and man's activities in family, State and culture establish limits beyond which a government cannot with impunity go; and
> *Whereas,* we further believe that respect for an observance of human rights constitutes an essential cornerstone for building a world society where peace and justice can prevail; and
> *Whereas,* the violation of human rights and fundamental freedoms in many parts of the world both degrade man and jeopardize world peace; therefore,
> be it
> *Resolved,* that the members of this Convention
>
> 1. Encourage and support full participation by the United States in international action through the United Nations to the end that the observance of human rights and fundamental freedoms for all men may be promoted, without distinction as to race, sex, language, or religion; and
> 2. Use every reasonable means to overcome longstanding discriminatory practices in our own land; and, particularly in these days when we seek to oppose the threat of totalitarianism from without, to guard against our own use of methods which we condemn in others.

At the same convention, the following resolution on racial discrimination was adopted:

Whereas, Christ teaches above all the Fatherhood of God, the consequent brotherhood of man and the oneness of the whole human family; and

Whereas, present-day developments, leading to an increasing interdependence of nations and peoples, are making ever clearer the necessity of Christ's way of brotherhood; and

Whereas, Christ's teaching is incompatible with every form of discrimination based on color or race both domestic and international;

and

Whereas, almost every country today, including our own, is guilty in greater or lesser degree of mass racial or color discrimination;

therefore, be it

Resolved, that we consistently oppose and combat discrimination based on color or race in every form, both within the Church and without, in this country and internationally.

These resolutions were passed at a time when civil liberties, human rights, and individual freedoms were very highly salient topics for Americans. It was a period during which Senator Joseph McCarthy was about at the height of his power and one in which concern with racial discrimination in America was beginning to grow.

The questionnaires touched on these issues in a variety of ways, enabling some assessment of both the direction and the degree of concern which Episcopalians were experiencing. On the whole, the clergy were considerably more concerned than the laity, as evidenced by their answers to two pertinent questions. More than 80 percent of the clergy expressed disagreement with the statements: "People who go around talking about equal rights for 'this group' and 'that group' are making a mountain out of a molehill," and "In this country people of different colors and religious beliefs are treated just about equally." In contrast, these statements met with disagreement among 46 percent and 52 percent of the laymen respectively. On the whole, laymen were about as likely to agree as to disagree with the statements. On balance, then, the clergy quite closely mirrored the concern expressed by the national Church; laymen were not especially prone to do so (Table 56).

The clergy, while much more perceptive about possible threats to civil liberties, were only slightly more likely to resist such

TABLE 56

CLERGY SHOW A GREATER CONCERN FOR CIVIL RIGHTS THAN DO PARISHIONERS

"People who go around talking about equal rights for 'this group' and 'that group' are making a mountain out of a molehill."	Bishops	Priests	Parishioners
Agree	6%	8%	39%
Disagree	83	83	46
Uncertain	11	9	16
100% =	95	252	1469
No answer	5	7	61
Total number	100	259	1530

"In this country people of different colors and religious beliefs are treated pretty much equally."	Bishops	Priests	Parishioners
Agree	10%	12%	42%
Disagree	81	85	52
Uncertain	9	3	6
100% =	97	259	1512
No answer	3	...	18
Total number	100	259	1530

threats. At least the percentage differences separating the views of the clergy and parishioners were smaller with regard to the defense of civil liberties than in the perception of possible threats. And, among the clergy, the bishops, in this instance, were more cautious than the priests (Table 57). The caution in these replies undoubtedly reflected the then prevailing general climate of opinion, and bishops, because of their position in the church, might have been particularly sensitive to the implications of such questions. It is doubtful that these questions would produce as much anti-civil-libertarian response today, even from the same respondents. This raises, of course, the fundamental question of the Church's ability to sustain the loyalty of its members under conditions whereby its values countervail those which are strongly held in the secular community.

TABLE 57

CLERGY ARE MORE LIKE PARISHIONERS IN RESISTING THREATS TO
CIVIL LIBERTIES THAN IN PERCEIVING THE THREATS

"It is all right for school boards to say what books on controversial issues their students should read in school."	Bishops	Priests	Parishioners
Agree	38%	28%	45%
Disagree	49	59	42
Uncertain	13	13	13
100% =	94	256	1473
No answer	6	3	57
Total number	100	259	1530

"The names of people receiving public relief should be made available for anyone who wants to see them."	Bishops	Priests	Parishioners
Agree	42%	35%	50%
Disagree	49	58	44
Uncertain	9	6	6
100% =	94	254	1486
No answer	6	5	44
Total number	100	259	1530

Judging from the present example, its power in such a situation seems severely taxed.

Interestingly enough, on a civil liberties issue which was peripheral to, if not wholly outside the debate generated by Senator McCarthy, clergy and parishioners show themselves to be much more staunch defenders of human rights. Thus, more than 90 percent of the clergy and over 70 percent of parishioners expressed the belief that people of different races should not be treated any differently in the Church (see Table 58).

The responses, for the most part, clearly affirm the forthright policy of the national Church. The minority of clergy favoring separate churches are primarily from the South, as are a substantial proportion of the laymen taking this position. It should be recognized, however, that in each instance, both clergy

TABLE 58

CLERGY ARE MORE STRONGLY OPPOSED TO SEGREGATED
CHURCHES THAN ARE PARISHIONERS

"People of different races should:"	Bishops	Priests	Parishioners
Not be treated differently	90%	91%	72%
Be seated in special sections	...	...	1
Have their own parish churches	10	9	27
100% =	100	255	1504
No answer	...	4	26
Total number	100	259	1530

and laity were clearly in accord with the prevailing secular climate of opinion. Outside of the South, overt proponents of racial segregation were certainly in a minority even by 1952. On the other hand, secular opinion was clearly divided on issues such as the rights of school boards to restrict the books made available to children. It is significant, therefore, that the least clergy and parishioner support for Church policy is found where the prevailing secular climate of opinion most openly contradicts that advocated by the Church.

Labor

Church policy on the issues considered thus far has been clearly partisan. While they have varied in forthrightness of expression, the resolutions have made reasonably clear just where the Church stands. This is not the case, however, with respect to the Church's stance vis-à-vis labor-management relations. Here, the church has tended to be equivocal rather than partisan; to adopt, in effect, the role of mediator. The following observation of an anonymous churchman typifies the equivocation with which this issue is treated: "The church is not a bystander but is not a partisan either. It is equally responsible for capital and labor and should strive to be an interpreter of one to the other and to serve as a mediator. Both capital and labor have rights to be respected as well as duties which must be performed."

It is almost self-evident that the Church does not expect its members to be equally equivocal in their feelings about labor-management problems. In this particular instance, the Church recognizes the possibility of conflict and calls upon its clergy to serve as arbitrators of dispute. Given the situation, we should expect the clergy to be more hesitant to take sides than parishioners.

The most overt attempt to force respondents into taking a stand in favor of labor or management misfired, at least in part, because of an error in question wording. The error, however, did not prove completely dysfunctional. It is still possible to discern the degree to which clergy and membership were pro-labor in outlook. The question asked respondents to express agreement or disagreement with the statement, "In disputes between management and labor, the unions seem to be right more often than management." An "agree" response can be reasonably interpreted as pro-labor. A "disagree" response, however, may represent either an unfavorable view of labor or simply the belief that labor and management are each right with about the same frequency. The responses are reported in Table 59.

TABLE 59

FEW RESPONDENTS TAKE A CLEARLY PRO-LABOR POSITION

"In disputes between management and labor, the unions seem to be right more often than management."	Bishops	Priests	Parishioners
Agree	9%	18%	15%
Disagree	49	46	57
Uncertain	42	36	28
100% =	96	255	1483
No answer	4	4	47
Total number	100	259	1530

Only a small minority are willing to answer this admittedly "loaded" question in labor's favor. The bishops are most cautious in this respect. The priests are most likely to be partisan in labor's favor but even they differ only slightly from parishioners —18 and 15 percent respectively. It is noteworthy, however, that the clergy are more likely than parishioners to express themselves as uncertain, to adopt, in effect, an equivocal attitude.

The bishops, again, show themselves to be more cautious than the priests.

Unfortunately, none of the other questions asked on this issue allow a judgment about the proportion of respondents who are basically inclined to management's point of view. Responses serve to provide more of a flavor of prevailing sentiment than a basis for predicting what decisions would arise if action were required. The rights of workers to organize into unions is generally defended even to the extent of accepting government intervention to protect this right (Table 60).

TABLE 60

MOST RESPONDENTS SUPPORT THE RIGHT OF LABOR TO ORGANIZE

"The government should protect the right of workers to organize into unions."	Bishops	Priests	Parishioners
Agree	93%	86%	65%
Disagree	4	9	21
Uncertain	3	5	14
100% =	94	249	1482
No answer	6	10	48
Total number	100	259	1530

While the clergy are more equivocal than the parishioners in identifying themselves with either labor or management in conflict, they exhibit a much greater propensity towards adopting a liberal position on the basic concept of organized labor. Almost all of the bishops and priests subscribe to the rights of workers to organize into unions. In contrast, about two-thirds of parishioners would outrightly defend this right.

Less support for labor unions is expressed by both clergy and laity in their responses to questions on which (1) there is not consensus of opinion among labor itself and (2) on which the issue not only invokes loyalties to management or labor but to other values as well. When confronted with the statement, "Workers should be allowed to strike in defense industries except in time of war," for example, they were more likely to agree than

TABLE 61

MOST RESPONDENTS SUPPORT THE RIGHT TO STRIKE

"Workers should be allowed to strike in defense industries except in time of war."	Bishops	Priests	Parishioners
Agree	63%	68%	48%
Disagree	22	22	39
Uncertain	15	10	13
100% =	93	256	1478
No answer	7	3	52
Total number	100	259	1530

disagree. Yet over one-fifth of the clergy and nearly two-fifths of the membership disagree, nonetheless (Table 61).

There is even greater resistance to the proposal that "Workers should be obligated to union membership if the majority of workers in a plant join one" (Table 62).

TABLE 62

THERE IS LITTLE SUPPORT FOR COMPULSORY UNION MEMBERSHIP

"Workers should be obligated to union membership if the majority of the workers in a plant join one."	Bishops	Priests	Parishioners
Agree	11%	20%	18%
Disagree	76	69	73
Uncertain	13	11	9
100% =	93	256	1483
No answer	7	3	47
Total number	100	259	1530

Here, the bishops are slightly more likely to take a conservative position than the laity; the priests are the most liberal, but the majority in all three groups take a stand in support of the open as against the closed shop.

These findings, however, cannot reasonably be interpreted as reflecting a basic antagonism to labor on the part of a majority of the respondents. In the case of the first question, considerations of the nation's security undoubtedly influence some of the negative response. And certainly the concept of individual freedom is clearly involved in responses to the second.

All in all, the structure of the questions dealing with this issue leaves something to be desired. But, the shortcomings notwithstanding, parishioners who felt strongly disposed one way or the other were afforded an opportunity to communicate their orientations. That so few accepted the opportunity to adopt a consistently pro- or anti-labor stance is indicative that Episcopalians, on the whole, are more prone to steer a middle course of mediating between the interests of labor and management than to commit themselves wholeheartedly to either side. As with the other issues already considered, there is no way of knowing how much of this tendency is related to, or is a function of, church membership per se.

Government Control

We now turn to an issue—government control of business—on which the General Convention has not adopted an official statement of policy. Clergy and laity are neither encouraged to take a partisan position nor are they instructed to consider the issue in an equivocal fashion. In examining the prevailing attitudes among clergy and parishioners on this issue, therefore, there is no official Church standard by which to evaluate the parishioners' acceptance or defiance. The primary purpose for presenting the data, therefore, is to set the stage for the later analysis of the relationship between involvement and social ideology. However, in their own right, the data are of intrinsic interest for what they reveal about the comparative views of clergy and parishioners on an issue for which the Church does not even provide an informal guideline.

Generally speaking, most respondents—both clergy and laity—are opposed, in principle, to government interference in business. The majority sentiment clearly supports the basic presuppositions of America's economic structure. However, support is definitely greater among laymen than among the clergy (Table 63). Over four-fifths of the laity subscribe to the proposal.

TABLE 63

THERE IS A GENERAL RESISTANCE TO GOVERNMENT CONTROL OF BUSINESS

"In peacetime, it is best if the federal government does not interfere with private enterprise."	Bishops	Priests	Parishioners
Agree	65%	61%	85%
Disagree	29	30	8
Uncertain	6	9	7
100% =	94	255	1484
No answer	6	4	46
Total number	100	259	1530

Slightly less than two-thirds of the clergy feel the same way. Thus, even in the absence of Church policy, the clergy tend to emerge somewhat more liberal in outlook than the laity.

But the laity as well as the clergy are willing to forego the laissez-faire principle during periods of national emergency. The intrusion of national security into the debate has the effect of leading a majority of both clergy and laity to compromise their values concerning the sanctity of the free enterprise system in peacetime (Table 64). Again, the clergy appear less committed to traditional economic values than the parishioners, but the

TABLE 64

THE MAJORITY OF CLERGY AND LAITY WOULD SUPPORT GOVERNMENT
CONTROL IN TIMES OF NATIONAL EMERGENCY

"In periods of national emergency like the present, industry should accept the need for more governmental control of its activities."	Bishops	Priests	Parishioners
Agree	65%	66%	58%
Disagree	21	22	29
Uncertain	14	12	13
100% =	100	259	1506
No answer	. . .	. . .	24
Total number	100	259	1530

distance separating them is considerably smaller than was true of their responses to the more general question.

Confirming our earlier observation of the equivocality of opinion on the issue of labor-management relations, we find that a substantial majority of both clergy and parishioners are inclined to establish the same standards for industry as they would for labor. While the clergy show a somewhat greater degree of support, still more than 70 percent of the parishioners subscribe to the proposal that, "If wages are controlled, then profits also should be controlled."

TABLE 65

MOST RESPONDENTS FAVOR EQUAL TREATMENT OF LABOR AND MANAGEMENT

"If wages are controlled, then profits also should be controlled."	Bishops	Priests	Parishioners
Agree	78%	85%	72%
Disagree	10	9	19
Uncertain	12	6	9
100% =	96	254	1477
No answer	4	5	53
Total number	100	259	1530

In and of themselves, these findings tell nothing about the bearing of church membership on the social ideology of either clergy or parishioners. And, on this particular issue, it is difficult to even speculate as to the relationship which should be expected. It is, however, of some interest that even when the Church offers no advice on an issue, the clergy continue to demonstrate a more liberal outlook than the parishioners.

Before turning to the effect of involvement on social ideology, we should attempt to place in perspective some of the broader implications of the findings just reported. Church policy on four of the issues is clearly in the liberal rather than the conservative direction. Given the greater influence of the clergy in policy formulation, it is not surprising that their attitudes correspond more closely to the official Church positions than is true of parishioners.

On the whole, the priests were found to respond very much like the bishops. To the extent that a pattern did emerge, the bishops exhibited a slight propensity to be more liberal on matters of principle while the priests were more prone to be so on matters of practice. On balance, however, the similarity in their responses was more impressive than the differences.

As compared to the clergy, there was much less consensus in the attitudes of parishioners on all of the issues. While in most instances a majority of the laity expressed an attitude which was in conformity with church policy, a substantial minority dissented. Dissent or conformity in this instance, however, cannot be interpreted necessarily as a reflection of general resistance to or identification with Church policy per se. The little evidence which was available indicated that only a third of the parishioners were informed as to actual Church policy.

INVOLVEMENT AND THE SOCIAL VALUES OF PARISHIONERS

The social policy of the Protestant Episcopal Church, as constituted in the social resolutions of the General Convention, clearly cannot be equated with church dogma. Parishioners are under no formal obligation to either know or abide by the social pronouncements of the Church. Nevertheless, the implicit expectation is that parishioners (and clergy) will be guided in their social thinking by the Church's deliberations and conclusions. The clear and explicit function of the Church's Christian Social Relations program is to inform Episcopalians of their Church's social policy with the expected consequence being that clergy and parishioners will lend it their support.

The foregoing descriptive account of Episcopalians' social attitudes does not permit any firm or precise conclusions as to the degree to which these expectations have been realized. It is clear, however, that the Church is far from securing complete consensus among parishioners even regarding those issues on which its stand is most explicit and partisan. In fact, the little evidence available suggests only a minority of parishioners are even informed about the Church's social policy. Hence, viewing the membership at large, it does not appear that social standards advocated by the Church are the primary referents for developing the social values of individual parishioners.

Such a broad generalization, however, overlooks the fact that the social values of some parishioners do correspond with those advocated by the church. The specific question to be explored now is whether the amount of concordance is related to the strength of the parishioner's ties to his church, that is, to his degree of involvement. If the Church does influence the social values of some parishioners, the effect should be most apparent among those with the deepest religious commitment. This, in essence, is the proposition to be tested.

Theoretically, a necessary precondition to being influenced by the Church's social policy is that one be correctly informed as to its content and meaning. However, it is not altogether clear what standards might best be applied in judging the state of a parishioner's knowledge. An Episcopalian who is overtly uninformed of the Church's social policy may, nevertheless, be covertly aware of its general direction. Furthermore, assuming the resolutions of the Church reflect basic Christian values such as charity, love of fellow man and the like, it is conceivable that as his devotion to the Church grows, a parishioner may come naturally to adopt these values, while being totally unaware that the specific attitudes he forms have been officially sanctioned by the Church. This then is the presumption with which we begin the analysis; later we shall return to this problem and determine whether our findings are affected when the parishioner's actual knowledge of Church policy is taken into account.

The present task is to determine whether and to what extent a parishioner's involvement in the church is related to his attitudes on issues such as the six identified in the preceding descriptive analysis. Insofar as there may be a relationship, it is most likely to occur with respect to the four issues on which Church policy is identifiably partisan and consistent with basic Christian values—the United Nations, immigration policy, conscientious objectors and human rights. These four will be considered first.

At no point in the questionnaire were parishioners asked to

evaluate specific policy actions of the Church. It is possible, however, to infer their leanings toward or away from Church policy on the basis of their answers to the specific attitudinal questions asked on each issue. Thus, for example, a parishioner who completely subscribes to Church policy on the United Nations should be expected to answer the United Nations questions in a supportive way. Hence, for each of the issues an attitudinal index has been constructed by combining responses to several relevant questions. The method of index construction adopted is described in detail in Appendix B. For present purposes, it need only be noted that each index permits the classification of parishioners along a continuum ranging from a conservative to a liberal orientation on a particular issue. Since Church policy is clearly liberal on each of the first four issues considered, we should expect a positive relationship between a parishioner's involvement score and the extent to which he exhibits a liberal posture on these issues; the deeper his involvement, the more liberal his attitudes should be.

The Church has taken no partisan stand on the two remaining issues—labor and governmental control. However, it will be recalled from Tables 60 and 63 that the clergy emerged generally more liberal on these issues than was true of the parishioners. This fact plus the Church's liberal posture on the four preceding issues leads us to expect that deep involvement by parishioners will be positively related to liberal attitudes on labor and governmental control as well. The strength of our expectations, however, must be less than if the Church had actually taken partisan positions in these instances.

In Table 66, the relationships between church involvement and attitudes on each of the six issues have been presented in two different forms. First, for parishioners at each level of involvement, mean scores were computed from their scores on each of the six indices. Thus, in the first row in Table 66, we may compare the mean scores on the United Nations index for parishioners at each level of involvement. Following the previous convention, all mean scores have been adjusted to fall within the range from 0.0 to 1.0. On the first four issues presented, a mean score of 1.0 would indicate that all the parishioners in

TABLE 66

CHURCH INVOLVEMENT HAS LITTLE, IF ANY, BEARING ON PARISHIONERS'
ATTITUDES ON THE SIX SOCIAL ISSUES

Issues	Mean scores Composite Index of Involvement						
	High					Low	
	5	4	3	2	1	0	Pearsonian r
United Nations	.66	.65	.63	.65	.63	.67	.050
Immigration policy	.58	.50	.50	.52	.48	.46	.087
Conscientious objectors	.59	.51	.46	.49	.45	.39	.131
Human rights	.53	.53	.52	.52	.55	.52	.072
Labor	.43	.50	.42	.50	.48	.51	−.060
Government control	.55	.56	.52	.59	.55	.52	.021
Total number	102	171	276	259	230	163	

a given group gave responses completely in agreement with the Church position on the issue. A mean score of *0.0*, on the other hand, would represent complete disagreement with the Church. On the last two issues, for which there is no clear Church policy, a mean score of *1.0* would represent an unequivocally liberal response by the parishioners in the given group, and a mean score of *0.0* indicates responses which are unequivocally conservative.

Second, Pearsonian *r* correlation coefficients have been computed as summary measures of the relationship between involvement and scores on each of the indices. It will be recalled that the correlation coefficient has a range from *−1.0* to *+1.0*. A correlation equal to *+1.0* would represent a perfect, positive relationship between involvement and taking the Church's (or the liberal) position on an issue. A correlation equal to *−1.0* would indicate a perfect, negative relationship. Finally, if a correlation of *0.0* appears, this would indicate there is no relationship between involvement and attitudes on the given issue.

The most reasonable conclusion to be drawn from Table 66 is that church involvement has very little effect on parishioners' social ideology. Or conversely, ideological concerns neither enhance nor discourage commitment to the church. While some small associations are indicated by the Pearsonian r computations, these do not, for the most part, warrant serious consideration.

Interestingly enough, involvement is the most strongly associated with the issue of conscientious objectors. Of the six issues, this one clearly has the greatest religious content. The association between involvement and attitudes toward the United Nations is the weakest among the four issues on which the Church has assumed a partisan position. Conceivably, this issue has the least religious relevance in the eyes of parishioners.

The second half of the table presents the two issues on which the Church has not taken a partisan stand. There is a slight, negative correlation between involvement and attitudes toward labor, but the relationship is too small to be considered significant. So is the slight, positive relationship between involvement and attitudes toward government control.

These figures alone seem to warrant the conclusion that involvement in the church, as it has been defined, bears little or no relationship to parishioners' social ideology. Furthermore, when Table 66 was recomputed for parishioners exhibiting different degrees of predisposition to involvement, the conclusion remained unchallenged. Whatever their motivation for becoming more or less involved, parishioners' actual involvement appears neither a source nor a consequence of their agreement with the Church on ideological matters.

Before moving on, however, there are two further possibilities to be explored: first, we shall return to the earlier notion that the association between involvement and social ideology may differ between those who are aware of the Church policy on a given issue, and those who are either uninformed or misinformed. Secondly, we shall attempt to determine whether a parishioner's church involvement bears any relationship to the extent of his agreement with his minister on social issues. It seems plausible that if the church exerts any influence on the parishioner's social values, it might be exerted through the parish priest. This seems especially important in view of the fact that contact with the church-at-large can only be indirect for most parishioners.

INVOLVEMENT, KNOWLEDGE OF THE CHURCH'S SOCIAL POLICY, AND EXTENT OF AGREEMENT

The questionnaire included only two questions assessing parishioners' awareness of the social policy positions advocated by the national Church. They were asked whether the Church had taken a strong stand in support of the United Nations, and in support of human rights. Being correctly informed, misinformed, or uninformed about the Church's action on these two issues is not related in any consistent way to the degree of involvement. Table 67 shows that those who are highly involved are about

TABLE 67

LEVEL OF INVOLVEMENT HAS NO EFFECT ON PARISHIONERS' KNOWLEDGE OF THE CHURCH'S POSITIONS ON THE ISSUES OF THE UNITED NATIONS AND HUMAN RIGHTS

| Knowledge of issues | Composite Index of Involvement | | | | | |
| | High | | | | | Low |
	5	4	3	2	1	0
United Nations						
Informed	32%	40%	40%	38%	41%	33%
Uninformed	57	50	54	54	50	61
Misinformed	11	10	5	7	9	6
100% =	97	161	258	248	222	156
No answer	4	10	20	11	8	7
Total number	101	171	278	259	230	163
Human Rights						
Informed	81%	65%	73%	69%	71%	65%
Uninformed	13	29	23	24	22	27
Misinformed	6	6	4	7	7	7
100% =	99	167	272	249	223	161
No answer	2	4	6	10	7	2
Total number	101	171	278	259	230	163

equally as well informed (and as badly informed) as those who score low on the involvement index. The absence of a relationship is, of course, significant in its own right since it conforms to the general tenor of the previous findings: namely, the involvement is not significantly related to the parishioner's social attitudes. Apparently involvement is not related to relative awareness of Church policy either.[3]

However, while involved parishioners are no better informed about the Church's social policy than the uninvolved, it is conceivable that among those who are correctly informed, involvement might be positively associated with a greater acceptance of the Church's social position. Therefore, the degrees of association between involvement and parishioners' attitudes on the United Nations and human rights have been computed separately for those who are informed or uninformed on each issue. The results are presented in Table 68; the measure of association is the Pearsonian *r*.

TABLE 68

THERE IS NO SIGNIFICANT ASSOCIATION BETWEEN INVOLVEMENT AND AGREEMENT WITH THE CHURCH'S SOCIAL POLICIES EVEN WHEN KNOWLEDGE OF THE CHURCH'S POSITION IS HELD CONSTANT

Issue	*Pearsonian r* Knowledge of Church position	
	Informed	Uninformed
United Nations	−.023	−.022
Human rights	−.015	.007

Again, all the correlations are relatively small and could easily fall within the realm of chance associations. On balance, the general conclusion that involvement does not lead Episcopalians to greater identification with the social values of the Church, or the converse, is again confirmed rather than denied. It does not appear that the Church could exert a major influence on its more involved parishioners simply by presenting its position to a larger audience.

[3] We note that the most involved parishioners are the best informed on human rights, and the least involved are among the most poorly informed. Nonetheless, involvement has no consistent effect other than that.

INVOLVEMENT AND THE SOCIAL VALUES
OF PARISHIONERS AND THEIR MINISTERS

It is not in the tradition of the Protestant Episcopal Church for its ministers to devote sermons primarily to discussions of contemporary social issues. However, sermons on such issues are not alien to the pulpit. And with the activation of the Church's Christian Social Relations program in 1950, there has been a more active encouragement to engage in such discussions, particularly with respect to the social policies of the Church as adopted at the General Convention. Our data provide a hint of the extent to which ministers have cooperated in this effort. Sixty-three percent of those who responded to the parish inventory[4] report that their parish had devoted one or more Sundays to a discussion of social issues during the preceding calendar year.

Despite this effort on the part of the national Church, as well as the cooperation extended by a substantial portion of the laity, there is nothing to suggest that ministers generally are militant social activists. However, the earlier comparison of ministers' and parishioners' attitudes on social issues showed that the clergy, on the whole, adopt a generally liberal position, not only in support of official Church policies, but on other issues as well.

In any event, our present concern is to determine the extent to which parishioners and their particular priests agree on social issues, and to test the more specific hypothesis that insofar as there is agreement, it will be greater among the more involved parishioners than among the less involved. Following the procedure adopted in the earlier analysis of the association between involvement and social ideology, the Pearsonian r will be used as the measure of association.

In making this comparison, it will be recalled that the questionnaire administered to parishioners was also sent to the priests from all those parishes represented in the parishioner sample. As is to be expected in a survey such as this, not all parishioners

[4] See the Preface and Appendix A for discussion of the parish inventories.

returned their questionnaires, nor did all the priests. However, out of the total of 1,530 parishioner questionnaires returned, parallel information was obtained from the priests of 69 percent of them. It is evident, as Appendix B points out, that these 1,058 parishioners do not wholly represent the total of 1,530, but the comparability is sufficient to permit the comparisons intended. Nonetheless, it should be recognized that the findings will not strictly represent the laity of the Church as a whole.

To begin the analysis, it is useful to measure the overall association between the attitudes of parishioners and their priests. The correlation coefficients on the six basic issues considered previously are reported in Table 69. The correlations are ex-

TABLE 69

THERE IS LITTLE IF ANY RELATIONSHIP BETWEEN THE ATTITUDES OF THE PRIESTS AND THOSE OF THEIR PARISHIONERS ON THE SIX SOCIAL ISSUES

Issues	Pearsonian r
United Nations	.039
Immigration	.007
Conscientious objectors	.014
Human rights	.048
Labor	.015
Government control	−.026

tremely small, for the most part, indicating that parishioners are not necessarily inclined to hold the same attitudes as their priests. However, there is some variation among the issues. To the extent that there is any consensus between parishioners and their priests, it is more evident on the issues of the United Nations and human rights. Still, as we have noted earlier, correlations of these magnitudes might very well be attributable to chance. And even in those instances where small associations do exist, it must be stressed these cannot be taken as indications that priests have influenced their parishioners, only that they agree.

Table 70 is a test of the hypothesis that parishioners with the strongest commitment to the church would be more influenced by their ministers' ideologies than would those with only marginal church ties. At each level of involvement, the correlation

TABLE 70

EVEN THE MOST INVOLVED PARISHIONERS DO NOT NECESSARILY AGREE
WITH THE SOCIAL IDEOLOGIES OF THEIR MINISTERS

Issues	Pearsonian r correlation between parishioners' and ministers' attitudes					
	Composite Index of Involvement					
	High					Low
	5	4	3	2	1	0
United Nations	.313	.026	.063	.091	.144	−.025
Immigration	.057	−.045	.024	.015	.001	.021
Conscientious objectors	−.132	−.047	−.140	.071	.117	−.025
Human rights	.018	−.114	.037	.003	.035	.116
Labor	.295	−.159	.019	.017	.176	−.098
Government control	.055	−.020	.032	.053	.015	−.154

between parishioners' and their ministers' attitudes on each issue
has been computed.

The data reveal no significant association between the attitudes of parishioners and of their ministers on the six social
issues—even among the most highly involved. Therefore, there
seems little reason to suppose that the social ideologies of the
priests are of very much importance in determining the corresponding attitudes among the members of their parishes.

SUMMARY AND CONCLUSIONS

The foregoing analysis has principally shown that involvement,
as it has been defined for this study, is not related in any significant way to parishioners' social ideologies. This means, in effect,
that parishioners are not prone, as a consequence of their involvement, to subscribe to social values of the Church, nor does
it indicate that those who subscribe to such values are more
likely to become deeply involved. In a word, the two tendencies
are irrelevant to one another.

The absence of any significant relationship raises an important
question as to the meaning of involvement. On the one hand,
it seems clear that a parishioner's involvement in his church is
determined by factors other than his concerns about the social
world in which he lives, his interests in reforming it within the

principles of Christianity. This reinforces, in a sense, the earlier conclusion that people are motivated to become deeply involved in a church out of primarily personal concerns; for example, the feeling of deprived status in the secular society.

On the other hand, the church has not succeeded on the whole in persuading its parishioners either to take a deep interest in social problems, nor to champion the causes advocated by the church. This is not completely unexpected, though, since the church as an institution has not appeared as a potent force in shaping the recent social life of the nation. Its advocacy of certain basic principles of social morality have not been translated effectively into a program of action. And, while its social pronouncements undoubtedly have some place and influence in the marketplace of ideas, they are neither expressed with sufficient force, communicated effectively, nor do they become the point of reference against which parishioners themselves judge their own values.

Chapter 8

Church Involvement and Religious Attitudes

That religion matters is generally just assumed. The church, of course, is grounded on this assumption for without it the entire Christian enterprise would be invalid. Students of religion also make this assumption else they would choose a different subject matter. Our own study at once both accepts the assumption and is concerned with testing it. The assumption is accepted in the sense that religion could not exist if it had no meaning for its followers; it is being tested to discover what that meaning is.

In Part One, religion was found to matter in providing comfort to the committed. In Part Two, thus far at least, it has not been found a significant referent for the committed parishioners' social values. While comforting its followers, the church, it would seem, does little to challenge them. Such a conclusion, however, may be premature. To be sure, one way in which the church may challenge its followers is to win them to accept the church's pronouncements on social issues, and the church's failure to do so may be regarded as a sign of impotence. This hardly warrants the generalization, however, that the church is altogether impotent except in the realm of comfort.

Unfortunately, the data available to us do not allow an exhaustive examination of the various ways that the lives of the committed may be influenced by their commitment. No information was collected, for example, on what church commitment means for the way individuals comport themselves in interpersonal relations or in the rearing of children. Conceivably, the committed may be more honest, more sensitive, kinder, and less

173

selfish than the less committed in their everyday lives. And, in child rearing, the committed may be more successful in instilling in their children a concern about the moral and ethical dimensions of life. Whether such effects follow from commitment cannot be tested with our data though, of course, such considerations would be necessary in a thoroughly comprehensive study of the consequences which follow from religious commitment.

While we must settle for less in our own inquiry, there are some additional questions about the effects of religious commitment which can be explored with the data at hand. These questions bear on the relation between church involvement and parishioners' attitudes on issues of more circumscribed religious content. While church involvement may be largely irrelevant to social ideology, it may conceivably be highly related to particular aspects of religious ideology.

In this realm, two hypotheses are subjected to test in this chapter. One of these is that deeply involved parishioners will be found to be more religiocentric than their less involved counterparts; the second is that they will also be found to be more denominationally parochial. By religiocentrism, we mean a tendency to view the world in primarily religious terms and to conceive religion and the church as miraculously capable of solving the world's problems. Denominational parochialism, in turn, signifies a tendency to be concerned about the integrity of one's own denomination, in the present instance, the Protestant Episcopal Church.

In pursuing these lines of inquiry, it should be noted in advance that the analysis may often stand on the brink of tautology. In some instances, it may appear that we have only discovered that involved parishioners are more religious than are the uninvolved. Still, the issues which will be examined in this chapter can provide further insight into the nature of church involvement itself.

RELIGIOCENTRISM

There are essentially two ways that the church may seek to exercise influence in shaping the secular world. One of these ways, examined earlier in the chapter on political permissiveness, is to participate actively in the world by vigorously expressing its positions on current social, political, and economic problems and by attempting to have these positions influence the ultimate resolution of the problems. A second route open to the church is to rely on the special power, often attributed to religion, to transform individual lives and, by extension, to transform society. The first of these orientations represents support of the church performing a challenging role in an active way. The second orientation, which we shall call *religiocentrism*, is its passive counterpart. The ultimate goal of both orientations is a society whose values and practices are based on Christian principles, but the means for achieving the desired end are importantly different.

In Chapter 6, the amount and quality of support for the first orientation was examined as well as its relationship to differential church involvement. Here, we wish to assess support for the second orientation and again to see how this is related to degree of involvement.

Two questions in the questionnaire dealt directly with the issue of religious efficacy per se. Since the study was conducted during the Korean conflict, respondents were asked to assess the power of prayers for peace and of the church as an institution to help prevent war. Table 71 presents the answers of clergy and parishioners to these questions.

With regard to the efficacy of special prayers for peace, bishops were nearly unanimous in their disagreement with the statement: "Special prayers for peace do not help to prevent war." Priests were the next most likely to disagree. While parishioners were the least convinced of the power of prayer, fully 70 percent disagreed with the statement.

A similar, though less striking, pattern appears with regard to the second item. While a small minority of the clergy feel that the church can do little to prevent war, over two-thirds of both the bishops and the priests indicate that the church can do "a great deal." Parishioners follow closely behind the clergy. Sixty-two percent of the parishioners feel the church can do a great deal to prevent war.

Table 72 shows the effect of parishioners' involvement on

TABLE 71

THE CLERGY ARE MORE LIKELY TO BELIEVE IN THE EFFICACY OF PRAYERS AND
THE CHURCH IN PREVENTING WAR THAN ARE PARISHIONERS

	Bishops	Priests	Parishioners
"Special prayers for peace do not help to prevent war."			
Agree	0%	6%	18%
Disagree	96	89	70
Uncertain	4	5	12
100% =	100	259	1500
No answer	...	...	30
Total	100	259	1530
"In helping to prevent war, the Church can do":			
Nothing	0%	0%	2%
Very little	5	7	12
Quite a bit	26	25	24
A great deal	69	68	62
100% =	98	256	1512
No answer	2	3	18
Total	100	259	1530

their responses to the two items.[1] Involvement, it will be recalled, was found earlier to be unrelated to political permissiveness and acceptance of the church's position on social issues. On the present matter of religious efficacy, however, involvement does make a difference. Involved parishioners are more convinced of the power of prayer than are the uninvolved, and also are more likely to feel the church can do a great deal to prevent war. In response to the second question, in fact, the more involved parishioners (scoring 4 and 5) are more likely to feel the church can do a great deal to prevent war than was even true of the clergy (recall Table 71).

As a follow up to the question on the church's role in preventing war, respondents were asked if they felt the church could do more than it was already doing. The clergy were more likely

[1] Since the issues considered in this chapter are directly relevant to understanding the nature of religious commitment, we shall examine the effects of involvement on each of the separate items.

TABLE 72

INVOLVEMENT IS POSITIVELY RELATED TO BELIEF IN THE POWER
OF THE CHURCH AND OF PRAYERS IN PREVENTING WAR

| | Composite Index of Involvement | | | | | |
| | High | | | | | Low |
	5	4	3	2	1	0
"Special prayers for peace do not help to prevent war."						
Agree	19%	13%	11%	16%	16%	31%
Disagree	79	81	78	72	68	55
Uncertain	2	6	11	12	16	13
100% =	96	167	273	258	225	163
No answer	6	4	3	1	5	...
Total	102	171	276	259	230	163
"In helping to prevent war, the Church can do":						
Nothing	2%	2%	3%	1%	2%	2%
Very little	5	7	9	15	13	15
Quite a bit	11	15	24	24	26	32
A great deal	82	76	64	61	59	51
100% =	99	168	275	258	228	163
No answer	3	3	1	1	2	...
Total	102	171	276	259	230	163

than parishioners to say they felt it could. Ninety percent of the
bishops and 84 percent of the priests answered yes, as contrasted
with one-half of the parishioners. Among parishioners, a strong,
positive correlation appeared between involvement and the belief
that the church could do more to prevent war.[2]

When asked what the church might do, parishioners tended
to suggest religious, rather than political, actions. Most common
were the suggestions that the church disseminate moral and religious principles among all people and that it seek to strengthen
the moral and religious fiber of the church and its members.
Some felt more prayer should be encouraged, others thought that
greater missionary activity would help. Less frequent were the
demands for direct political action by the church. Those highest

[2] See Appendix B.

on involvement were clearly the most likely to suggest "religious" action.[3]

The finding that involved parishioners are more convinced of the efficacy of religion may, as suggested earlier, border on tautology. Nonetheless, the data just examined highlight the distinction between political permissiveness and religiocentrism. Involvement is not related to the desire for the church to actively seek an informing role in the secular world. It is clearly associated, however, with the belief that religion per se is powerful enough to transform the world in a miraculous way.

Religiocentrism is not only comprised of a belief in the power of religion to effect change. It also includes a conception that religion warrants a privileged, indeed a "sacred" status in society. This element in religiocentrism is captured in the responses to two other issues dealt with in the questionnaire, both of which were under public scrutiny at the time of the study and remain so today.

The first of these issues is government aid to parochial schools on which the Episcopal General Convention took the following unequivocal position in 1949.

> Resolved, That this Convention fully endorses the principle that sectarian schools be supported in full from private sources or from a Church, and be it further
> Resolved, That we stand unalterably against the use of Federal or State funds for the support of private, parochial, or sectarian schools.

Respondents, when asked to agree or disagree with the statement "Government funds should be used for support of parochial or religious schools," overwhelmingly express their support for the Church's official position by expressing disagreement (Table 73). Bishops are the most likely to oppose the use of government funds for the support of parochial schools, and priests are next. While parishioners are the least likely to support the Church's position, still, nearly eight parishioners in ten disagree with the statement.

In Table 72, it will be recalled, the most involved parishioners closely resembled the clergy in their belief in the efficacy of prayer and of the church's power to prevent war. In the present

[3] See Appendix B.

TABLE 73

FEW AMONG THE CLERGY OR LAITY FEEL GOVERNMENT FUNDS SHOULD
BE USED TO SUPPORT PAROCHIAL SCHOOLS

"Government funds should be used for support of parochial or religious schools."	Bishops	Priests	Parishioners
Agree	0%	10%	13%
Disagree	96	85	79
Uncertain	4	5	8
100% =	95	250	1502
No answer	5	9	28
Total	100	259	1530

instance, quite the opposite is true. Parishioners highest on involvement are more likely to differ from the clergy and from the official Church position than the relatively uninvolved (Table 74).

Eighty-six percent of the least involved parishioners support the unequivocal Church position; this is comparable to the 85 percent of the priests who do so. Yet, as involvement increases, disagreement with the statement decreases. While involvement is not related to support for government aid to parochial schools, the most involved parishioners are the most inclined to take an equivocal stand of uncertainty. We would suggest that this reflects a propensity on the part of the most involved to assign a

TABLE 74

INVOLVEMENT IS NEGATIVELY RELATED TO DISAGREEMENT WITH THE STATEMENT
PROPOSING GOVERNMENT AID TO PAROCHIAL SCHOOLS

"Government funds should be used for support of parochial or religious schools."	Composite Index of Involvement					
	High					Low
	5	4	3	2	1	0
Agree	11%	10%	11%	15%	11%	10%
Disagree	75	77	80	79	82	86
Uncertain	14	13	9	7	7	4
100% =	98	167	269	254	224	159
No answer	4	4	7	5	6	4
Total	102	171	276	259	230	163

special status to religion in the society. While the Church and its clergy surely would not demean the importance of religion, they oppose the suggested measure on the basis of the separation of church and state. Most parishioners, involved or not, agree. Relatively, however, it is the more involved who are the least likely to deny religion's special significance to them even if this threatens the separation of church and state in the process.

This same religiocentric orientation is found even more clearly in connection with the issue of religious instruction in public schools. It seems safe to assume that sensitivity on this issue has increased significantly, since the study was conducted prior to the Supreme Court's ban on prayers in schools. The issue was nevertheless salient at the time of the study and was also the subject of a resolution passed at the 1949 General Convention.

> *Resolved,* That the fifty-sixth General Convention of this Church affirms anew its belief in our traditional separation of Church and State, but that traditional American doctrine in this matter does not preclude but rather would encourage religious instruction in the public schools where such is arranged by the local school authorities and is on a voluntary basis. . . .

For the purposes of the present analysis, the critical phrase in this resolution is "on a voluntary basis." In the study, respondents were asked whether they believed religious instruction in public schools should be forbidden, voluntary, or compulsory. As was true of the responses to the issue of government aid to parochial schools, the vast majority of parishioners and clergy agreed with the Church's position—religious instruction should be voluntary (Table 75).

Bishops are nearly unanimous in their conviction that religious instruction should be offered on a voluntary basis in the public schools, available to those who want it but not thrust upon those who do not. Interestingly, more bishops would have religious instruction totally forbidden than would have it compulsory for all children, 5 and 1 percent respectively. Among priests and parishioners the opposite is true. While 85 percent of the priests subscribe to the Church position of voluntary instruction, the remainder are two-to-one in favor of making religious instruction compulsory rather than prohibiting it. A comparatively smaller 71 percent of parishioners support the

TABLE 75

PARISHIONERS AND CLERGY ALIKE MODALLY FEEL THAT RELIGIOUS
INSTRUCTION IN THE PUBLIC SCHOOLS SHOULD BE "VOLUNTARY"

"Religious instruction in public schools should be":	Bishops	Priests	Parishioners
Forbidden by law	5%	5%	10%
Voluntary for children whose parents approve	94	85	71
Compulsory	1	10	20
100% =	98	254	1498
No answer	2	5	32
Total	100	259	1530

Church position, and the dissenting laity are, like the priests, two-to-one in favor of compulsory instruction. For present purposes, the most interesting finding of Table 75 is that one out of five parishioners would favor making religious instruction compulsory for all students, regardless of their own desires or those of their parents.

Support for compulsory religious instruction seems another clear evidence of the religiocentric orientation under discussion. And as Table 76 shows, it is more typical of involved parishioners than of the uninvolved. Parishioners scored lowest on involvement are about as likely to favor compulsory religious in-

TABLE 76

CHURCH INVOLVEMENT IS ASSOCIATED WITH SUPPORT FOR COMPULSORY
RELIGIOUS INSTRUCTION IN THE PUBLIC SCHOOLS

"Religious instruction in public schools should be":	Composite Index of Involvement					
	High					Low
	5	4	3	2	1	0
Forbidden by law	2%	5%	7%	7%	12%	13%
Voluntary for children whose parents approve	66	67	64	75	74	76
Compulsory	32	28	19	18	14	11
100% =	97	168	272	257	222	162
No answer	5	3	4	2	8	1
Total	102	171	276	259	230	163

struction as are the priests. As involvement increases, we note a commensurate increase in the proportion of parishioners assuming the religiocentric posture.

Church involvement is also negatively related to support for prohibiting religious instruction, as one might imagine. Nevertheless, the strongest and clearest association is with regard to holding the religiocentric position: compulsory instruction. Ironically, the net effect of involvement is such as to produce a negative association with support for the Church policy of voluntary instruction. This is the same effect noted with regard to the issue of government aid to parochial schools (Table 74).

The relationships observed in Tables 74 and 76 emphasize the distinction between religiocentrism and political permissiveness. We have already noted that involvement and permissiveness are not related to one another. It may also be recalled from Table 45 (Chapter 6) that political permissiveness was not related to attitudes regarding government aid to parochial schools and religious instruction in public schools. Thus the view that the Church should seek an informing role in society is quite distinct from the view that it should be accorded such a role. While church involvement is apparently irrelevant to the former, active orientation, it is clearly associated with the latter, passive one.

Finally, another item in the questionnaire may be used to further elucidate the religiocentric orientation. The value placed on charity is not unique to the Episcopal Church nor even to Christianity. It is an important element of many religions. As such, the performance of charitable acts is commonly regarded as a consequence or evidence of religious commitment. To examine this possible effect, respondents were presented with a list of common charitable activities and organizations and asked which, if any, they had supported during the two years prior to the study.

The participation of clergy and parishioners in each of the charitable activities is presented in full in Appendix B. For present purposes, it is sufficient to make two observations. First, bishops and priests generally reported a greater participation than was true of the laity. Second, when parishioners' involvement is taken into account, it has little overall effect on the degree of charitable activities. In most cases, there is no discernible relationship between involvement and charitable acts. In some cases, a negative relationship appears. (For example, 12 percent of the most involved parishioners report giving blood to the Red Cross, as contrasted with 23 percent of the least involved.) Among parishioners, then, church involvement does not have the necessary consequence of increasing their concern for charity.

While this general observation applies to most of the charitable activities in the list, there are notable exceptions. In particular, church involvement is positively related to participation in charitable activities which have a religious affiliation. As Table 77 shows, involved parishioners are more likely to report contributions to Church World Service and to have contributed clothing to Korea, a program carried on by the Church at the time of the study.

TABLE 77

PARISHIONERS SCORING HIGHEST ON INVOLVEMENT ARE THE MOST LIKELY TO PARTICIPATE IN CHARITABLE ACTIVITIES WHICH HAVE SOME RELIGIOUS AFFILIATION

| | Composite Index of Involvement | | | | | |
| | High | | | | | Low |
	5	4	3	2	1	0
Percentage who, in the preceding two years:						
Contributed to Church World Service	58	58	49	54	44	34
Contributed clothing to Korea	40	44	36	35	23	20
Total number	102	171	276	259	230	163

This latest finding can also be located within the context of religiocentrism. The data introduced thus far in the present chapter indicate that church involvement is related to a tendency to view the world in a religious perspective. Although involved parishioners are no more or less supportive of an active political role for the church, they have, nonetheless, demonstrated a greater conviction that religion is potentially powerful (e.g., in preventing war) and deserving of special consideration in American life (e.g., religion in schools). It was noted in passing that involved parishioners also were most prone to believe that the

Church could be most effective when it acted in a clearly "religious" manner—through prayers and moral instruction. The relationship between involvement and charity fits neatly into the same religiocentric orientation. Overall, church involvement does not bring about greater charitability, contrary to what one might have imagined. Yet, when a particular charitable act is identified as religious, involvement matters.

The most involved parishioners, then, are the most ready to support and defend the special efficacy of religion to deal miraculously with world problems and also to conceive of religion as deserving a privileged status in society. Since issues such as the United Nations and immigration are not immediately religious in content, they are irrelevant to church involvement. Even charitable activities not affiliated with the church appear to fall into the same category.

Since we shall wish to consider religiocentrism in another context, later in this chapter, it will be useful to create a composite index to reflect its several aspects. To construct such an index, parishioners were given one point for each of the following responses in the questionnaire:

(1) Responding that the Church could do "a great deal" to help prevent war. (Examined in Tables 71 and 72.)

(2) Responding that religious instruction in public schools should be compulsory. (Examined in Tables 75 and 76.)

(3) Reporting a contribution to Church World Service. (Examined in Table 77.)

The resultant scores on the composite index of religiocentrism, then, ranged from a high of 3 to a low of 0. To insure that the index could be used as a valid representation of religiocentrism, scores on the composite index were compared with responses to other items which reflect the religiocentric orientation, but which were not included in the composite measure. The items appropriate for this test are:

(1) Responses to the statement: "Special prayers for peace do not help to prevent war." (Examined in Tables 71 and 72.)

(2) Attitudes toward government assistance to parochial schools. (Examined in Tables 73 and 74.)

(3) Responses to the question: "Can the Church do any-

TABLE 78

VALIDATION OF THE RELIGIOCENTRISM INDEX

| | Composite Index of Religiocentrism | | | |
| | High | | | Low |
	3	2	1	0
Percentage disagreeing with the statement: "Special prayers for peace do not help prevent war."	85	79	68	54
	(94)	(484)	(570)	(256)
Percentage who do not disagree with government assistance to parochial schools	36	20	19	15
	(94)	(474)	(569)	(257)
Percentage who felt the church could do more than it was doing to prevent war	70	65	48	22
	(96)	(481)	(577)	(262)

thing more than it is already doing to prevent war?" (Discussed earlier in the chapter.)

Table 78 presents the relationships between the composite index of religiocentrism and each of the validating items.

In each instance, the index of religiocentrism predicts religiocentric responses to the validating items. With the validity of the composite measure thus established, the question remains as to whether church involvement is related to the accumulation of religiocentric responses. Table 79 presents the mean scores on religiocentrism for parishioners at each level of involvement. (As in previous presentations, the mean scores have been adjusted to represent a range from *0.0* to *1.0*.)

TABLE 79

CHURCH INVOLVEMENT IS CLOSELY RELATED TO RELIGIOCENTRISM

| | Composite Index of Involvement | | | | | |
| | High | | | | | Low |
	5	4	3	2	1	0
Mean scores on religiocentrism	*.58*	*.54*	*.44*	*.44*	*.39*	*.32*
	(99)	(167)	(269)	(256)	(220)	(161)

As the data indicate, involvement is strongly related to the accumulation of religiocentric responses as well as to the individual items comprising the index. Parishioners highest on involvement have a mean score of .58 on religiocentrism, as contrasted with .32 for those lowest on involvement.

In summary, parishioners' church involvement is closely related to the religious perspective we have referred to as religiocentrism. Those deeply committed to the church exhibit the greatest faith in the potential power of religion and are the most concerned for granting religion a special place in the social order. As noted earlier, all this is true even though involved parishioners are no more interested than the uninvolved to have the church participate actively in the secular society.

DENOMINATIONAL PAROCHIALISM

Despite the current excitement about the ecumenical movement in the United States and elsewhere, social scientists have begun to note the existence of strong, countervailing tendencies.[4] Many church members across the country no doubt subscribe to the principle of interfaith cooperation. There are some, nonetheless, who are very concerned with the maintenance of particularistic denominational identities.

On the question of interfaith cooperation, the majority of both the clergy and laity feel their church should support the local, national, and world councils of churches. When asked if they favored parish cooperation with interfaith organizations for purposes of social planning, civic improvement, and fellowships, 66 percent of the bishops and priests and 50 percent of the parishioners approved.

In absolute terms, these figures do not represent anything approaching a consensus, but they do indicate fairly substantial support for interfaith cooperation nonetheless.

In such instances, religious cooperation is normally a means for promoting generally religious programs such as charity, welfare, and brotherhood. On the whole, there is a fair amount of

4 For example, see Charles Y. Glock and Rodney Stark, "The New Denominationalism," *Religion and Society in Tension* (Chicago: Rand McNally, 1965), pp. 86–122.

support among Episcopalians for their Church to participate alongside other religious bodies. Yet, when interfaith cooperation is focused on specifically, and intimately, religious matters, many among the clergy and laity express a concern that cooperation may threaten the integrity of their particular denomination. For the purpose of the present analysis, this latter orientation will be referred to as *denominational parochialism*.

Before turning to the specific issues reflecting this orientation, it is necessary to note a peculiar aspect of the Protestant Episcopal Church which should inform the analysis. Episcopalians are the first to admit that their Church represents a curious, religious composite—half Protestant and half Catholic. Historically, the Anglican Church was established as the Apostolic Successor to the Catholic Church in Rome. The term *Protestant* Episcopal Church was chosen at a time when "Protestant" meant "non-Roman." Historically, however, the Church viewed itself as separate from the Protestant Reformation.

At the present time, the Catholic and Protestant tendencies are preserved, respectively, in the "high church"/"low church" dualism. Unfortunately, the questionnaire did not ask respondents to identify themselves in these terms, although such information would have been of obvious value in understanding parishioners' attitudes toward interfaith cooperation. While this represents a deficiency in the data available for analysis, there are grounds for believing parishioners themselves tend to identify more with Protestantism than with Catholicism. For example, when asked the advisability of their parish cooperating with various non-Episcopalian religious groups, 68 percent of the parishioners said cooperation with Protestant Churches was all right; 32 percent favored cooperation with Roman Catholic Churches. A similar distinction was made by bishops and priests.

Nevertheless, the reader should bear in mind that the Protestant Episcopal Church, strictly speaking, does not fall wholly within either Catholicism or Protestantism. In this section, we shall examine respondents' attitudes toward interaction with both Protestants and Roman Catholics. First, we shall focus on the question of ritual cooperation with Protestant churches and clergy, and second, on the question of intermarriage with Roman Catholics.

Two questions in the questionnaire focused on ritual cooperation between Episcopal parishes and Protestant churches. First,
respondents were asked whether they favored "joint worship
services with Protestant churches of any denomination." To distinguish the degree of ritual intimacy they would favor, clergy
and parishioners were asked to indicate if joint worship services
would be all right (1) including Holy Communion, (2) exclud-
ing Holy Communion, or (3) under no circumstances. The
overall distribution of responses is presented in Table 80. Bishops

TABLE 80

CLERGY ARE MORE LIKELY THAN PARISHIONERS TO RULE OUT JOINT
WORSHIP SERVICES WHICH WOULD INCLUDE HOLY COMMUNION

"It is all right for my church to hold joint worship services with Protestant churches of any denomination":	Bishops	Priests	Parishioners
Including Holy Communion	18%	20%	47%
Excluding Holy Communion	78	70	42
Under no circumstances	4	10	11
100% =	90	251	1447
No answer	10	8	83
Total	100	259	1530

and priests were most likely to favor joint services which would
exclude Holy Communion; parishioners are not as likely to make
this ritual distinction—being about evenly divided between the
two types of service. Few respondents would rule out joint services altogether, although priests and parishioners are the most
likely to do so.

Church involvement seems to have little effect on parishioners'
responses to joint worship services. The least involved are the
most favorable to including Holy Communion, but other than
that, involvement appears to be irrelevant (Table 81).

On the whole, it can be concluded that most Episcopalians—
clergy and laity—support the idea of joint worship services
with Protestant churches. Regarding the intimacy of ritual cooperation, however, the clergy are modally opposed to sharing
the sacrament of Holy Communion with non-Episcopalians,
while parishioners are about evenly divided.

TABLE 81

INVOLVEMENT HAS LITTLE OR NO EFFECT ON ACTIVITIES TOWARD
JOINT WORSHIP SERVICES

"It is all right for my church to hold joint worship services with Protestant churches of any denomination":	Composite Index of Involvement					
	High					Low
	5	4	3	2	1	0
Including Holy Communion	46%	47%	43%	43%	45%	55%
Excluding Holy Communion	42	44	44	44	44	38
Under no circumstances	12	9	13	12	11	7
100% =	100	163	260	252	215	156
No answer	2	8	16	7	15	7
Total	102	171	276	259	230	163

The second question on ritual cooperation asked whether it was all right for a Protestant minister to preach in one's parish church. Relatively, both clergy and parishioners are more favorable to a visiting minister than to sharing Holy Communion with members of a Protestant denomination. Again, however, bishops and priests are less open to the proposal than parishioners (Table 82).

Slightly more than half of the clergy say it is all right for a minister of a Protestant church to preach in the local parish church; 80 percent of the parishioners say it is all right. The data do not tell us why this should be so. Perhaps parishioners are less sensitive to the implications of modifications in church

TABLE 82

PARISHIONERS ARE MORE LIKELY TO ACCEPT A VISITING MINISTER
FROM A PROTESTANT DENOMINATION THAN ARE THE CLERGY

"It is all right for a minister of a Protestant church to preach in my local church."	Bishops	Priests	Parishioners
Agree	56%	54%	80%
Disagree	31	39	14
Uncertain	12	8	6
100% =	89	248	1482
No answer	11	11	48
Total	100	259	1530

ritual than are the clergy. Whatever the reasons for their over-whelming agreement with the proposal, however, involved parishioners are less likely to accept a visiting Protestant minister than are the uninvolved (Table 83).

TABLE 83

CHURCH INVOLVEMENT IS NEGATIVELY RELATED TO ACCEPTANCE
OF A VISITING PROTESTANT MINISTER

"It is all right for a minister of a Protestant church to preach in my local parish church."	Composite Index of Involvement					
	High					Low
	5	4	3	2	1	0
Agree	72%	78%	80%	79%	83%	87%
Disagree	20	15	16	15	13	7
Uncertain	7	7	4	6	4	6
100% =	98	167	270	256	222	159
No answer	4	4	6	3	8	4
Total	102	171	276	259	230	163

Comparatively, even the most involved parishioners are more likely to accept a visiting Protestant minister than was true of the clergy. Nevertheless, the effect of involvement on parochialism in this instance is relatively consistent.

Joint worship services with Protestant churches and preaching by a visiting Protestant minister are very weak encroachments on the denominational integrity of the Protestant Episcopal Church. The questions regarding interaction with Roman Catholics strike a more sensitive nerve. The official Church position on this matter was stated in a resolution by the 1949 General Convention.

> *Resolved,* That this Convention earnestly warns members of our Church against contracting marriages with Roman Catholics under the conditions imposed by modern Roman Canon Law, especially as these conditions involve a promise to have their children brought up in a religious system which they cannot themselves accept. . . .

Respondents to the present study were asked to agree or disagree with two statements regarding intermarriage with Roman Catholics.

(1) "Protestant and Roman Catholics should be allowed to intermarry freely."

(2) "It is all right for an Episcopalian who marries a Roman Catholic to agree to let their children be brought up as Roman Catholics."

Table 84 presents the responses of bishops, priests and pa-

TABLE 84

CLERGY ARE MORE RESISTANT TO INTERMARRIAGE WITH
ROMAN CATHOLICS THAN IS TRUE OF PARISHIONERS

"Protestants and Roman Catholics should be allowed to intermarry freely."	Bishops	Priests	Parishioners
Agree	33%	37%	57%
Disagree	55	51	29
Uncertain	12	11	14
100% =	92	247	1475
No answer	8	12	55
Total	100	259	1530

rishioners regarding the first statement: intermarriage with Roman Catholics. The clergy are again more parochial in their responses than are the parishioners. Approximately half of the clergy support the Church policy by disagreeing with the statement; only about one-third take a position opposed to the Church's. The majority of parishioners, however, agree with the statement, feeling that Protestants and Roman Catholics should be permitted to intermarry if they wish; only 29 percent disagree.

The influence of church involvement on this issue is immediately apparent in Table 85. Forty-two percent of the most involved parishioners support the official Church position, as contrasted with 19 percent of the least involved. The responses of the most involved parishioners more closely approximate—although they do not match—the responses given by bishops and priests.

Both the clergy and parishioners make a sharp distinction between intermarriage and raising the children of such marriages within the Roman Catholic faith. Bishops and priests are still more resistant than parishioners, but still only a minority of the

TABLE 85

HIGH CHURCH INVOLVEMENT IS RELATED TO A GREATER RESISTANCE
TO INTERMARRIAGE BETWEEN PROTESTANTS AND ROMAN CATHOLICS

"Protestants and Roman Catholics should be allowed to intermarry freely."	Composite Index of Involvement					
	High					Low
	5	4	3	2	1	0
Agree	41%	47%	53%	63%	62%	69%
Disagree	42	38	31	25	26	19
Uncertain	17	14	16	12	12	13
100% =	97	169	270	254	221	159
No answer	5	2	6	5	9	4
Total	102	171	276	259	230	163

latter agree with the second statement. Four percent of the bishops, 6 percent of the priests and 21 percent of the parishioners feel it is all right for an Episcopalian, married to a Roman Catholic, to agree to have his children raised as Roman Catholics. The clergy are nearly unanimous in their disagreement, while 16 percent of the parishioners say they are uncertain (Table 86).

Once again, church involvement is associated with the orientation of denominational parochialism. As Table 87 shows, involved parishioners are the most likely to disapprove of raising the children of mixed marriages as Roman Catholics. Those low-

TABLE 86

FEW EPISCOPALIANS FEEL THE CHILDREN OF MIXED MARRIAGES
SHOULD BE RAISED AS ROMAN CATHOLICS

"It is all right for an Episcopalian who marries a Roman Catholic, to agree to let their children be brought up as Roman Catholics."	Bishops	Priests	Parishioners
Agree	4%	6%	21%
Disagree	93	92	64
Uncertain	2	2	16
100% =	91	252	1469
No answer	9	7	61
Total	100	259	1530

TABLE 87

INVOLVEMENT IS RELATED TO ATTITUDES ON RAISING THE CHILDREN
OF MIXED MARRIAGES AS ROMAN CATHOLICS

"It is all right for an Episcopalian who marries a Roman Catholic, to agree to let their children be brought up as Roman Catholics."	Composite Index of Involvement					
	High					Low
	5	4	3	2	1	0
Agree	17%	13%	16%	20%	24%	30%
Disagree	69	72	68	64	63	52
Uncertain	15	15	16	17	13	18
100% =	96	168	269	253	222	159
No answer	6	3	7	6	8	4
Total	102	171	276	259	230	163

est on involvement are the most likely to agree with the statement, although less than one-third do so.

On a variety of issues, then, we have noted that some Episcopalians exhibit a certain wariness about interfaith contacts and mixing. Some are reluctant to share the sacrament of Holy Communion with non-Episcopalians, some disapprove of a Protestant minister preaching in an Episcopalian parish, and many are opposed to intermarriage with Roman Catholics. For the most part, this orientation of denominational parochialism is positively associated with high church involvement.

In the examination of religiocentrism, it was noted that parishioners tended to see the obligation of charity in rather restricted, religious terms. Involvement seemed to have little effect on charitable activities of Episcopalians with the exception of those programs which bore a religious stamp. Thus, while involvement was unrelated to participation in secular charities, high church involvement was seen to encourage contributions to Church World Service and contributions of clothing to Korea.

Among the charitable activities listed in the questionnaire, one referred specifically to an Episcopalian program: the Presiding Bishop's Fund. In terms of the preceding discussion of denominational parochialism, one should expect involvement to be related to participation in this particular charity. Such an expectation is definitely confirmed by Table 88.

Eighty-three percent of the most involved parishioners report

TABLE 88

INVOLVEMENT IS STRONGLY RELATED TO PARTICIPATING
IN THE PRESIDING BISHOP'S FUND

	Composite Index of Involvement					
	High					Low
	5	4	3	2	1	0
Percentage who report contributing to the Presiding Bishop's Fund	83	80	69	61	55	35
	(102)	(171)	(276)	(259)	(230)	(163)

contributing to the Presiding Bishop's Fund as contrasted with little more than a third of the least involved. Such a finding might seem rather trivial if it were not for the previous observation that involvement has little or no effect on charitability in general. Involvement only matters when a charity is identified as religious (Table 77), and it matters most when that charity is Episcopalian.

The implication of the data examined in this section is that a certain parochial tendency exists among Episcopalian parishioners. In some instances, this tendency is supported by official Church policy; in other cases it is not. On the whole, denominational parochialism represents a tendency to preserve and protect the individual identity of a specific religious group and to view the religious world in terms of that group. In its extreme, denominational parochialism was best characterized by Henry Fielding who had Reverend Thwackum say in *Tom Jones*: "When I mention religion I mean the Christian religion; and not only the Christian religion, but the Protestant religion; and not only the Protestant religion, but the Church of England." [5]

Such a position is surely characteristic of few if any contemporary Episcopalians. Still, denominational parochialism is sufficiently in evidence to warrant the construction of a composite index for future consideration in the analysis. In creating such an index, one point was given parishioners for each of the following responses.

(1) Disagreeing with the suggestion that a Protestant minister

[5] Henry Fielding, *Tom Jones* (New York: The Modern Library, 1950), p. 84.

preach at the local parish church. (Examined in Tables 82 and 83.)

(2) Disagreeing with the statement: "Protestants and Roman Catholics should be allowed to intermarry freely." (Examined in Tables 84 and 85.)

(3) Reporting a contribution to the Presiding Bishop's Fund. (Examined in Table 88.)

By combining the responses in this manner, each parishioner was assigned a score on the composite measure ranging from the highest denominational parochialism (3) to the lowest (0). Once again, several other items were available for use in testing the appropriateness of the composite measure. In this instance, they were:

(1) Attitudes toward joint worship services with other Protestant denominations. (Examined in Tables 80 and 81.)

(2) Attitudes toward the raising of children from mixed marriages as Roman Catholics. (Examined in Tables 86 and 87.)

(3) Response to the statement, "There is no room in the church for people who believe in communism." (Agreement with this statement was felt to represent another kind of parochialism and exclusivism with regard to the integrity and composition of the Episcopal Church.)

(4) Attitudes toward the United States sending an ambassador to the Vatican. (At the time of the study, President Truman had appointed Mark Clark to that post, and it was reasoned that parishioners most resistant to strengthening the position of the Roman Catholic Church would disagree with the action.)

In each instance, those parishioners scoring higher on the index of denominational parochialism were more likely to choose parochial responses to the additional questions (Table 89). Having thus validated the composite index, denominational parochialism mean scores were computed for parishioners at each level of church involvement. The resulting data are presented in Table 90 and clearly demonstrate the effect of involvement on the accumulation of parochial responses.

The findings of Table 90 further substantiate the observations made earlier in this section. Parishioners highest on involvement are the most likely to resist anything which would weaken the denominational integrity of the Protestant Episcopal Church.

TABLE 89

VALIDATION OF THE DENOMINATIONAL PAROCHIALISM INDEX

| | Composite Index of Denominational Parochialism | | | |
| | High | | | Low |
	3	2	1	0
Percentage objecting to joint worship services including Holy Communion	72 (72)	70 (304)	66 (627)	54 (403)
Percentage disagreeing with the raising of children as Roman Catholics	54 (72)	45 (303)	38 (630)	33 (404)
Percentage agreeing there is no room in the church for communists	87 (71)	82 (304)	61 (632)	48 (404)
Percentage disagreeing with the decision for U.S. to send an ambassador to the Vatican	96 (69)	62 (295)	47 (608)	46 (389)

TABLE 90

RESPONDENTS SCORING HIGHEST ON CHURCH INVOLVEMENT ARE MOST LIKELY
TO SCORE HIGHER ON DENOMINATIONAL PAROCHIALISM

| | Composite Index of Involvement | | | | | |
| | High | | | | | Low |
	5	4	3	2	1	0
Mean scores on denominational parochialism:	.49 (98)	.44 (165)	.39 (268)	.34 (254)	.31 (219)	.20 (158)

While parishioners generally are willing to support interfaith co-operation aimed at achieving mutually desirable religious objectives, it is important to recognize the countervailing orientation which may limit the possibilities for ecumenical action.

THE PROTECTION OF RELIGIOUS INSTITUTIONS

Implicit to the analysis thus far has been the contention that religiocentrism and denominational parochialism are in essence the same quality, differing only in level of specificity. Religiocentrism represents an overriding concern for the assertion and maintenance of religion in American life generally, while denominational parochialism refers more specifically to the concern for protecting the integrity of the Episcopal Church in particular. At this point we are in a position to put that assumption to an empirical test. If the two measures are different aspects of the same quality, it should be expected that scores on one index would predict scores on the other. Table 91 presents the data from that test.

For purposes of the present analysis, denominational parochialism has been presented as the independent variable and is used to predict scores on the religiocentrism index, although no causal or temporal association is assumed to exist between the two. As the table shows, 56 percent of those scoring highest (3) on denominational parochialism scored either 3 or 2 on religiocentrism, as contrasted with 28 percent of those scoring lowest (0) on parochialism.

The data presented in Table 91 demonstrate the empirical

TABLE 91

PARISHIONERS SCORING HIGHEST ON DENOMINATIONAL PAROCHIALISM
ALSO SCORE HIGHEST ON RELIGIOCENTRISM

| | Denominational Parochialism | | |
| | High | | Low |
	3	2	1	0
Religiocentrism:				
High 3	11%	8%	8%	3%
2	45	38	37	25
1	35	38	39	46
Low 0	8	15	16	27
100% =	71	299	618	394

relationship between religiocentric and parochial orientations among Episcopal parishioners. This is clearly in accord with the contentions derived from the *Comfort Hypothesis*. If church involvement results primarily from the need for personal comfort to alleviate the deprivations experienced in secular society, it follows that involvement for this reason engenders a greater belief in the efficacy of religion generally and a greater concern for the continued recognition of its importance. However, the formation of this kind of religious perspective is closely tied to the protection of denominational integrity. Parishioners who receive comfort from the Episcopal Church have a vested interest in maintaining the religious institution through which their comfort is derived.

If this line of reasoning is correct, religiocentrism and denominational parochialism are two aspects of the same religious orientation, which in turn is associated with the comfort which church involvement affords. With this in mind, parishioners' scores on the two indices were combined to produce a measure of what we shall call *parochial religiocentrism*[6]—reflecting a religious perspective which is conditioned by a particularistic concern for maintaining denominational integrity. If this overall religious orientation is actually associated with the church's comfort function, we should expect a strong association between involvement and scores on the new index.

Table 92 confirms the expectation. Parishioners scored highest on involvement have a mean score of *.70* on parochial re-

TABLE 92

CHURCH INVOLVEMENT IS STRONGLY ASSOCIATED WITH PAROCHIAL RELIGIOCENTRISM

	Composite Index of Involvement					
	High					Low
	5	4	3	2	1	0
Mean scores on parochial						
religiocentrism	.70	.61	.48	.46	.39	.24
	(96)	(162)	(261)	(251)	(210)	(156)

[6] First, parishioners' scores on religiocentrism and denominational parochialism were combined, producing a range of composite scores from *0* to *6*. Since we wish to compare the effect of involvement on the composite index with its effect on the two separate indices, the composite scores were collapsed in such a way as to produce a distribution on parochial religiocentrism roughly comparable to the distribution of scores on religiocentrism and denominational parochialism.

ORIGINAL SCORES	COLLAPSED SCORES
0,1	*0*
2	*1*
3	*2*
4,5,6	*3*

ligiocentrism. Those lowest on involvement have a mean score of *.24.* Moreover, the relationship between involvement and the composite measure is consistent. Each increase in involvement is associated with a commensurate increase in parochial religiocentrism.

Given the fact that parishioners involve themselves in the church for different reasons, Table 92 was recomputed for parishioners at different levels of predisposition to involvement. The previous relationship is repeated among the highly predisposed, the moderately predisposed and the undisposed. Furthermore, as one might expect, parishioners most predisposed to involvement (assumed to be the most deprived) generally score higher on parochial religiocentrism at each level of involvement (Table 93).

TABLE 93

AT EACH LEVEL OF PREDISPOSITION, INVOLVEMENT IS
ASSOCIATED WITH PAROCHIAL RELIGIOCENTRISM

| | Composite Index of Involvement | | | | | |
| | High | | | | | Low |
	5	4	3	2	1	0
Mean score on parochial religiocentrism among the:						
Highly predisposed	*.71*	*.65*	*.54*	*.49*	*.54*	*.44*
	(42)	(55)	(71)	(42)	(16)	(13)
Moderately predisposed	*.72*	*.60*	*.45*	*.45*	*.35*	*.23*
	(52)	(94)	(163)	(174)	(143)	(100)
Undisposed	*.33*	*.54*	*.51*	*.44*	*.44*	*.22*
	(2)[a]	(13)	(27)	(35)	(51)	(43)

[a] Note the small number of cases upon which score is based.

When the individual sub-indices of involvement were substituted for the composite measure, essentially the same findings were forthcoming. Parochial religiocentrism is most closely related to intellectual involvement, while the relationship is weakest in the case of organizational involvement. On the whole, then, church involvement as it has been considered throughout the book is also associated with the orientations of religiocentrism and denominational parochialism.

SUMMARY AND CONCLUSIONS

In Chapters 6 and 7, it appeared that church involvement has little or no influence on the way parishioners live their lives. By turning our attention to the more narrow, religious sector of their lives, it has become evident that some consequences may be discerned.

First, involved parishioners are more likely to believe in the power of religion and of the Church. They, more than the uninvolved, feel that prayers for peace can prevent war and that the Church can be an effective force in this regard. Furthermore, the involved are more likely to feel religion deserves a special place in American life; they are more likely to favor government aid to parochial schools and to demand religious instruction in public schools. They are committed to the preservation of religious institutions and seem willing to carry out what they consider religious work (participating in religious charities). This religiocentric orientation, while related closely to involvement, is distinct from political permissiveness.

While the politically permissive Episcopalians desire their Church to play actively a challenging role in society, the more religiocentric take a passive view of how the church ought to satisfy its commitment to challenge. Here the motif is that the Church should rely on the efficacy of religion itself to transform the individual and by extension the society; the Church may intervene in secular affairs (e.g., war and peace) but it should do so through prayers and moral instruction, not through actively endorsing partisan positions.

An orientation toward denominational parochialism was also found among Episcopalians, and this, too, was related to church involvement. Involved parishioners are more likely to protect the integrity of their own particular denomination. While they generally support interfaith cooperation to achieve religious goals, they are wary of more intimate religious contacts. The deeply involved are the most likely to oppose having a Protestant minister preach in their parish and are basically unwilling to condone intermarriage with Roman Catholics.

Finally the measures of religiocentrism and denominational

parochialism were combined in a composite measure representing a religious perspective conditioned by a particularistic commitment to the Episcopal Church. This composite measure was very highly related to involvement.

While the observed consequences of church involvement are narrowly religious in substance, they should not be ignored for that reason. The religiocentric and parochial qualities of involvement provide a new insight into the basic nature of religion in contemporary American society. The implications of this insight and of the findings more generally for the role of the contemporary church are considered in Chapter 9.

Chapter 9

To Comfort and to Challenge

Like General Custer, the contemporary church finds itself encircled by angry critics. Church leaders have good reasons to believe that any action they take will produce a hostile reaction from some quarter. Such attacks may take the form of critical books and tracts, reduced pledges, empty pews or public demonstrations. Some churches have been picketed for favoring racial segregation while others have been bombed and burned for favoring integration. Churches and churchmen have been condemned for entering public controversies and damned for staying out. On every side, concerned men and women stand ready to tell the church what to do and where to go.

The present study has not avoided joining the critics, perhaps, but this was not its motivation. Whatever the church is to be, it seemed a prerequisite to gain a better understanding of what it is now. This essentially is what we have sought to discover. Having completed the examination, it seems appropriate to return to the criticism and to reconsider it in light of what has been learned. Given the source of our data, the conclusions can be said only to apply directly to the Protestant Episcopal Church and indeed, the Protestant Episcopal Church as it existed in 1952. We suspect, however, that the portrait to be drawn reasonably characterizes the church-at-large, then and now.[1]

[1] More recent studies in the Survey Research Center's *Research Program in Religion and Society* confirm this suspicion. These new studies will be reported in a three-volume series to be published by the University of California Press beginning in Fall, 1967.

Additional confirmation may be found in the initial findings of a 1966 survey of Episcopal Churchwomen in the California Diocese. This latest

202

At the root of the criticism of the church, as well as our examination of it, is a problem as old as the church itself, namely, a definition of its role. What ought the church's role in society be? The answer, of course, is that the church has many roles. First, it has many specialized religious roles. It is the primary agency for providing the sacraments, the focus of ritual life. It carries the burden of responsibility for religious education. Its missionaries circle the globe winning converts to Christianity. From an eschatological perspective, the church's most important role lies with the preparation of its followers for the Final Judgement. However, the church has played many nonreligious or quasi-religious roles as well. Sociologists generally attribute to religious institutions a major share in the task of generating and perpetuating the general principles and values upon which societies are based. In some countries, the church has been the center of established political control—in others, the seat of revolution.

While a variety of societal roles have been and might be played by the church, there are two which are especially relevant to an understanding of the current criticism of the church in America. These two roles are responses to the imperfections of the temporal order and represent two distinct historical orientations. From the time of Christ, the church has sought both to comfort and to challenge; to care for the "halt, the lame, and the blind" and those who are "weary and heavy laden," but also to make the church meaningful and influential in daily life. The contemporary church still seems committed to serve both functions. Like its forebear, however, it finds itself on the horns of a dilemma as to how to do so effectively.

The church's dual commitment to these two functions makes it unique among social institutions. Its commitment to comfort

survey, which was completed just prior to publication of the present book, was designed as a test of the comfort/challenge theses developed above. The conclusions are clear. Episcopal women in the California Diocese, at least, have not changed from the general orientations observed in the data from the 1952 national survey. While they readily turn to the church for personal comfort and see its pastoral function as very important, they are not especially concerned to seek its advice in the solution of social problems. See Earl R. Babbie, "A Religious Profile of Episcopal Churchwomen," *Pacific Churchman* 97 (January, 1967).

distinguishes the church from the political party and the social reform movement. Its commitment to challenge, on the other hand, distinguishes it from the rest home and social club. Yet, it is the church's explicit commitment to both functions which has generated much of the controversy in which it is presently embroiled.

As regards comfort, the church is committed first of all to the belief that the Christian faith itself possesses the power to surmount the trials and tribulations of daily life. For many Christians, this is no doubt an accurate appraisal; the centrality of their commitment to Christ is sufficient to enable them to transcend the slings and arrows of earthly existence. At the same time, however, the church has recognized that faith alone is not enough for all men. Thus it has also rendered more worldly assistance through efforts to collect and distribute clothing and food to the poor, to minister to the sick and to extend pastoral counseling to the anguished.

At first glance, the church's role as comforter seems incontrovertible. Comfort for those in need of it has always been an integral part of Christian love and compassion. That the church continues to provide comfort today should, it would seem, come as no surprise, nor evoke a critical reaction. Yet, some of the church's contemporary critics do question the church's wisdom. In their eyes, the church has become so much a captive of its commitment to comfort as to overshadow and nearly overwhelm the exercise of its commitment to challenge.

This criticism of the church as comforter is important and should be understood for what it is. None of the critics would deny the church's obligation to ease the burdens of those who suffer; they uniformly agree the church *should* act on this obligation. However, the critics' demand is for the church to actively seek to abolish suffering, rather than simply to make it more bearable. By helping people to cope with an imperfect society, the critics charge, the church becomes an accomplice to the preservation of the injustice and inequality which constitute the imperfection.

Thus, when the church helps the impoverished to tolerate their deprivations, it implies that involuntary poverty itself is tolerable in Christian eyes. Or, while the church may have provided valuable spiritual support for Negroes in America, many observers feel it has done so at the cost of "keeping Negroes in their place." In teaching men to live with their worldly sufferings, then, the church has run the risk of preserving suffering itself.

There are two aspects of this criticism of the church's comforting function. First, comforting the oppressed may prevent them from seeking or demanding something better from themselves in this life. By helping to make this life bearable through promising a greater reward "across Jordan," the church may effectively quell protestations for social change from the bottom of the social structure. Second, the critics fear that the values of social harmony and tranquility which make the "comfortable pew" so comfortable will have the effect of preventing movements toward social justice from originating at the top of the social structure. Thus, when the more fortunate parishioners feel they have helped to make life more tolerable for the suffering, they may be less zealous in bringing down the structures which foster suffering. In this sense, the church may ease the guilt and soothe the consciences of its more socially esteemed (hence, more influential) members, and prevent or inhibit them from acting on any natural inclinations to strive for social justice.

The data examined in the present study permit an empirical test of many of the critics' observations and assertions. First, the contention that the contemporary church is largely a comforting institution seems to be confirmed by the facts. In Part One it was discovered that parishioners whose personal attributes were the most devalued by the secular society were the most likely to become deeply involved in the church. Women, the elderly, the famililess, and parishioners of relatively low social status were all found to be more involved than their more esteemed counterparts. It was concluded, therefore, that parishioners deprived of status gratification in the secular society turned to the church for alternative rewards, for comfort and consolation. In short, dispensing comfort seems a major function of the contemporary church.

Furthermore, the critics are at least partly correct in their assessments of the church's attempt to challenge. In Part Two it was observed that involved parishioners were no more or less likely to favor such efforts on the church's part. They did not differ significantly from the less involved in their support for having the church actively challenge the values and practices of the secular society. At the very least, it was evident that social concern was not a motivation to deep commitment to the church. Furthermore, degree of involvement was not related to agreement with those social and economic positions which the church did take. On the whole, what the church had to say seemed irrelevant to parishioners' social values.

Thus, the critics are not wholly correct. Involvement does not make parishioners less politically permissive. It simply has no effect. However, this observation does not rule out the possibility that a positive relationship between involvement and permissiveness might exist if the church did not emphasize its comforting function. On balance, the arguments made to support this notion still seem quite reasonable, although the present data do not permit an empirical test.

The analysis in Chapter 8 does permit a further elaboration of the church's failure to challenge, however. If anything, church involvement seems to go hand-in-hand with a narrowly religious perspective. By their religiocentric commitment, involved parishioners appear to have defined more direct social action by the church as irrelevant or superfluous. Having asserted that religious instruction could prevent war, they are not especially concerned, on religious grounds, with the possible value of a United Nations. Having expressed their belief that religion should be taught to children in schools, they do not feel their religious commitment entails support for a politically active church among adults. Having participated in religiously sponsored charities, they do not feel religiously constrained to support other, secular, charitable activities.

This belief in the miraculous power of faith, then, constitutes an alternative to social action as a means for dealing with the problem of suffering. It is not necessary to deal directly with injustice in society. Win men to Christ, and injustice and suffering will automatically disappear. From this viewpoint, if all men truly subscribed to the teachings of the Christian faith, there would be no need for civil rights demonstrations, for there would be no discrimination. There would be no need for peace protests, for there would be no war. In the minds of many churchmen then, the solution to all social problems lies in spreading the Christian faith.

That Christian faith has the power to transform individual lives is evidenced by Christian saints and martyrs of the past and present. There is less evidence, however, that it applies whole-sale and that the vast body of persons calling themselves Christians have been so transformed. Nonetheless, this is the orientation which many parishioners feel the church should take in confronting the problems of secular society.

Perhaps this is all the church can or ought to do. Perhaps more active and partisan efforts to challenge its followers should be abjured, and it should concentrate even more on its task of alleviating human misery, thereby winning men to Christ. This would be one solution to the church's present dilemma. Nevertheless, if the church were to withdraw from direct social action and concentrate its energies on providing comfort, the probable changes in the nature of the church would be severe. Surely there will always be suffering in the world, and the church would never want for people to comfort. However, a church limited exclusively to such concerns would differ little from a rest home. Furthermore, this orientation would, in effect, deny a traditional Christian commitment. Those clergymen and parishioners who feel their church must challenge the imperfections of society would probably desert.

To adopt the alternative route, to become exclusively an institution devoted to social protest and social reform, would be equally disastrous. It, too, would require an explicit denial of a traditional Christian concern, in this case, the commitment to comfort. Moreover, were the church to follow this course, it could not even count on the support of its most committed members—those who have turned to the church for relief. We have already seen that moderate efforts at challenge are largely ineffective. For the church to even hope to be influential, its stands on issues would have to be much stronger and its demands on parishioners much more persistent.

Past experience already sounds a warning against this orientation. Where the church has become actively engaged in controversial and unpopular issues, it has all too often alienated its membership, losing their moral and economic support. When the church has been critical of the abuses of capitalism, it has alienated the businessmen among its constituency. When it has pointed to inconsistencies in the practices of unions, it has lost the loyalty of union members. The condemnation of racial segregation estranges the prejudiced, and a strong pacifist position might produce apostasy among defense workers in the church. In short, when the church calls for specific social change, it must face the fact that it will lose support among those who are living comfortably within the existing conditions.

While some may feel that this is the price which the church must expect to pay, this orientation represents a losing proposition ultimately. First, while church leaders with strong social consciences may justifiably resent being supported financially by hypocritical parishioners, the complete withdrawal of such finances could render the church wholly impotent. While a destitute church might know in its heart that it was right, it would be forced to admit in its head that it could accomplish nothing.

Second, an uncompromising reorientation of the church to work exclusively for social justice would represent a denial of the church's responsibility for those who would leave the church. In facing hypocrisy among its members, the church must decide whether it is to rid itself of the hypocrites or attempt to make them less hypocritical. Those most impatient with hypocrisy will surely answer that it is better to know one's enemies than to be deceived with half-way friends. Others, however, would argue that by losing its audience the church would lose effectively its potential to communicate.

A final problem is the old one of obtaining consensus about the constitution of a Christian society. The New Testament affords room for a variety of interpretations. Feudal societies and communal ones, democracies and dictatorships, socialism and capitalism have at different times and places all been espoused as reflecting the Christian ideal. Walter Rauschenbusch, not so long ago, thought that he had discovered the true social meaning of the Gospels; and the contemporary critics feel that they have rediscovered it for the modern age. The fact of the matter is that there are no systematic prescriptions in the New Testament for the organization of society. There are clues, of course, and it is these which have inspired men to ponder their meaning. But history has not demonstrated that a consistent interpretation is possible. It seems wishful thinking at best to conceive that an interpretation about which all men can agree can still be attained.

In sum, for the church to opt for either comfort or challenge as its principal task seems unreasonable. One might suggest, then, that the church seek to redress the balance between the two functions. Since the church's performance of a comforting role now overshadows its efforts to challenge, why not try to put a little more backbone in the latter, while maintaining a commitment to the former? That there is a receptivity to having the church become more active in challenging its constituency and the society is evident in the response to the contemporary critics of the church. One sign is the sale of the critics' books and the generally favorable reception these have received in the religious press. Another is the inspiration these writings have given to a spate of new experimental programs in the churches. Still another is the greater active involvement of clergy and laity alike in social protest.

Nonetheless, redressing the balance is no simple solution. First, the attempt to strengthen the church's challenge would probably engender many of the same problems discussed in connection with an exclusive concern for social change. The second difficulty lies with the incompatibility of the two functions. If making life more bearable for the deprived can prevent them from achieving more just conditions, the converse also seems true. To some extent, certainly, the open turmoil which would be produced by more intensive efforts to challenge would work against the church's continuing efforts to afford comfort. Those who come to the church in search of relief and tranquility are not likely to find it by embroiling themselves in demands for social change. Challenging social imperfections requires the taking of unpopular stands and those who would march with the church would have to anticipate ridicule and reprisals.

This fact is nowhere clearer than in the history of the Negro civil rights movement in the South. Negroes who have learned to survive in the past by a shuffle and a spiritual hymn now discover that standing fast with the radical church and with the

Movement is anything but comfortable. Furthermore, to the extent that greater efforts to challenge would alienate the support of more prosperous parishioners, their paternalistic efforts—and these do provide a modicum of comfort—would have to be written off. In sum, redressing the balance between the church as comforter and as challenger seems a difficult solution at best.

Thus far we have dwelt on the gloomy aspects of the church's dilemma. The discussion has been aimed at elaborating the severe difficulties which confront the church as it seeks to meet its commitment to the two functions of comfort and challenge. However, in the belief that the ultimate hope for the church lies in a greater balance between the functions, we shall turn now to some of the positive solutions which are suggested by the data and by the preceding discussion. There are three proposals which the church might well consider.

1. A REEVALUATION OF DEPRIVATION

Despite the heated criticism of the church's support for the status quo, there are many ways in which the church extends comfort to its followers which are acceptable even to its harshest critics. The comfort afforded by the church to those who have lost a beloved parent, for example, is a case in point. The need for comfort in this instance is inevitable, and no amount of social change can abolish the problem. Similarly, it seems likely that the elderly will always be disadvantaged, and although their lot can be improved through financial assistance, the special, spiritual support which the church can offer seems of continued importance. A similar defense can be made for comforting the physically and mentally handicapped.

It should be clear then that many of the deprivations which the church seeks to alleviate cannot easily be abolished by social change. Many of man's sorrows are inherent in his being. Others are based on more or less rational grounds. If the elderly and the physically handicapped are denied the status afforded the young and the well, there seems little the church can do other than ease the pain. Whether comfort in these circumstances supports the status quo seems irrelevant.

On the other hand, many of the deprivations of social life are notably irrational. Attaching more prestige to a white skin than a black one is a classic example. The belief that the impoverished deserve to live in poverty is another. For the church to condone and perpetuate the status quo in these regards is indeed unacceptable. Not only are such deprivations as these irrational at base, but it is evident that they are subject to abolition through programs of social change. What is called for here is challenge, not comfort.

The church must decide when to comfort and when to challenge. The church—and its critics—must admit that some of the circumstances which plague man cannot be changed, but must be lived with. Others, however, can be changed and should not be lived with in any society which is informed by Christian principles. The current problem of the church is that it has indiscriminantly meted out its comfort without an informed consideration of whether its action would be beneficial or detrimental in the long run.

We should not be misled to think that the reevaluation of the many forms of deprivation provides an easy solution to the problem. Not the least of the difficulties to be faced is that of reaching agreement as to the forms of deprivation which ought to be comforted primarily and those which should be challenged and abolished. With regard to aging for example, while there are inherent disadvantages to being elderly, many irrational deprivations are often added to the burden. It might be deemed necessary by some to seek to generate more respect for the elderly in society, or to break down discrimination against the aged in hiring. Similarly, while being female entails a number of inherent disavantages in secular life, some members of the church might feel it important to whittle away at the less reasonable restrictions which women face. There is no clear scheme for ultimately classifying all forms of deprivations into those to be comforted and those to be challenged. Nevertheless, an overt attempt at such a rethinking of the church's comforting activities can at least single out the less ambiguous instances and clarify the choices for the more ambiguous ones.

Another difficulty, of course, is that it cannot be assumed that all individuals who are deprived on irrational grounds would want their situations changed. As difficult as it may be to accept ideologically, there are those who are content to live with their deprivations within the status quo and who would prefer the comfort which the church now offers over the strife and turmoil which social change would require. Ultimately it would seem necessary for the church to be willing to continue providing comfort in such instances, even though the bulk of its efforts is given to helping abolish the source of the deprivation.

In sum, what seems called for is that the church become more self-conscious about the implications of its actions—both manifest and latent. If its response to deprivation were informed by a more sophisticated understanding of the nature of human suffering, it is even possible that the church might be able to take considerably more pride in what it does both to comfort and to challenge. One senses a certain embarrassment on the part of churchmen when confronted with assertions that the church is the society's principal agent for providing comfort. Insofar as the comfort provided may help perpetuate the existence of intolerable social conditions, embarrassment is probably the appropriate response. However, pride rather than embarrassment should attend on the church helping people to live with unfortunate circumstances which cannot be changed.

2. A DUAL STRUCTURE FOR THE CHURCH

There are grounds for suggesting that the attempt to achieve a more effective balance between the two commitments might also call for a consideration, at least, of some modification in the organizational structure of the church. Through personal and continuing contacts, clergy and lay leaders in the local parish can best appreciate the idiosyncratic needs of parishioners. Moreover, the parish priest is in an excellent position to render spiritual first aid to those who face immediate and personal problems. In these situations where comfort is called for, it seems best provided through the familiar network of friends and clergy within the parish.[2]

[2] Peter Berger and others have suggested that the parish church is in a particularly advantageous position to comfort. See, for example, Berger's discussion of *Christian diaconate* in *The Noise of Solemn Assemblies* (Garden City, N.Y.: Doubleday, 1961), pp. 140–143.

The parish might not be the most effective setting for mobilizing parishioner support on social issues, however. The parish priest, it will be recalled from data presented in Chapter 7, has little success in winning parishioners to his views on social issues. This function could be better served perhaps by non-parish organizations—voluntary and/or interfaith.

First, a voluntary social action group can clearly be more effective in mobilizing its members than could ever be the case of the parish church whose ultimate aims are primarily religious. Thus a church-sponsored civil rights group can reach agreement on a program of action much more readily than would be possible in the parish. It is not surprising, then, to find increasing numbers of clergy and laymen (perhaps out of despair) forming and joining problem-oriented groups which deal with issues such as civil rights, peace, slums, homosexuality, labor relations, and so forth. Just as the parish priest can perhaps best determine the idiosyncratic needs of his own parishioners, these groups seem better equipped to form and carry out a challenging program to abolish the forms of deprivations which concern them.

From the church's point of view, interdenominational and interfaith groups are perhaps the most appropriate vehicle for meeting its commitment to challenge. The social problems which ought to be challenged and abolished are not the unique possession of any religious group. While each church might comfort its own members, the broader social issues carry a moral responsibility for all the churches. The formation of an Episcopal solution, a Presbyterian solution, a Congregational solution and a Lutheran solution to the problem of poverty would probably end in no solution. In this regard, interfaith cooperation seems essential. Such cooperation provides greater financial and intellectual resources and, by its representativeness, commands broader public attention and respect.

Although the data do not show that parishioners unanimously support such interfaith groups, it was evident that substantial support does exist. Furthermore, to the extent that support for such organizations—though not necessarily personal participation—can be presented as a religious act, parishioner response might be enhanced.

3. BROADENING RELIGIOUS HORIZONS

The proposal to make the parish the church's primary instrument of comfort is not intended also to mean the abdication of challenge at the parish level. On the contrary, even with a parallel institutional structure oriented to challenge, the potential would exist for doing more at the parish level than is currently being done. As we have already seen, parishioners generally, and the involved particularly, stand ready to carry out what they consider "religious" work. Most parishioners would support the church in speaking out on prayers in school; church involvement is an effective mobilizing factor in obtaining gifts to the Presiding Bishop's Fund and to Church World Service. Even in regard to less clearly religious matters, parishioners tend to favor "religious" action such as prayers and moral instruction.

This narrowness of perspective has probably generated the greatest impatience among the critics of the church. Many actions in daily life have important moral and ethical implications which should be informed by religious faith, yet the church has not succeeded in bringing the faithful to recognize this. For most parishioners, issues such as race relations, poverty, war and immigration still are purely secular, to be decided on other than religious grounds.

The church's past program of challenge, it would seem, has helped to perpetuate this myopic view of the implications of faith. While church leaders have often recognized the need for Christian action on social issues, their attempt to challenge church members has been directed, at once, at both a too abstract and a too concrete level. The church proclaims "Peace on Earth" as a Christian ideal and encourages churchmen to support the United Nations, but the links between the two messages are all too often not elaborated. The painful result is that while church members may applaud the church's abstract position, many feel no constraint to accept the concrete proposals. Thus, for many parishioners, the road from "Peace on Earth" to the United Nations is not immediately clear, and the church has not been successful in showing the way. By not specifying the links which connect the general with the specific, the church has failed to generate support for its concrete proposals and has, thereby, endangered the realization of its principles.

Three measures seem called for. First, the church should continue to seek consensus on general Christian principles. As suggested earlier, this represents a hopeful beginning, although it is not a sufficient accomplishment. Second, the church must undertake a conscious educational program through which to point out the ethical implications of daily actions in secular life. A simple concern for peace is not sufficient. All parishioners ought to realize, for example, that the Christian ideal of peace may often conflict with nationalistic and economic interests. The reasons for and instances of such conflicts should be understood. Furthermore, church members should be encouraged to examine the ways in which their own personal interests are at stake in the issue, and they should be led to realize the many ways in which their daily actions may influence the ultimate achievement of peace. In short, the church must convince its members that although secular factors are introduced into the consideration of social issues, religious concerns do not become any less relevant.

Third, we feel that an educational program which would enhance parishioners' understanding of the religious implications of their daily lives would be more successful if partisan positions were not taken by the church.[3] The basis of any educational pro-

[3] The logic of my co-authors on this matter seems compelling; however, I feel impelled to take exception to the conclusions drawn. In my estimation, the church, even on the parish level, should take partisan stands on the more morally urgent issues of the day. If it avoids doing so merely because many of its parishioners hold a contrary view, it would then be less than true to the fulfillment of one of its major missions in society: namely that of exhorting man to act in accordance with basic moral and other ideals, and it would thereby deprive mankind of a major agency for motivating people to do what they should do instead of merely doing what is expedient or what they want to do.

To paraphrase the eminent sociologist Vilfredo Pareto, no one expects a person to act only in reference to his ideals, but the absence of a clear-cut statement of these ideals would result in the person's failure to take even a step in the direction of their fulfillment. And so may it well be with the church. An explicit statement of its convictions may have little immediate influence on the secular behavior of its parishioners, but it nevertheless reminds them of the disparity between their behavior and the ideals that represent the moral conscience of the religious community.

Benjamin B. Ringer

gram ought to be the presentation of both sides of an issue. Past experience has shown, moreover, that when the church has taken a strong and unequivocal position on an issue, it has alienated members whose nonreligious interests are threatened and has led them to suspect the motives, logic and wisdom of the church's actions. There is no evidence that taking an unpopular stand has changed the thinking of many parishioners. Forcing them to recognize that the Christian principles which they profess are involved in the stand which they themselves take, however, seems potentially more fruitful.

To many, we suspect, such an approach will appear compromising and to beg the question. For them, the moral urgency of some of today's problems demand a more forthright response from the church and in their eyes, there is no question about what that response should be. The church's task, however, seems to be not so much one of reinforcing those who are now morally sensitive as making morally sensitive those who now are not. This is more likely to be accomplished, we would aver, through the church helping its followers to analyze and interpret the values which undergird both sides of a controversial issue than by stumping for one side in an unequivocal way.

A case in point is the problem of gaining equality for Negroes in our society. This is one of those morally urgent questions which seem to call for no other than a partisan stand. By and large, this is the stand which American churches have adopted, but with what effect? Seventy million church members devoted to the Negroes' cause, it would seem, ought to be able to move mountains. But, of course, mountains are not being moved, only hills and at a much slower pace than many would like.

Whether or not the church has the capacity to play this special kind of educational role is, of course, an open question. It would call upon churchmen to transcend their own partisan commitments in the interests of the larger cause. Moreover, it would require on their part a sensitivity to not only the values of both sides but an understanding of how these values came into being. Here, perhaps, we are counting on the possibility of another kind of miracle. Still, in the long run, this route seems more promising than any other for the church's commitment of challenge at the parish level.

APPENDICES

APPENDIX A: *The Sample Design*

The manner in which the sample was selected for this study was based on the several applied goals of the National Council of the Protestant Episcopal Church. One of these goals was to assess the extent to which Episcopalian parishes across the country were implementing the Church's Social Education and Community Action program. To this end, it was necessary to select a representative national sample of parishes. Since the Church was also interested in examining the attitudes of its parishioners and clergy, the design had to provide representative samples from these groups as well. Thus, a procedure was devised to provide samples from three separate universes: local parishes, clergy and parishioners.

SAMPLE DESIGN AND COLLECTION OF DATA

First, all parishes were stratified into seven groups according to size. Then, an 8 percent sample was selected from all but the two extreme strata. The largest-sized parishes—those with 1,501 parishioners or more—were overrepresented in order to insure adequate coverage for this study. The smallest-sized parishes—those with 150 parishioners or less—were underrepresented because of time and cost factors. The total number of congregations in our sample, therefore, came to 299 instead of the 536 which would have resulted from a uniform 8 percent sample. Table A-1 describes the distribution of parishes within the sample and universe.

Within each of the seven categories, the specific parishes were selected on a random basis. Every *n*th church—the specific *n* depending on the proportion desired from that category—was chosen with the starting number being randomly selected. For categories II through VI, this meant every 12th or 13th church was included;

TABLE A-1

Sample Design for Selection of Parish Units

Group	Size of parish	Parishes (local units)	Percentage of total churches in each group	Approximately 8% of parishes to be chosen for sample	Actual number of parishes chosen
I	1–150	3,777	56.6	303[a]	54[a]
II	151–350	1,452	21.75	117	120
III	351–500	497	7.40	40	41
IV	501–750	474	7.10	38	39
V	751–1,000	210	3.14	17	17
VI	1,001–1,500	193	2.89	15	16
VII	1,501[a]	71	1.06	6[b]	12[b]
Totals		6,674	99.94	536	299

[a] Two adjustments were made in the number of local units selected in group I. (1) Since the number of communicants in so many of these units was less than 50, the data to be obtained from surveying each of these 303 did not justify the cost. The number was, therefore, cut one-fourth, to a total of 77. (2) When these 77 were chosen on a random basis, it was found that 23 had less than 25 communicants. These 23 were, therefore, dropped from the sample. The adjusted number for group I is, therefore, 54.

[b] On the basis of the sample design only 6 local units were allocated to group VII. This number was increased for the actual sample to 12.

for category I, every 48th; and for category VII, every 6th. Table A-2 reports the procedure for selecting the individual parishes.

Once the 299 congregations were selected, the parish priests were sent a questionnaire (Parish Inventory) which sought information on the characteristics of the parish church: its size, wealth, surroundings, and so forth; on the nature of its community activities; and on the extent of and kinds of participation in the Social Education and Community Action Program of the church.

TABLE A-2

Procedure for Selection of Parishes

Size Category	Starting number[a]	Interval
I	5	every 48th
II	1	every 12th
III	3	every 12th
IV	9	every 12th
V	7	every 12th
VI	5	every 13th
VII	2	every 6th

[a] Starting number selected at random.

The second phase of the sample design involved the selection of the lay sample. Since the interrelationships between a parishioner's and his priest's attitudes as well as those between institutional and personal variables were considered primary foci of the study, the lay sample was selected from the membership lists of the sample parishes. The total number sought was 3,020. This number was distributed among the 299 parish units according to (a) the proportion of total communicants found in the universe of churches in the various categories—I through VII—and (b) the actual number of parishes from each size category included in the parish sample.

To arrive at the number of lay persons to be included from a specific parish, we multiplied 3,020 by (a) and then divided the product by (b). For example, 9 percent of all communicants belong to churches in category VII. As a result, we wanted 9 percent of our lay sample of 3,020, or approximately 272 respondents, to come from this kind of church.

TABLE A-3

SAMPLE DESIGN FOR SELECTION OF LAY SAMPLE

Group	Size of parish	Communicants (population)	Parishes (local units)	Percentage of total communicants in each group	Actual number of parishes in parish sample	Average number of communicants per parish	Total number of lay persons sought	Number of lay persons per parish
I	1–150	221,063	3,777	14	54	58	432	8
II	151–350	344,877	1,452	21	120	237	600	5
III	351–500	208,303	497	13	41	419	410	10
IV	501–750	289,704	474	18	39	611	546	14
V	751–1,000	181,782	210	11	17	865	340	20
VI	1,001–1,500	231,160	193	14	16	1,197	416	26
VII	1,501+	142,814	71	9	12	2,011	276	23
Totals		1,619,703	6,674	100	299		3,020	

A description of the lay universe and sample is offered in Table A-3. Since 12 parishes of this size were included in our parish sample, we divided the number 272 equally among them. This gave us 22⅔ parishioners per parish. We then rounded the number to eliminate the fraction, making it 23 per parish. This, then, became the number of parishioners we sought to include in our sample from each parish in category VII. The same procedures were followed for all other categories.

The lay persons selected from these sample parishes as well as the parish priests were sent a questionnaire (see Appendix C) designed to measure their attitudes on social problems and on public issues—

particularly those upon which the church had taken an official stand —to obtain information about the kind of role they would have the church play in public affairs, and to identify, in the case of parishioners, the nature and kinds of ties they have to the church.

Both the Parish Inventory and questionnaire were self-administered. In the case of the former, the National Council sent the instrument directly to the parish priests and asked them to fill out the schedule and to return it to the National Council. The same procedure was followed for the questionnaire which the priest himself was to answer. However, the distribution of questionnaires to the laity followed a somewhat more circuitous route. The latter was distributed by the priest who was instructed to select every nth parishioner from his list starting from a randomly chosen number. Both the n and starting number were provided him by the directors of the study— the specific n depending on the factors discussed above. The parishioners, in turn, were requested to mail the questionnaire back to the National Council in a self-addressed, stamped envelope. For purposes of comparison, questionnaires were also sent to all the bishops of the Church.

RETURNS

In view of the procedures used to distribute and to collect the data, it is not surprising to find that not all who were included in the original samples returned their questionnaires. Of the 299 Parish Inventories and questionnaires distributed to the priests, 235 of the former (79 percent) and 259 of the latter (87 percent) were returned. Of the 3,020 questionnaires distributed to the laity, 1,530 (51 percent) were returned.

Though a relatively large number did not return questionnaires— particularly among the laity—the distribution of lay respondents according to size of parish, nevertheless, corresponds closely to the distribution of communicants in these parishes. As can be seen in Table A-4, the maximum difference between the two is 2.7 percent.

This close correspondence between communicants and respondents lends confidence that the results obtained from respondents are representative of the universe of Episcopalian parishioners as of the time, 1952, that the data were collected. It is not possible with the data at hand to provide an absolute test of representativeness, however. In this regard, it is to be noted that insofar as a sample may be non-representative, this has a greater effect on the distribution of responses to individual questions than on the relationships between

TABLE A-4

DISTRIBUTION OF LAY RESPONDENTS AND COMMUNICANTS
ACCORDING TO SIZE OF PARISH

Group	Size of parish	Percentage of total communicants in each group	Percentage of respondents in each group	Differences between communicants and respondents
I	...–150	14	16.7	+2.7%
II	151–350	21	20.9	−.1
III	351–500	13	15.1	+2.1
IV	501–750	18	15.4	−2.6
V	751–1,000	11	12.4	+1.4
VI	1,001–1,500	14	11.3	−2.7
VII	1,500 or more	9	8.2	.8
		100 (1,619,703)	100 (1,530)	

responses to different questions. To be sure, the strength of the relationships may be different in the sample than the universe. It is unlikely, however, that the direction of the relationships will be different. Possible non-representativeness, then, constitutes less of a problem in a study such as the present one where the analysis is primarily relational than in a study whose primary purpose is description.

As regards the additional question of whether or not results based on data collected from a sample of Episcopalians in 1952 may be representative of Episcopalians today, we can only say that specific attitudes may very well have shifted in the ensuing years. It is less probable, however, that the basic dynamics of church involvement have changed.

APPENDIX B: *Methodological Notes*

This section is designed as a methodological supplement for the reader who desires a more detailed description of the methods employed in the analysis. The appendix contains descriptions of index and scale construction, plus some commentaries regarding the reasons for selecting some methods over others. Also presented are some supplementary, substantive data which we felt might be irrelevant or distracting in the main text but which should be of interest to some readers. For ease of reference, the appendix begins with some general notes and then is arranged in terms of the specific chapters to which the notes and comments refer.

GENERAL NOTES

Protocol for Table Computations

In presenting the proportional distribution of responses to a particular questionnaire item, percentages have been based on the number of persons who gave some meaningful response. For example, if only 1,500 of the 1,530 parishioners answered a given question, the percentages who said "yes," "no," and so forth are based on those 1,500. In most instances, the number of respondents upon which percentage distributions are based is indicated by the notation "100% =." Whenever the number of non-respondents on a given item seemed intrinsically interesting, this additional datum has been presented beside the label "no answer."

An abbreviated format has been used in certain cases. First, when mean scores on an index or scale have been presented, the number of non-respondents has been omitted as having little direct meaning. Second, whenever non-response is, in fact, a response to a dichotomous variable (e.g., not reporting a contribution to Church World

224

Service), the base for percentage computation is automatically the total number of parishioners being examined. Finally, whenever the inclusion of non-response information would confuse or clutter the main presentation, it has been omitted. In most of these exceptional cases, the number of respondents upon which percentages or mean scores are based has been presented in parentheses.

All percentage computations have been rounded off to the nearest whole percent. Computations carried out to several decimal places seem to promote a false sense of rigor and precision which is generally unwarranted in survey analysis. Moreover, it is our feeling that any conclusion which stands or falls on the difference of one percentage point either way should be seriously reconsidered, and we have sought to invoke somewhat higher standards. The reader should be aware, however, that the rounding off process occasionally results in a column of percentages which add to 101 percent or 99 percent.

Treatment of Non-responses in Indexing and Scaling

In creating a composite measure of some variable, the researcher faces the perennial problem of what to do with respondents who failed to answer one or more of the questions being considered. There are many different solutions to this dilemma. The primary factor distinguishing them is the extent to which the investigator is willing to speak on behalf of the respondents. For the most part, we have tended to be conservative in this regard.

In some fortunate instances, it has been possible to discern a rational and consistent pattern among the responses to a given set of items (e.g., political permissiveness) and scaling procedures have been used. Thus, it has sometimes seemed very reasonable to infer certain data which were missing from an otherwise consistent response pattern. More often than not, however, scaling procedures were unwarranted and simple indices were constructed. When indices have been constructed to measure a given variable, respondents who failed to answer one or more of the relevant questions were not scored. (See notes for Chapter 5, below, for the one exception.)

It should be noted that in failing to score some respondents on a given index any tables which utilize that index are necessarily incomplete. Strictly speaking, such tables do not wholly reflect the sample of parishioners who responded to the questionnaire. It is conceivable that the findings of those tables might be biased by virtue of their failure to include those parishioners not scored on the index. Wherever possible, we have tested for bias and have found that the omission of non-respondents does not affect the conclusions being drawn in a given instance. Of course, it is not always possible to conduct this test, but we have chosen to run this risk rather than taking the liberty of filling in answers where none existed.

The problem of non-respondents is most salient in the consideration of priests' influence on the attitudes of their parishioners. Since not all of the parish priests responded to the survey, this part of the analysis was limited to approximately two-thirds of the parishioner sample. The discussion of this problem is presented separately in the Chapter 7 notes below.

CHAPTER 1: MEASURING RELIGIOUS INVOLVEMENT

As discussed in the text, we believe religiosity must be regarded as a multidimensional phenomenon. The ways in which a person may be religious are manifold, and there is surely no single measure which would satisfactorily reflect this general concept. It was our intention, then, to tap as many meaningful dimensions of religiosity as the data in the survey would permit. After examining the information available on the Episcopalian parishioners, three dimensions seemed most appropriate for consideration: ritual, organizational, and intellectual involvement.

Ritual Involvement

The questionnaire provided two measures of ritual involvement: attendance at Sunday worship services, and participation in Holy Communion. It will be recalled from Table 1 that responses to the two questions were highly related, as one might expect. In view of this very high degree of association, it was decided that church attendance alone would serve as a sufficient measure. Furthermore, since nearly two-thirds (66 percent) of the parishioners reported attending church "almost every Sunday," this response was designated as "high" ritual involvement. Respondents attending church less frequently were scored "low" on this dimension.

Organizational Involvement

As noted in the text, two types of scoring procedures were available for measuring organizational involvement. First, it would have been possible to assign scores according to the degree of church-related activity. By such a procedure, parishioners would have been scored on the basis of the number of church-related organizations to which they belonged—the more religious organizations, the higher the score.

As explained in Chapter 1, however, we felt a superior measure of organizational involvement would be one which reflected the saliency of the church in providing a focus for parishioners' organizational interests and energies. Logically, it seemed that the church's organizational life was not as salient for the person who belonged to ten organizations, of which two were religious, as it was for a person whose sole extra-curricular activity was church-related. Following this line of reasoning, the organizational involvement index was constructed to reflect the proportion of a parishioner's activities which were church-related. The percentage scores which parishioners received were then divided into four levels of organizational involvement. (Parishioners who reported they belonged to no organizations— either secular or religious—could not be scored on this dimension.)

Score on Index of Organizational Involvement	Percentage of parishioners' organizational memberships which were church-related
High	75–100
Moderately high	50–74
Moderately low	1–49
Low	0

Intellectual Involvement

While ritual and organizational involvement dealt primarily with institutional life in the church, intellectual involvement was designed to indicate the tendency among parishioners to turn to the church and to religion for information, advice and guidance in their daily lives. Several questions in the questionnaire referred to this aspect of involvement.

First, respondents were asked to list all the magazines which they regularly read. These, in turn, were coded as to type of publication; one category was "religious." As in the case of organizational involvement, there were two possibilities for scoring parishioners on the basis of magazine reading. They could have been scored according to the number of religious magazines which they read or according to the proportion of their reading which was religious. Again, the latter procedure seemed superior. We recall from Chapter 1, however, that 77 percent of the respondents reported they read no church publications, and a bare 5 percent depended on the church for more than half of their magazine reading. Hence, it was necessary to supplement this item with others which reflected intellectual involvement.

Another question asked parishioners whether they would turn to religious sources for the solutions to a difficult community problem.

Of the possible answers, two involved reading religious books. Selecting either of these was taken as a further indication of intellectual involvement.

Finally, parishioners were asked for a subjective evaluation of the extent to which the Church had influenced their opinions. Those who replied "Yes, the church has changed my opinions a great deal," were assumed to have demonstrated a greater reliance on the church for information and advice than was true of those who did not feel this was the case.

Given the overall distribution of responses to these three items, it was decided that a typology of responses would provide the best measure of intellectual involvement—ranging from those who were heavily reliant on the church to those who would hardly ever turn to the church for information and advice. The letter-symbols below represent the four responses used in scoring parishioners on intellectual involvement.

Symbol	Item
a.....	50–100% of the parishioner's total magazine consumption was church-related.
b.....	1–49% of the parishioner's total magazine consumption was church-related.
c.....	The parishioner responded: "Yes, the church has changed my opinions a great deal."
d.....	In seeking advice or information concerning a community problem, the parishioner said he would "read the Bible" and/or "read a religious book."

The following chart shows the several response patterns which were converted to scores on this index. In each case, the response patterns shown represent the minimum required for the corresponding score.

Response patterns	Intellectual involvement scores
(a).................	High
(c + d)............	High
(b + c)............	Moderately high
(b + d)............	Moderately high
(b).................	Moderately low
(c).................	Moderately low
(d).................	Moderately low
None..............	Low

Composite Index of Involvement (C.I.I.)

Although we felt it important to measure church involvement along several dimensions, a Composite Index of Involvement was also created to facilitate the analysis. The C.I.I. combined the ritual, organizational and intellectual dimensions and ranged from a low of 0 to a high of 5. Scores on the composite index were assigned as follows:

	Scores on C.I.I.
Ritual Dimension	
High	1
Low	0
Organizational Dimension	
High or moderately high	2
Moderately low	1
Low	0
Intellectual Dimension	
High or moderately high	2
Moderately low	1
Low	0

CHAPTER 3: MEASURING ANOMIE

The Anomie Scale was constructed from the following five items:

Item 1: Nowadays a person has to live pretty much for to-day and let tomorrow take care of itself.

Item 2: These days a person doesn't really know on whom he can count.

Item 3: It is hardly fair to bring children into the world the way things look for the future.

Item 4: In spite of what some people say, the lot of the average man is getting worse, not better.

Item 5: There's no use writing to public officials because they are not really interested in the problems of the average man.

Responses to these items were so highly intercorrelated that we were able to devise a two-point scale using latent structure analysis. On the basis of computations which determined the latent class parameters and the probabilities of a person with a given response pattern being in either of the two classes, we included in the "high anomie" class those who agreed with at least three of the above items. In addition, so great was the discriminatory power of Items 2 and 4 that we also included in the "high" class those who agreed with both, irrespective of how they answered the other items. The rest of our respondents were included in the "low anomie" class.

CHAPTER 4: INVOLVEMENT AND SOCIAL CLASS

Measuring Social Class

The questionnaire contained four types of information relevant to determining parishioners' social class: education, income, occupation, and self-evaluation of class standing. Of these, the first two were selected as the most appropriate for inclusion in the class index.

Occupation was especially difficult to use for two reasons. First, respondents were asked to write in their occupation in a blank space. To score respondents on the basis of their answers would require the classification of a multitude of different occupations in terms of the status they carried more than a decade ago. Second, married and employed female parishioners were asked to indicate their own occupations as well as those of their husbands. It would have been necessary therefore to reconcile the two occupations in arriving at a single class score for the woman. Furthermore, male parishioners were not asked if their wives were employed, hence the scoring of men and women respondents could not have been wholly comparable.

When asked if they thought of themselves as being of "the working class, the upper class, the lower class, or the middle class," the vast majority of respondents placed themselves in the middle class.

TABLE B-1

VALIDATION OF THE SOCIAL CLASS INDEX

Self-evaluation of social class:	Index of Social Class				
	Low				High
	0	1	2	3	4
Upper class	5%	8%	7%	16%	24%
Middle class	47	54	72	78	76
Working class[a]	48	38	21	6	0
100% =	155	361	419	263	80

[a] Includes 6 respondents who chose "lower class."

TABLE B-2

WOMEN: CLASS, AGE AND RITUAL, ORGANIZATIONAL
AND INTELLECTUAL INVOLVEMENT

| | Index of Social Class | | | | |
| | Low | | | | High |
	0	1	2	3	4
Mean scores on ritual involvement among women aged:					
Under 30	.78	.69	.51	.39	.50
	(9)[a]	(45)	(41)	(18)	(2)[a]
30 to 49	.68	.66	.61	.70	.60
	(22)	(92)	(150)	(76)	(20)
50 and over	.79	.70	.73	.70	.86
	(64)	(91)	(62)	(40)	(7)[a]
Mean scores on organizational involvement among women aged:					
Under 30	.80	.46	.50	.35	.25
	(5)[a]	(34)	(30)	(17)	(2)[a]
30 to 49	.56	.68	.59	.61	.55
	(18)	(85)	(143)	(75)	(20)
50 and over	.64	.74	.59	.68	.50
	(48)	(76)	(59)	(41)	(7)[a]
Mean scores on intellectual involvement among women aged:					
Under 30	.29	.28	.13	.11	.50
	(7)[a]	(43)	(41)	(18)	(2)[a]
30 to 49	.45	.34	.29	.26	.25
	(22)	(86)	(149)	(76)	(20)
50 and over	.55	.48	.46	.35	.29
	(63)	(87)	(62)	(40)	(7)[a]

[a] Note the small number of cases on which scores are based.

As a result, this question did not provide sufficient variation to be a meaningful and useful measure of social class.

Ultimately, education and income were accepted as the clearest signs of status. Both items were in the form of "closed-ended" question and required no personal interpretation by the investigators. Moreover parishioners varied widely on both items. Although both education and income have been up-graded in the ensuing years, the relative ranking of parishioners on these two aspects of social class seems appropriate to the analysis. Respondents were scored as follows:

Score on Index of
Social Class

Annual family income:
$4,000 or less..................................... *0*
$4,001 to $10,000............................... *1*
$10,001 or more................................ *2*

Education:
Did not graduate from high school.................. *0*
Graduated from high school and/or some college..... *1*
Graduated from college.......................... *2*

Scores on the index of social class ranged, then, from a low of *0*
to a high of *4*. The most appropriate test of the validity of the index
is its effectiveness in predicting parishioners' self-evaluation of their

TABLE B-3

MEN: CLASS, AGE AND RITUAL, ORGANIZATIONAL
AND INTELLECTUAL INVOLVEMENT

| | Index of Social Class | | | | |
| | Low | | | | High |
	0	1	2	3	4
Mean scores on ritual involvement					
among men aged:					
Under 30	*.88*	*.70*	*.69*	*.25*	*.00*
	(8)[a]	(30)	(29)	(12)	(1)[a]
30 to 49	*.33*	*.52*	*.69*	*.54*	*.38*
	(18)	(52)	(84)	(74)	(26)
50 and over	*.70*	*.59*	*.74*	*.66*	*.44*
	(30)	(46)	(47)	(50)	(25)
Mean scores on organizational					
involvement among men aged:					
Under 30	*.58*	*.39*	*.26*	*.56*	*.00*
	(6)[a]	(22)	(21)	(8)[a]	(1)[a]
30 to 49	*.22*	*.23*	*.32*	*.27*	*.39*
	(16)	(43)	(74)	(64)	(22)
50 and over	*.42*	*.12*	*.34*	*.24*	*.21*
	(19)	(39)	(40)	(44)	(21)
Mean scores on intellectual in-					
volvement among men aged:					
Under 30	*.36*	*.17*	*.40*	*.14*	*.00*
	(7)[a]	(29)	(29)	(11)	(1)[a]
30 to 49	*.28*	*.24*	*.19*	*.17*	*.07*
	(16)	(45)	(81)	(73)	(27)
50 and over	*.40*	*.39*	*.33*	*.22*	*.20*
	(25)	(36)	(43)	(51)	(25)

[a] Note the small number of cases upon which scores are based.

social class. While the latter did not provide enough variation to be useful in creating the index itself, it still may be used to demonstrate the validity of the index (see Table B-1, p. 230).

Class, Sex, Age and Involvement

The joint effects of sex, age and social class on the Composite Index of Involvement were presented in the main text. Tables B-2 (p. 231) and B-3 (p. 232) present the relationships with respect to the three sub-indices of involvement.

CHAPTER 5: MEASURING PREDISPOSITION TO INVOLVEMENT

In constructing the predisposition index, an exception was made to the general rule of omitting parishioners who failed to answer any of the relevant questions. There were two reasons for making an exception in this instance. First, since the index was based, ultimately, on responses to six questions, it became apparent that the general rule would result in too few parishioners being scored. Second, the nature of the questions themselves and the basic scoring procedure readily suggested reasonable inferences which might be made in the cases of missing data. The following procedures were followed.

Sex: Men received 0 and women received 2. Parishioners who did not indicate their sex were given the intermediate score of 1. This scoring procedure was selected as the one which introduced the least amount of distortion. Whatever the non-respondent's sex, the score assigned was very close to the score which was actually appropriate.

Age and social class: Non-respondents on these items were also scored 1 for the same reasons discussed under sex.

Marital status and number of children: It will be recalled that being single and being childless were each scored 1 point. Those who were married and who reported having children were scored 0 on both counts. It was not possible in this case to assign an intermediate score without hopelessly complicating the index. Upon reflection, however, it was concluded that respondents who did not indicate whether they had any children simply skipped the question as being irrelevant to them. Similarly, it was reasoned that single parishioners would be more likely to skip over the question of marital status than would those who were married. Thus non-responses to both of these questions were scored *1*. While the scoring was surely not one hundred percent accurate in this respect, it represented the best possible inference.

One further comment is in order regarding the treatment of age and family status. It will be recalled (Chapter 3) that the discussion of family deviants was limited to those parishioners who had passed the normal age for marriage and childbearing. The conclusion drawn was that parishioners thirty years of age or older who lacked spouses and/or children shared a somewhat devalued social status in that they had violated social norms regarding family life. This form of deprivation, then, was reflected in a greater degree of church involvement.

The question arose as to whether younger parishioners should be scored on the basis of family status. The ultimate decision to give all parishioners—regardless of age—predisposition points for incomplete families was based on both theoretical and empirical considerations. First, in the discussion of age and social values, it was pointed out that "responsible youth" is highly valued in American society. The commensurate devaluation of the elderly is clear. However, it should also be apparent that adolescents share in this devaluation. As long as they are regarded as children, young people are somewhat restricted in their activities and are denied the serious consideration which is the mark of status as we have used that term. Anyone who has escaped the fetters of adolescence to find himself treated as a responsible citizen is surely aware of this situation. However, the transition from adolescence to adulthood seems less a matter of age itself than of the assumption of responsibilities—in particular, family responsibilities. Therefore, while older parishioners with incomplete families are regarded as family deviants, younger parishioners without family responsibilities are treated as children who have not reached the stage of adult participation in society.

Second, this line of reasoning is substantiated by the available empirical data—on Episcopalians and others. Figure 1 (Chapter 2) corresponds closely to the findings of Argyle and others in that the very young are quite high on religious involvement. The lowest level of involvement for both men and women occurs upon marriage and childbearing. Similarly, when this issue was examined in detail, the same effects of family status on involvement were discovered among younger parishioners as appeared among those past the normal age of marriage. Therefore, all parishioners were scored on the basis of family status, whatever their age.

CHAPTER 7: SOCIAL IDEOLOGY AND INVOLVEMENT

In examining the effects of church involvement on social ideology, it was useful to construct scales and indices representing parishioners' ideological positions on each of the six issues. The different patterns of responses to the several issues dictated varying means of measurement, and all of these are described in detail below. In each instance, higher scores are taken to represent the Church's official, or inferred, position.

United Nations

Item	Response	Score
"It is all right for United States troops to serve under officers of another country appointed by the UN."	Agree	2
	Uncertain	1
	Disagree	0
"It would be a good thing if the UN were some day replaced by some kind of world government."	Agree	2
	Uncertain	1
	Disagree	0
"The United Nations is not worth the money we in the United States have spent on it."	Disagree	2
	Uncertain	1
	Agree	0

Immigration Policy

Item	Response	Score
"The immigration laws should be changed so that the quota system does not favor certain nations as opposed to others."	Agree	2
	Uncertain	1
	Disagree	0
"The United States has already admitted too many refugees since the end of World War II."	Disagree	2
	Uncertain	1
	Agree	0

Conscientious Objectors

Item	Response	Score
"Episcopalians should recognize the right of conscientious objectors to refuse to bear arms."	Agree	2
	Uncertain	1
	Disagree	0

Item	Response	Score
"Episcopalians have a moral obligation to give financial and other assistance to conscientious objectors who need it."	Agree........ Uncertain.... Disagree.....	2 1 0

Human Rights

Item	Response	Score
"The names of people receiving public relief should be made available for anyone who wants to see them."	Disagree..... Uncertain.... Agree........	1 1 0
"It is all right for school boards to say what books on controversial social issues their students should read in school."	Disagree..... Uncertain.... Agree........	1 1 0
"Have you done any of the following things to express your opinion about the activities of people who try to suppress free speech?"	Discussed it with friends or wrote a letter.........	1
"People who go around talking about equal rights for 'this group' and 'that group' are making a mountain out of a molehill."	Disagree..... Uncertain.... Agree........	1 0 0
"In this country people of different colors and religious beliefs are treated pretty much equally."	Disagree..... Uncertain.... Agree........	1 0 0

Labor Attitudes Scale

The nature of responses to the questions regarding labor were such as to permit the construction of a Guttman scale. Below, we have used letter-symbols to indicate the pro-labor responses included in each of the scale-types. Parishioners were assigned scale designations corresponding to the scale-type most closely approximating their own response-patterns. The coefficient of reproducibility obtained by this scaling procedure was 95 percent.

Symbol	Response
A......	*Agree* that "If the majority of workers in a plant decide to join a union, then the others should join too."
B......	*Agree or uncertain* that "In disputes between management and labor, the unions seem to be right more often than does management."
C......	*Agree or uncertain* that "Workers should be allowed to strike in defense industries except in times of war."
D......	*Agree or uncertain* that "The government should protect the rights of workers to organize into unions."

Scale-type	Response-pattern
Highest pro-labor......................................	ABCD
Second highest..	BCD
Third highest...	CD
Fourth highest..	D
Lowest pro-labor...........................	None of the responses

Government Control of Business

As with Labor attitudes, the responses to questions dealing with the governmental control of business were such as to permit the construction of a Guttman scale. The coefficient of reproducibility in this instance was 95.4 percent.

Symbol	Response
A......	*Disagree* that "In peacetime, it is best if the federal government does not interfere with private industry."
B......	*Agree* that "In periods of national emergency like the present, industry should accept the need for more governmental control of its activities."
C......	*Agree or uncertain* that "In time of war, the government should have the right to tell industry what prices they can charge for their products."
D......	*Agree or uncertain* that "If wages are controlled then profits also should be controlled."

Scale-type	Response-pattern
Most in favor of government control.....................	ABCD
Second most favorable................................	BCD
Third most favorable.................................	CD
Fourth most favorable................................	D
Least favorable..........................	None of the responses

Priests' Influence on Parishioners' Ideologies

Having discovered that involvement did not affect the likelihood of parishioners agreeing with the official Church position on matters of social ideology, it was suggested that the parish priests might exercise some influence. It will be recalled from Appendix A that in each parish selected for the survey parish priests were asked to complete the same questionnaire which was given to parishioners. In the analysis, the information provided by participating parish priests was transferred to the IBM cards of all their parishioners, permitting us to test the extent of agreement.

However, of the 299 priests who were contacted, only 259 completed and returned their questionnaires. This meant that many parishioners could not be examined on this issue. Of the total 1,530 parishioners who responded, the priests of only 1,058 replied. Thus, 472 parishioners were omitted from the examination. To place the resultant conclusions in their proper perspective, it is necessary to compare the 1,058 parishioners examined with the 472 who were omitted. If the two groups differ radically, it will be necessary to restrict the generalizability of the findings.

In Table B-4, the two groups are compared in terms of three variables that might have an effect on the extent to which parishioners might be influenced by their priests.

(1) Education. Conceivably, those parishioners with less education might be more susceptible to influence than those with more education.

(2) Political sophistication. Education was combined with several questions which measured political knowledge to provide a general measure of political sophistication. It seems possible that the least sophisticated parishioners would be the most susceptible to influence.

(3) Church involvement. Although involvement was not related to ideological positions, it is important to be aware of any differences in involvement between the two groups. If differences exist, it might be necessary to reevaluate the representativeness of the basic findings.

TABLE B-4

THERE ARE NO RELEVANT DIFFERENCES BETWEEN PARISHIONERS WHOSE PRIESTS RESPONDED TO THE QUESTIONNAIRE AND THOSE WHOSE PRIESTS DID NOT RESPOND

	Parishioners whose priests:	
	Responded	Did not respond
Parishioner's education:		
Grammar school	9%	11%
High school	39	32
College	40	45
More than college	12	13
Mean scores on political sophistication	.50	.52
Mean involvement scores (C.I.I.)	.46	.47

CHAPTER 8: RELIGIOUS ORIENTATIONS

The Church and War

When respondents were asked if they felt the Church could do more than it was already doing to prevent war, the clergy appeared considerably more optomistic than parishioners, as Table B-5 demonstrates.

TABLE B-5

CLERGY ARE MORE LIKELY TO FEEL THE CHURCH CAN DO MORE
TO PREVENT WAR THAN ARE PARISHIONERS

"Can the Church do anything more than it is already doing to prevent war?"	Bishops	Priests	Parishioners
Yes	90%	84%	50%
No	2	2	13
Uncertain	8	14	37
100% =	97	253	1501
No answer	3	6	29
Total	100	259	1530

Among parishioners, the feeling that the Church could do more was associated with high church involvement. Sixty-eight percent of the most involved said "yes" as compared with 47 percent of the least involved (see Table B-6).

TABLE B-6

INVOLVEMENT IS RELATED TO THE BELIEF THAT THE CHURCH
CAN DO MORE TO PREVENT WAR

"Can the Church do anything more than it is already doing to prevent war?"	Composite Index of Involvement					
	High					Low
	5	4	3	2	1	0
Yes	68%	63%	55%	48%	48%	47%
No	8	8	12	10	13	15
Uncertain	24	29	33	42	38	39
100% =	101	166	273	253	229	161
No answer	1	5	3	6	1	2
Total	102	171	276	259	230	163

Those who said the Church could do more were then asked what they felt should be done. Their responses generally fell into two categories: political action and religious action.

Political action: (a) contacting public officials;
                        (b) more active role in discussion of public affairs;
                        (c) encourage parishioners to take more active roles in public affairs;
                        (d) sponsoring public forums for education in peace.

Religious action: (a) disseminate moral and religious principles among all people;
                        (b) moral and religious training for the young;
                        (c) increased missionary activities;
                        (d) intra-church and inter-faith harmony;
                        (e) strengthen the moral fiber of the Church and its believers;
                        (f) more prayers.

Overall, parishioners were more likely to suggest religious actions than political actions. Furthermore, church involvement strongly influenced the type of action suggested. As Table B-7 shows, involvement is strongly associated with the suggestion of religious actions, while there is only a weak, negative relationship between involvement and the suggestion of political actions. This latter observation is in keeping with the lack of relationship between involvement and political permissiveness. (Since some parishioners gave more than one answer to the question, the percentages do not add to one hundred percent.)

TABLE B-7

CHURCH INVOLVEMENT IS ASSOCIATED WITH THE FEELING THAT THE CHURCH SHOULD TAKE RELIGIOUS ACTIONS TO HELP PREVENT WAR

| | Composite Index of Involvement | | | | | |
| | High | | | | | Low |
	5	4	3	2	1	0
Percentage who suggested a religious action	95	89	86	74	74	58
Percentage who suggested a political action	30	33	31	38	36	41
Total number	57	83	122	101	95	64

Charitable Activities

Table B-8 shows the percentages of bishops, priests and parishioners who reported performing a variety of charitable acts during the two years preceding the study. Table B-9 examines the activities of parishioners at each level of involvement.

TABLE B-8

CHARITABLE ACTIVITIES OF BISHOPS, PRIESTS AND PARISHIONERS

	Bishops	Priests	Parishioners
Percentage who have:			
Contributed clothing for Korea	39	53	30
Contributed to Church World Service	67	65	45
Sent a CARE package overseas	48	31	16
Purchased a UNESCO gift coupon	4	1	2
Given money to the Presiding Bishop's Fund	75	81	58
Contributed blood to the American Red Cross	91	95	90
Given money to the local Community Chest	87	81	82
Served as a volunteer in a social service agency	28	44	28
100% =	100	259	1530

TABLE B-9

CHURCH INVOLVEMENT INCREASES THE LIKELIHOOD OF A PARISHIONER PERFORMING A CHARITABLE ACT WHICH BEARS A RELIGIOUS STAMP

	Composite Index of Involvement					
	High					Low
	5	4	3	2	1	0
Percentage who have:						
Contributed clothing to Korea	40	44	36	35	23	20
Contributed to Church World Service	58	58	49	54	44	34
Sent a CARE package overseas	20	16	17	17	17	18
Purchased a UNESCO gift coupon	2	1	1	3	1	2
Given money to Presiding Bishop's Fund	83	80	69	61	55	35
Contributed blood to the American Red Cross	12	19	16	15	23	23
Given money to the local Community Chest	69	82	88	87	88	85
Served as a volunteer in a social service agency	28	27	31	38	36	34
100% =	102	171	276	259	230	163

APPENDIX C: *The Questionnaire*

Your World

YOU HAVE BEEN SELECTED

to render a very important service to the Church and to the whole Christian community. You are being asked to take part in an important churchwide study being made for the National Council of your Church, the Episcopal Church. A national committee of bishops, other clergy, and laity is co-operating with the Department of Christian Social Relations in making this study. In addition, a group of top-flight social research experts is helping, so that our methods and findings will be in keeping with the highest scientific standards.

You have been chosen according to a scientific plan, to fill out this *Opinion Poll.* Your answers, together with those of a large group of church members all over the country chosen in the same way, will help point the way to what we as church people have done and should do to make our world a more Christian one. When you fill out all the questions inside, you will render, therefore, a great service to the Church. You are part of this scientifically chosen group, therefore we need your answers to guarantee that this important study will be sound. No substitute will do.

Absolutely Confidential

This Poll is as secret as your ballot. You will not be identified personally in any way. Nobody will know your answers but you. We want to know exactly what you think about each question or statement, but *we do not want to know your name.* So, please do not write your name on it anywhere. Only your clergyman or whoever hands you this poll will know that you filled it out, but *even he will*

242

not know what your answers are, because you will mail the poll directly to the National Council in the attached, self-addressed envelope. No postage is required—do not put a stamp on the envelope.

How to Fill Out the Poll

The mechanics of the poll are simple. You only mark most of the questions whether you *Agree,* or *Disagree* with a statement, or you may mark that you are *Uncertain* how you feel. There are also some checklist questions, and the directions given with each such question will tell you what to do. Please give to each question only the answer that you really believe, not what you think may be the *correct* or *Christian* answer. Your own opinion is what really counts. If you do not know you will always have the choice of marking *Don't Know* or *Uncertain.* But please mark each question, even if you have to guess. Do not write anything else.

There is no rating for this. There is no high score or low score, or good or bad or average. It is simply an expression of what you think and what you feel.

We want to thank you for agreeing to take part in this important experiment on behalf of the whole Church.

It is not as long as it looks. A number of people tested it for us. Some persons filled it out in 30 minutes; others took 45 minutes. No matter how much time they took, all persons who tried it out for us said they enjoyed it. Take all the time you need. *Just be sure to mail it back to the National Council the same day you get it.*

We hope you enjoy it!

THE NATIONAL COUNCIL
Department of Christian Social Relations
281 Fourth Avenue, New York 10, N. Y.

> *Here is some fun with a purpose! This is not exactly a game, but everyone who has seen it has said right off,* I'd like to fill that out. It looks like it would be fun!

INSTRUCTIONS

ON the next few pages are listed a number of statements on current affairs, with which some people agree and some disagree. Please indicate how you feel about each one of them:

	A	D	U
If you **Agree** *with a statement, check the box under the column headed* **A**	x	□	□
If you **Disagree** *with a statement, check the box under the column headed* **D**	□	x	□
If you are **Uncertain** *about a statement, check the box under the column headed* **U**	□	□	x

That is all you have to do. Please do not skip any. Check the column which is closest to how you feel. The numbers and letters beside each box are to help tabulate the answers. Please disregard them.

WAR & PEACE

	A	D	U
War is justified when other ways of settling international disputes fail	□$^{5-1}$	□^{2}	□^{3}
It is all right for United States troops to serve under officers of another country appointed by the UN	□^{4}	□^{5}	□^{6}
Military action is justified to stop aggression as in Korea	□^{7}	□^{8}	□^{9}
The USA and Russia cannot live side by side without fighting	□^{0}	□^{X}	□^{Y}
War is justified when one has been attacked . . .	□$^{6-1}$	□^{2}	□^{3}
Special prayers for peace do not help to prevent war	□^{4}	□^{5}	□^{6}
War is never justified under any conditions	□^{7}	□^{8}	□^{9}
The USA has done all it can to make peace with Russia	□^{0}	□^{X}	□^{Y}
War cannot be avoided in our present time	□$^{7-1}$	□^{2}	□^{3}

WORLD PROBLEMS

	A	D	U
It would be a good thing if the UN were someday replaced by some kind of world government . . .	□^{4}	□^{5}	□^{6}
The United Nations is not worth the money we in the United States have spent on it	□^{7}	□^{8}	□^{9}
The United States should not spend money to help "under-developed countries" raise their standards of living	□^{0}	□^{X}	□^{Y}

	A	D	U
The Church should actively encourage its members to support the UN.....................	□ 8–1	□ 2	□ 3
The spread of international communism would not be stopped even by finding new ways to bring social justice to all people..............	□ 4	□ 5	□ 6
The immigration laws should be changed so that the quota system does not favor certain nations as opposed to others........................	□ O	□ X	□ Y
The United States should appoint an ambassador to the Vatican.............................	□ 9–1	□ 2	□ 3
The United States has already admitted too many refugees since the end of World War II..	□ 4	□ 5	□ 6

NATIONAL PROBLEMS

	A	D	U
Nowadays people are more afraid to speak their mind on controversial social issues...........	□ O	□ X	□ Y
The names of people receiving public relief should be made available for anyone who wants to see them...............................	□ 10–1	□ 2	□ 3
There is no room in the Church for people who believe in communism......................	□ 4	□ 5	□ 6
It is all right for school boards to say what books on controversial social issues their students should read in school......................	□ 7	□ 8	□ 9
Episcopalians should recognize the right of conscientious objectors to refuse to bear arms.....	□ O	□ X	□ Y
Episcopalians must take a bold stand in protecting freedom of speech even for people whose views are unpopular........................	□ 11–1	□ 2	□ 3
Episcopalians have a moral obligation to give financial and other assistance to conscientious objectors who need it......................	□ 4	□ 5	□ 6

COMMUNITY PROBLEMS

	A	D	U
Aside from preaching, there is little that the Church can do about social and economic problems....................................	□ 7	□ 8	□ 9

	A	D	U
Government funds should be used for support of parochial or religious schools.............	□ O	□ X	□ Y
The most important thing to teach children is absolute obedience to their parents...........	□ 12–1	□ 2	□ 3
Poverty tends to weaken the faith of the Christian..................................	□ 4	□ 5	□ 6
The main responsibility for giving children a moral and ethical education rests with the church school rather than with parents..............	□ 7	□ 8	□ 9
The Church should have a special missionary program for workers in industrialized areas....	□ O	□ X	□ Y
It is right to expect a higher standard of behavior from public officials than from private citizens..	□ 13–1	□ 2	□ 3
The Church should stick to religion and not concern itself with social and economic problems..	□ 4	□ 5	□ 6
Alcoholism is caused by moral weakness......	□ 7	□ 8	□ 9
People who go around talking about equal rights for "this group" and "that group" are making a mountain out of a molehill................	□ O	□ X	□ Y
It is proper for the Church to state its position on practical political issues to the local, State, or the national government..................	□ 14–1	□ 2	□ 3
Alcoholism is a disease and should be treated as such.....................................	□ 4	□ 5	□ 6
Protestants and Roman Catholics should be allowed to intermarry freely.................	□ 7	□ 8	□ 9
It is all right for a minister of a Protestant Church to preach in my local parish church....	□ O	□ X	□ Y
It is all right for an Episcopalian who marries a Roman Catholic, to agree to let their children be brought up as Roman Catholics...........	□ 15–1	□ 2	□ 3

MAKING A LIVING

	A	D	U
The Church has no responsibility to try to bring about more active co-operation between labor and management.............................	□ 4	□ 5	□ 6

	A	D	U
If the majority of workers in a plant decide to join a union, then the others should join, too..	$\square^7$	$\square^8$	$\square^9$
White collar workers should be encouraged to organize for their economic security..........	$\square^0$	$\square^X$	$\square^Y$
Workers should be allowed to strike in defense industries except in time of war.............	$\square^{16-1}$	$\square^2$	$\square^3$
The government should protect the right of workers to organize into unions.............	$\square^4$	$\square^5$	$\square^6$
It's a good idea for people to work even if they don't have to do so for a living.............	$\square^7$	$\square^8$	$\square^9$
If wages are controlled, then profits also should be controlled.............................	$\square^0$	$\square^X$	$\square^Y$
In peacetime, it is best if the federal government does not interfere with private enterprise......	$\square^{17-1}$	$\square^2$	$\square^3$
In disputes between management and labor, the unions seem to be right more often than does management.............................	$\square^4$	$\square^5$	$\square^6$
In time of war, the government should have the right to tell industry what prices they can charge for their products.........................	$\square^7$	$\square^8$	$\square^9$
In periods of national emergency like the present, industry should accept the need for more governmental control of its activities..............	$\square^0$	$\square^X$	$\square^Y$
In time of war, labor unions must expect the government to control wages................	$\square^{18-1}$	$\square^2$	$\square^3$

GENERAL

	A	D	U
There's no use writing to public officials because they are not really interested in the problems of the average man..........................	$\square^4$	$\square^5$	$\square^6$
What this country needs most is a few courageous, tireless, devoted leaders in whom the people can put their faith, MORE than it needs laws and political movements................	$\square^7$	$\square^8$	$\square^9$
Alcoholics Anonymous is doing what the Church ought to be doing to help alcoholics..........	$\square^0$	$\square^X$	$\square^Y$
Nowadays a person has to live pretty much for today and let tomorrow take care of itself.....	$\square^{19-1}$	$\square^2$	$\square^3$

	A	D	U
No weakness or difficulty can hold us back if we have enough will power.................	□4	□5	□6
These days a person doesn't really know on whom he can count.......................	□7	□8	□9
In this country, people of different colors and religious beliefs are treated pretty much equally	□0	□X	□Y
It is hardly fair to bring children into the world the way things look for the future............	□20–1	□2	□3
Any good leader should be strict with people under him in order to gain their respect.......	□4	□5	□6
The true American way of life is disappearing so fast in the USA that force may be necessary to preserve it.............................	□7	□8	□9
In spite of what some people say, the lot of the average man is getting worse, not better.......	□0	□X	□Y
In order for us to do good work, it is necessary that our superiors outline in detail what is to be done and exactly how to go about it..........	□21–1	□2	□3

HERE are a few more questions about some of the things already touched upon. Your opinion is needed on these also. Since these are presented in a different form, they were not included with the Agree-Disagree questions you have just answered. In answering these, please follow instructions included in each question.

In helping to prevent war, the Church can do   (*Check one*)

Nothing...................................... □21–4
Very little.................................... □5
Quite a bit.................................... □6
A great deal.................................. □7

Can the Church do anything more than it is already doing to prevent war?   (*Check one*)

Yes.. □21–9
No... □0
Uncertain.................................... □X

If you check *yes*, write what you think the Church can do....   22

....
....
....

Which of the following countries should be helped by the United States Government to get on its feet economically? (*Check those which should be helped*)

India.. ☐²³⁻¹
England....................................... ☐²
Western Germany.............................. ☐³
Iran.. ☐⁴
Puerto Rico................................... ☐⁵
Japan... ☐⁶
Liberia, Africa............................... ☐⁷
None of these countries....................... ☐⁸

Religious instruction in public schools should be: (*Check one*)

Forbidden by law............................. ☐²³⁻⁹
Voluntary for children whose parents approve.... ☐⁰
Compulsory................................... ☐ˣ

We would all agree that many factors weaken the foundations of family life. Which *one* in the following list do you consider most important?

(*Check one*)

Poor housing................................. ☐²⁴⁻¹
Low income................................... ☐²
The bad example of parents................... ☐³
Indifference to religion...................... ☐⁴
None of these................................ ☐⁵

The Church should actively support the following organizations:

(*Check the ones you approve*)

Local Council of Churches.................... ☐²⁴⁻⁷
National Council of Churches of Christ......... ☐⁸
World Council of Churches.................... ☐⁹

People of different races should: (*Check one*)

Not be treated any differently in the Church...... ☐²⁵⁻¹
Be seated in special sections of the church........ ☐²
Have their own parish churches................ ☐³

The sale of alcohol should be: (*Check one*)

Unregulated but licensed...................... ☐²⁵⁻⁵
Regulated.................................... ☐⁶
Prohibited................................... ☐⁷

Compared with the general population, the ethics of most government officials are: (*Check one*)

    Higher.. □ 25–9

    Lower.. □ o

    About the same.............................. □ x

The Episcopal Church is best described as a Church for the:

                                                  (*Check one*)

    Upper class.................................. □ 26–1

    Middle class................................. □ 2

    Working class............................... □ 3

    Lower class................................. □ 4

    No one of these............................. □ 5

Individual parishes often co-operate with other churches in civic affairs and social service programs. Do you think your church should go beyond this and do any of the following: It is all right for my church to hold joint worship services with Protestant churches of any denomination   (*Check one*)

    Including Holy Communion.................... □ 27–7

    Excluding Holy Communion.................. □ 27–8

    Under no conditions......................... □ 27–9

In this country the schools, the federal government, the Churches, the labor unions and industry—each has a different job to do. In general, would you say each is doing an excellent, a good, a fair or a poor job:

                        (*Please check your answer for each of the following*)

	Excellent	Good	Fair	Poor	Don't Know
Schools.................	□ 27–1	□ 2	□ 3	□ 4	□ 5
Federal Government.....	□ 7	□ 8	□ 9	□ o	□ x
Church.................	□ 28–1	□ 2	□ 3	□ 4	□ 5
Unions.................	□ 7	□ 8	□ 9	□ o	□ x
Industry...............	□ 29–1	□ 2	□ 3	□ 4	□ 5

The United States Government policy with respect to refugees of World War II has been: (*Check one*)

    To refuse admission to all refugees.............. □ 31–1

    To limit the number of admissions.............. □ 2

    To admit anyone who wants to come............ □ 3

Have you read anything or attended a lecture on any of the following topics: (*Check each one you did*)

    The appointment of an ambassador to the Vatican.. □ 31–5

    Public funds for parochial schools.............. □ 6

The Ecumenical Movement..................... □⁷
Corruption in Government..................... □⁸

The Church nationally has taken a strong stand in support of the United Nations.

Yes.............. □⁹
No.............. □⁰
Don't know....... □ˣ

The quota system in the USA immigration law permits entrance of:
(*Check one*)

An equal number of persons from each nation.... □³²⁻¹
A number in proportion to the population of their
native country............................... □²
A number in proportion to the number of their
fellow countrymen in the USA prior to 1890...... □³
Don't know....... □⁴

Do you know the name of the man nominated by President Truman to be Ambassador to the Vatican?

Yes.............. □⁵
No.............. □⁶

If yes, what is his name?..

How actively do you feel you participate in the life of the community:
(*Check one*)

Very actively............................... □³²⁻⁸
Fairly actively............................... □⁹
To some extent............................... □⁰
Hardly at all............................... □ˣ

Many parishes co-operate with other churches and religious groups for social planning, civic improvement, and for fellowship. Do you think your church should co-operate in this way with any of the following:
(*Check each one you approve*)

Interfaith organizations........................ □³³⁻¹
Your local council or federation of churches...... □²
Jewish congregations.......................... □³
Eastern Orthodox Churches..................... □⁴
Roman Catholic Churches..................... □⁵
Protestant Churches.......................... □⁶

UNESCO stands for   (*Check one*)
Union of National Episcopal Service Clubs and
Organizations............................... □³⁴⁻¹

United Nations Economic and Social Conference
Organization................................. $\Box^2$

United Nations Educational, Scientific and Cultural
Organization................................. $\Box^3$

United National Employment Service Council
Office....................................... $\Box^4$

NATO stands for   (*Check one*)

National Advertising and Technical Organization.. $\Box^6$
North Atlantic Treaty Organization............ $\Box^7$
North Atlantic Transport Organization......... $\Box^8$
North American Tabulating Office............. $\Box^9$

The Church nationally has taken a strong stand for freedom of conscience, speech, and worship.

Yes.............. $\Box^0$
No.............. $\Box^X$
Don't know....... $\Box^Y$

Which of the following would you say has had most influence on your
social ideals or opinions?   (*Check only one*)

Just going to church......................... $\Box^{35-1}$
Listening to sermons......................... $\Box^2$
Attending lectures or discussion groups at church.. $\Box^3$
Reading a non-religious book.................. $\Box^4$
Other, please say what....................... ^{5}
.... ^{6}

In this election, some important problems will face the country. Which
two of the following are *most important* to you in making up your mind
how to vote? *Which two are least important?*

	Most	Least
How our relations with Russia should be handled...............................	$\Box^{36-1}$	$\Box^{36-7}$
How relations between labor and business should be handled......................	$\Box^2$	$\Box^8$
How to keep the cost of living from going up more.............................	$\Box^3$	$\Box^9$
Whether the Government should control business more.........................	$\Box^4$	$\Box L$
How to keep the United Nations a going concern...............................	$\Box^5$	$\Box^X$

Everyone's ideas change from time to time. Would you say that your Church has played any part in changing your opinions?   (*Check one*)

Yes, the Church has changed my opinions a great deal... □ 37–1

Yes, the Church has changed my opinions somewhat...................................... □ 2

I don't know whether the Church has changed my opinions.................................... □ 3

No, I don't think the Church has changed my opinions.................................... □ 4

It is proper for your parish to: (*Check* Yes *or* No *for each statement*)

	Yes	No
Encourage its members to study political issues and candidates...........................	□ 37–6	□
Encourage groups within the Church to engage in political action........................	□ 7	□
Urge citizens to vote......................	□ 8	□
Permit candidates to speak in the parish house	□ 9	□
Have some effort on the Sunday before Election Day to get out the vote................	□ O	□
Endorse candidates for office..............	□ X	□
Encourage the minister to discuss political issues from the pulpit.....................	□ Y	□

Is it all right for the clergy to speak out on:

(*Check* Yes *or* No *for each statement*)

	Yes	No
Birth control............................	□ 38–1	□
Labor legislation like the Taft-Hartley Law..	□ 2	□
Political corruption.......................	□ 3	□
Prayers in schools........................	□ 4	□
Anti-Semitism in the community............	□ 5	□

YOU, YOUR CHURCH, AND YOUR COMMUNITY

Is there a Christian Social Relations group in your local parish church?

Yes.............. □ 38–6

No.............. □ 7

Don't know....... □ 8

If so, are you a member of this group?

Yes.............. ☐⁹
No.............. ☐⁰

How frequently do you attend the meetings of this group?   (*Check one*)

Every meeting............................. ☐³⁹⁻¹
Occasionally................................ ☐²
Rarely.. ☐³

Are you active in the program of the group when you do attend?

Yes.............. ☐³⁹⁻⁵
No.............. ☐⁶

Does your parish church provide any special services for the aged?

Yes.............. ☐⁴⁰⁻¹
No.............. ☐²
Don't know....... ☐³

If yes, what services are provided?   (*Check each service provided*)

Visiting...................................... ☐⁴⁰⁻⁴
Providing supplies............................ ☐⁵
Financial aid................................. ☐⁶
Books.. ☐⁷
Entertainment................................ ☐⁸

Have you done any of the following things to express your opinion about the activities of people who try to suppress free speech:

(*Check what you did*)

Written a letter.............................. ☐⁴¹⁻¹
Discussed it with friends...................... ☐²
Other: please say what:...................... ☐³

....
....
....

Did you vote in the last presidential election in which Truman and Dewey were running?   (*Check one*)

Yes.............. ☐⁴²⁻¹
No.............. ☐²
Don't remember... ☐³

Did you vote in the last local election?

Yes.............. ☐⁴²⁻⁵
No.............. ☐⁶
Don't remember... ☐⁷

Have you done anything yourself which you think would help prevent war, even little things?

Yes.............. □ 42–9

No.............. □ 0

If yes, what have you done?....................................
.... 43
....

Have you done any of the following in the past two years:

(*Check* Yes *or* No *for each*)

	Yes	No
Contributed clothing for Korea.............	□ 44–1	□
Contributed to Church World Service.......	□ 2	□
Sent a CARE package overseas.............	□ 3	□
Purchased a UNESCO gift coupon..........	□ 4	□
Given money to the Presiding Bishop's Fund..	□ 5	□
Contributed blood to the American Red Cross	□ 6	□
Given money to the American Red Cross....	□ 7	□
Given money to the local Community Chest..	□ 8	□
Served as a volunteer in a social service agency	□ 9	□

As you read the newspapers, do you find news of the United Nations:

(*Check one*)

Very interesting.............................. □ 45–1

Mildly interesting............................ □ 2

Not interesting at all......................... □ 3

Is there a group in your community which actively supports the UN:

(*Check one*)

Yes............,..... □ 45–5

No.............. □ 6

Don't know....... □ 7

If so, are you a member of this group?

Yes.............. □ 45–9

No.............. □ 0

Has your parish or any group in the parish participated in voluntary community efforts to improve or affect social relations or conditions in the following areas?   (*Check*)

Slums...................................... □ 46–1

Health facilities.............................. □ 2

Intergroup relations.......................... □ 3

In which of these did you personally participate?

(Check the ones you did)

Slums...................................... □ 46—5
Health facilities.............................. □ 6
Intergroup relations.......................... □ 7

The services provided by my parish church for the aged   *(Check one)*

Are as good as can be expected................ □ 46—9
Should be improved.......................... □ °

Have you read any pamphlets or books on Christian Social Relations topics?

Yes.............. □ 47—1
No.............. □ 2

If so, can you name one or two that you have liked especially?

.... □ 48

....

Do you belong to any group interested in promoting better relations between racial and religious groups?

Yes.............. □ 49—1
No.............. □ 2

Have you attended any lecture, discussion group on a social topic in your parish church within the last two years?

Yes.............. □ 49—4
No.............. □ 5

Comments, if any: ....

....

....

If you wanted advice or information about a difficult community problem (not necessarily a family problem), would you do any of the following?   *(Check each one you would do)*

Go to your minister.......................... □ 50—1
Read the Bible.............................. □ 2
Pray....................................... □ 3
Read a religious book........................ □ 4
Go to Communion more often................. □ 5
None of these.............................. □ 6

What magazines do you read more or less regularly? *(Write the names of the magazines below)*

....51

....

. . . .
. . . .
. . . .
. . . .
. . . .
. . . .

Are there any clubs or associations that you belong to or attend:

(*Check one*)

Yes. . . . . ☐ [52–1]

No. . . . . ☐

What kinds of clubs and other organizations do you belong to in the Church, such as Woman's Auxiliary, Brotherhood of St. Andrew, Altar Guild, etc., and in the community, such as trade union, political club, sports, Community Chest, Red Cross, hobby clubs, PTA, and so on? Please list the clubs and organizations you belong to:

(*Full name*)

1. . . . . [53]

2. . . . .

3. . . . .

4. . . . .

5. . . . .

6. . . . .

Check proper box below for each organization listed above.

How frequently do you attend meetings?			Do you hold any office in the club?			
Regularly	Irregularly	Never	At present?		Have you ever?	
1. ☐	☐	☐ [54]	☐ YES	☐ NO	☐ YES	☐ [55] NO
2. ☐	☐	☐	☐ YES	☐ NO	☐ YES	☐ NO
3. ☐	☐	☐	☐ YES	☐ NO	☐ YES	☐ NO
4. ☐	☐	☐	☐ YES	☐ NO	☐ YES	☐ NO
5. ☐	☐	☐	☐ YES	☐ NO	☐ YES	☐ NO
6. ☐	☐	☐	☐ YES	☐ NO	☐ YES	☐ NO

How often do you attend church?   (*Check*)

    Almost every Sunday.......................... ☐ 56—1

    About twice a month.......................... ☐ 2

    About once a month.......................... ☐ 3

    Hardly ever except Christmas and Easter......... ☐ 4

How often do you take Holy Communion?   (*Check*)

    More than once a week...................... ☐ 56—6

    About once a week.......................... ☐ 7

    2 or 3 times a month......................... ☐ 8

    About once a month.......................... ☐ 9

    Less than once a month....................... ☐ 0

    Every 3 or 4 months......................... ☐ X

What is your membership in the Church?   (*Check*)

    A lay person (layman or laywoman)............ ☐ 57—1

    A priest

        Parochial.................................. ☐ 2

        Non-parochial.............................. ☐ 3

        Cathedral Dean............................ ☐ 4

        Seminary professor......................... ☐ 5

        Social relations officer...................... ☐ 6

        Other..................................... ☐ 7

    A bishop

        Active.................................... ☐ 8

        Retired................................... ☐ 9

Have you ever held an office in the Church, as layman, or as clergyman?

                            Yes.............. ☐ 1

                            No............... ☐ 2

If so, what office?...................................... ☐ 58

About when?........... ☐ 59   For how long?.......... ☐ 60

Are you a member of any of the following?   (*Check*)

    Rotary.................................... ☐ 61—1

    Chamber of Commerce...................... ☐ 2

    Lions..................................... ☐ 3

    Kiwanis................................... ☐ 4

    Exchange.................................. ☐ 5

    Other..................................... ☐ 6

Are you a member of a labor union?

Yes.............	☐ 62–1
No..............	☐ 2

If so, is it   (*Check*)

CIO.......................................	☐ 62–4
AFL.......................................	☐ 5
Other; please give name......................	☐ 6

Is any member of your family a member of a labor union?

Yes.............	☐ 63–1
No..............	☐ 2

If so, is it   (*Check*)

CIO.......................................	☐ 63–4
AFL.......................................	☐ 5
Other; please give name of union..............	☐ 6

SELF PORTRAIT

LET'S paint a picture of you in facts and figures. Our panel of experts tells us that the following information about each person is absolutely necessary if we are to understand the answers you and the others who take part in this experiment give. *There is nothing here which will tell who you are or where you are.* So, please fill out each of the following or else our whole project falls down. (*Check the correct answer on all the following*):

Male.......................................	☐ 65–1
Female.......................................	☐ 2
Married.......................................	☐ 4
Single (*Check Single if widowed or divorced*)......	☐ 5

How many children are in your family?

None.......................................	☐ 65–7
1.......................................	☐ 8
2.......................................	☐ 9
3–5.......................................	☐ 0
6 or more.......................................	☐ X

How many of these children are twelve years of age or younger?

None.......................................	☐ 66–1
1.......................................	☐ 2
2.......................................	☐ 3
3–4.......................................	☐ 4
5 or more.......................................	☐ 5

Are you gainfully employed?

Yes.............	☐ 66–7
No.............	☐ 8

Are you a housewife?

Yes.............	☐ 66– 0
No.............	☐ x

What is your present occupation? Please say what you actually do and give your job title... 67

. . . .

What was your father's occupation when you were about fifteen years old?... 68

If you are not employed, are you (*Check one of the following*)

A student.....................	☐ 69–1
Retired.......................	☐ 2
Old age pension...............	☐ 3
Public assistance.............	☐ 4
Unemployed: seeking work......	☐ 5
Unemployed: ill...............	☐ 6

If you are not head of your home (household), is the head now employed?

Yes.............	☐ 69–8
No.............	☐ 9

If head of household is working, what is his present occupation?

. . . . 70

Your annual income falls roughly into which of the following:

$2,000 or less................	☐ 71–1
$2,001 to $4,000..............	☐ 2
$4,001 to $6,000..............	☐ 3
$6,001 to $7,500..............	☐ 4
$7,501 to $10,000.............	☐ 5
$10,001 to $15,000............	☐ 6
$15,001 to $25,000............	☐ 7
Over $25,000..................	☐ 8

Your education was:

Some grammar school...........	☐ 72–1
Finished grammar school.......	☐ 2
Some high school..............	☐ 3
Finished high school..........	☐ 4

Some college.................................. ☐⁵
Finished college............................. ☐⁶
More... ☐⁷

In what country were you born?

The USA.................................... ☐⁷³⁻¹
Other; give the name.................................

Did you grow up in a city, town, village or on a farm?   (*Check one*)

On a farm................................... ☐⁷⁴⁻¹
Village of 2,000 or less........................ ☐²
Town of over 2,000 to 10,000.................. ☐³
Small city over 10,000 to 100,000............... ☐⁴
Large city, over 100,000....................... ☐⁵

In what country was your father born?

The USA.................................... ☐⁷⁵⁻¹
Other; give name of country.........................

Have you lived in the community where you now are all your life?

Yes.............. ☐⁷⁶⁻¹
No.............. ☐²

If not, how long have you lived here?   (*Check one*)

Less than 4 years.......................... ☐⁷⁶⁻⁴
4 to 9 years............................... ☐⁵
10 to 19 years............................. ☐⁶
20 years or more........................... ☐⁷

Which of the following is your age group?   (*Check one*)

21 and under............................... ☐⁷⁷⁻¹
22 to 29................................... ☐²
30 to 39................................... ☐³
40 to 49................................... ☐⁴
50 to 59................................... ☐⁵
60 or over................................. ☐⁶

By and large, do you think of yourself as being of the working class, the upper class, the lower class, or the middle class? Of which of these groups do you consider yourself a member?   (*Check one*)

Working.................................... ☐⁷⁸⁻¹
Upper...................................... ☐²
Lower...................................... ☐³
Middle..................................... ☐⁴

Index

Activity, index of, 32–33. *See also* Intellectual involvement; organizational involvement

Age and involvement, women, 48–54, 57–59, 65, 67, 71, 73, 87–88; men, 53–59, 71, 72, 95–96; general, 62–63, 103, 234

Alcoholism and Church, 138

Altar Guilds, 21

American Institute of Public Opinion, 76, 77

Anglican Church of Canada, 5

Anomie and involvement, 68–70, 73; scale of, defined, 229–230

Anti-Semitism, and Church stand, 121–123, 129

Argyle, Michael, 41n., 46n., 234

Babbie, Earl R., 203n.

Baptist church, 80, 81

Berger, Peter, 3–4, 212n.

Berton, Pierre, 3, 5–6, 7

Birth control, and Church, attitudes on, 121–123, 129

Bishops, Episcopalian, 8, 142; and public affairs, 120–125, 135, 143–162 *passim*, 175–184 *passim*, 239; and charity, 182–183, 241; and interfaith cooperation, 186–192 *passim*

Bishops, House of, 142

Bultena, Louis, 77, 82

California Diocese, 1966 survey of Episcopal Churchwomen, 202–203n.

California, rural, study of social class in denominations in, 81

Capitalism, and Church, 118, 121, 138, 155, 161. *See also* Government control of business, and Church; Labor, and Church; Social adjustment, and Church; Upper class and involvement

Catholic Digest, social class poll in, 77–78

Catholic church. *See* Roman Catholic church

Census of Religious Bodies, 1936, 41n.

Challenge, social, and Church's role, 203–216. *See also* Church, Christian, criticism of; Comfort, and Church's role

Charity and involvement, 182–184, 193–194, 241

Children, effect on parent's involvement, 46–47, 49–53, 55–59, 62–65, 66, 70–74; lack of, effect on involvement, 63, 66–74

Children of mixed marriages, attitudes toward, 192–193, 196

Christian Social Relations program. *See* Social Relations, Christian, Department of

Church Association for the Advancement of the Interests of Labor, 118

Church, Christian, criticism of, 1–8, 76, 202–216 *passim;* ideals of, 2–3, 6, 137; and social adjustment, 3–7, 138; and secular society, 6–7; effectiveness of, 7, 113–218 *passim;* and membership, 14–16; and family status, 43–45, 60–65; and economic life, 44–45; and social class, 75–98 *passim;* historic role of, in America, 116–118; and role in society, 203

Church Hypothesis, 125–126

Church of England, 117, 142

Church-State relations, 130–131, 180. *See also* Public affairs, and Church; Social issues, and Church

263